Additional Praise for *Net Zero Business Models*

"Finally a book that recognizes and separates reality from fiction in what it will really take to achieve net zero carbon emissions. Montgomery and Van Clieaf make clear that, for companies with high carbon intensity footprints, contracts for renewable resources (solar or wind) alone do not provide 24x7 electricity or steam needed for their operations. We are proud to be recognized as one of the solutions to achieve the 2040 net zero emissions target as outlined by the International Energy Agency. Net Zero Business Models is brilliant because it concisely outlines the foundation of the future energy system required for a net zero world: Smart Power Grids powered by 100 % Carbon Free Energy and 24/7/365 electric power reliability."

Chris Colbert, CFA,
Chief Financial Officer, NuScale Power Corporation

"Transitioning the North American power system over the next 20 years to a 100% carbon free energy (CFE) and a SMART power grid that delivers 24/7/365 power reliability is the engine to achieve the net zero global economy. Net Zero Business Models provides C-Suites, Boards, and Regulators four net zero navigation pathways and five core eco-efficiency processes, based on best-in-class research from companies executing a net zero business model strategic intent. Adopting a long-term energy strategy that identifies the requisite strategic leadership capacity, including the three domains of systems thinking and innovation required, reduces the friction to transition to a net zero economy."

Aurora Geis, PCC
Former Board Chair, CPS Energy, San Antonio, Texas
America's largest electric and gas municipal utility

"Given the widespread evidence of climate change, the need to create a net zero economy is a global imperative. What's been missing is a clear roadmap for companies to achieve this goal. Net Zero Business Models: Winning in the Global Net Zero Economy, *by John Montgomery and Mark Van Clieaf, lays out the practical steps companies need to take—and boards need to monitor—to ensure a successful transition to the net zero economy. It provides invaluable insights for corporate leaders and investors alike."*

Chris Librie, Global Director,
ESG and Sustainability Strategy, Applied Materials
Original contributor to the Green House Gas (GHG)
Corporate Accounting and Reporting Standard

"As companies and investors wake up to the reality that "net zero" is more than a marketing strategy or a compliance exercise, Net Zero Business Models *provides an excellent guide to understanding not only what it means but also how to get there with practical, phased recommendations to change the scaffolding that determines how companies operate, grow, and adapt to impending radical change. Thank you!"*

Susan MacCormack, Partner and Chair ESG, Social Enterprise and
Impact Investing and Energy practices, Morrison & Foerster

"An Extraordinary Book!"

Michael Hugman, Director, Climate Finance,
Children's Investment Fund Foundation

"An excellent book that offers detailed pathways to net zero business models, a necessary step on society's longer journey to a net negative *future where a regenerative and distributive economy will counteract the damage wrought to our climate regulation and human systems since the Industrial Revolution."*

Bill Baue, Senior Director, r3.0
(Redesign for Resilience & Regeneration) and
Original Instigator, Science Based Targets initiative

"The world is being challenged, businesses are being challenged, and we need to educate future business leaders to address these challenges. Net Zero Business Models *is the blueprint for doing that!"*

Dean Thomas Horan, School of Business
and Society, University of Redlands School of Business

"A must read for all businesses in this era of climate transition!"

Christopher Marquis, Sinyi, Professor of Chinese Management,
Cambridge Judge Business School, and
author of *Better Business: How the B Corp Movement Is
Remaking Capitalism* and *Mao and Markets: The Communist Roots
of Chinese Enterprise*

"Achieving a net zero economy has become a global necessity. Net Zero Business Models *documents the challenges corporations face in attaining this goal in a sober, proactive manner. Net zero must become a core part of each company's long-term strategy. Four net zero pathways are described in detail with excellent examples given for each pathway. For some companies, the change will be transitional and for others transformational. Change management is an essential ingredient. The authors go to great pains to point out that winning business models must be net zero* and *commercial successes. Corporate strategy and finance must act together.*

Winners will be companies that can make the net zero transition integral to their core business strategy and a competitive advantage while generating returns on capital that exceed the cost of capital and future cost of carbon. The enormity of the challenge should not be underestimated. The authors provide a comprehensive playbook for not only meeting the net zero challenge but making it an economic success."

David Holland, Fractal Value Advisors and
Co-Author "Beyond Earnings"
Former Managing Director, Credit Suisse HOLT,
Company Valuation and Analytics

"Finally, a book that transcends the climate change debates to provide a roadmap for companies and their investors to successfully navigate perhaps the greatest business opportunity and challenge of the twenty-first century. The authors offer insights on real-world economic risks and industry sector net zero business strategy benchmarks. They also provide best in class examples and metrics from their research, that goes beyond the International Sustainability Standards Board (ISSB), Glasgow Financial Alliance for Net Zero (GFANZ), UK Transition Plan Task Force (UK-TFT), Climate Action 100 + (CA-100) net zero guidance frameworks from which to evaluate the viability of company net zero transition plans.

This book is a "must read" for legal counsel, advisors, executives, directors, and managers with fiduciary-related accountability for companies or institutional investors."

Keith Johnson, Former Chief Legal Counsel,
State of Wisconsin Investment Board (SWIB)
Co-Editor, Cambridge Handbook of Institutional Investment
and Fiduciary Duty
National Association of Public Pension Attorneys, Former President

NET ZERO BUSINESS MODELS

NET ZERO BUSINESS MODELS

Winning in the Global Net Zero Economy

John Montgomery and Mark Van Clieaf

WILEY

For general information on our other products and services or for technical support, please contact our Customer Care Department within the United States at (800) 762-2974, outside the United States at (317) 572-3993 or fax (317) 572-4002.

Wiley also publishes its books in a variety of electronic formats. Some content that appears in print may not be available in electronic formats. For more information about Wiley products, visit our web site at www.wiley.com.

Library of Congress Cataloging-in-Publication Data is Available:

ISBN 9781119895060 (Hardback)
ISBN 9781119895084 (ePDF)
ISBN 9781119895077 (epub)

Cover Design and Image: © Denise Bonte
John Montgomery/Photo Credit: © Todd Pickering
Mark Van Clieaf/Photo Credit: © Leino Ole - Halton Headshots

SKY10039803_120922

CONTENTS

Contents

Contents

Contents

Contents

LIST OF EXHIBITS

LIST OF APPENDICES

PROLOGUE

Inverness, California, and Toronto, Ontario
29 September 2022

During our collaboration on a project to make the strategic duties of corporate directors explicit under Delaware law, we noted that BlackRock Chairman Larry Fink's 2021 letter to CEOs demanded that businesses prepare plans to conform their business models to a net zero emissions economy but the letter had little guidance on how to do so. We suspected that most companies would grossly underestimate the magnitude of the transformation required to conform their business models to a net zero emissions economy and be commercially successful.

To test this hypothesis, Credit Suisse HOLT® helped Mark and his FutureZero team stress-test over 14,000 public companies with available carbon data for a hypothetical carbon price of $75 per metric ton of CO_2 emissions. The stress-test revealed that every industrial sector except energy has material capital markets securities mispricing risk relative to the prospective carbon shock. This stress test scenario analysis only included Scope 1 and Scope 2 emissions. The analysis suggested that more than 40% of the companies analyzed will require a complete transformation of their business models to achieve net zero.

The stress-test showed a clear need for *Net Zero Business Models* because the prevailing conversation greatly underestimates the risk to individual companies, specific industries, and the overall financial system posed by a potential real carbon cost and does not recognize the need to integrate reducing greenhouse gas emissions with companies' core business strategies and business model design. In October 2021, Mark, the FutureZero team, Sustainalytics, and Credit Suisse HOLT® held a virtual conference on net zero business models that attracted over 2,000 people from 38 countries and over $50 trillion in assets under management. The audience for this event was four times larger than expected, which confirmed the urgent need for *Net Zero Business Models*.

During this time, James (Jim) Goodfellow, a corporate director and former vice chairman of Deloitte & Touche, LLP (Canada) and Alan Willis, a corporate sustainability advisor and former Deloitte partner, began to collaborate with us on this book and particularly on the strategic options available to companies to conform their business models to a net zero economy.

Jim and Alan provided critical strategic advice on the four transformational Pathways described in Part III, wrote an outline for each chapter in Part III, developed the questions for corporate directors and institutional investors to ask management about the Pathways included in the Appendices for Part III, and provided editorial input on Chapter 14, Telling the Net Zero Story. Their contributions to *Net Zero Business Models* were legion. They brought clarity and precision to the concept of the four Pathways and brought a unique combination of experience, wisdom, and levity to the writing process.

To help ensure the narrative voice of this book is authentic and credible, John decided to conform his life and consulting business to the net zero emissions economy to better understand the kind of transformation that this entails.

During the Covid-19 pandemic, John had already reduced his flight miles from 50,000 per year to zero, curtailed his driving in an electric Chevrolet Bolt to 4,000 miles per year, and given up a small office in Point Reyes Station to work from home. John discovered, however, that he had a long way to go to conform his business and personal lives to a net zero emissions economy. John and his wife, Maggie, installed a solar power system and a rain catchment system to irrigate the garden. They replaced the remaining incandescent bulbs in their house with low watt-age LED lights and are replacing a propane furnace that heats a radiant water heating system with a heat pump powered by the new solar system.

Mark and his wife, Susan, have been on a similar personal journey to create a smart and sustainable home. This included complete LED lighting with indoor and outdoor lighting automation and internet-enabled ther-mostats to control heating and cooling, which resulted in improved energy efficiency and energy conservation for their home. Mark uses a 56-volt electric powered lawnmower, leaf blower, and snowblower; all are powered by the Ontario electric power grid, whose power generation mix is 93% carbon free energy.

John enrolled in Being First's course: Leading Transformational Change. Being First's co-founders, Dean and Linda Anderson, are two of the world's foremost experts on corporate transformation and co-authors of *Beyond Change Management* and *The Change Leader's Roadmap*.[1,2] Dean and Linda's life work helped us see that conforming a company's business model to a net zero economy will often require an epic transformation of the entire company. Their work helped us refine the narrative arc of *Net Zero Business Models*, provided us with many useful insights to frame some of the concepts in this book, and provided much of the foundation for Chapter 12, Preparing to Lead the Transformation.

The last three years also dispelled whatever residual skepticism John may have had about the reality of climate change. During the 2019 Kincade Fire that burned 77,000 acres in neighboring Sonoma County, John and Maggie were without power and water for six days and sheltered six evac-uees and their six pets until they could return home safely. The Woodward Fire, which burned nearly 5,000 acres in the Point Reyes National Seashore in 2020, came within a mile of their house and put them on evacuation standby for three weeks. And 2021 was the second consecutive year of severe drought and brought water rationing to their hamlet. As we write this, a heat wave that brought record temperatures of 115°F (46°C) to Sonoma County is finally subsiding.

What really motivated us to write this book, however, was not the fires and drought but observing John's new greenhouse. Growing tomatoes in the cool, foggy coastal climate of Northern California is almost impossible. In his greenhouse, however, tomatoes thrive. The greenhouse gets so hot in the summer that they must open the windows and doors to prevent the tomatoes from wilting to death. His greenhouse made the urgency of our climate crisis real to us: there are no windows and doors in our atmosphere to let out the extra heat trapped by greenhouse gases as there are in John's greenhouse.

Today, we are excited to share this book and provide insights about best practices and direction for the global conversation about net zero and to help companies compete to win in the emerging global net zero emissions economy. We are optimistic that collectively we can innovate and transform the global economy into a net zero emissions one in time for our children, grandchildren, and future generations to inherit a habitable, healthy, and sustainable planet.

John Montgomery and Mark Van Clieaf

NOTES

1. Anderson, D. and Anderson, L. (2010). *Beyond Change Management: How to Achieve Breakthrough Results Through Conscious Change Leadership*. San Francisco: Pfeiffer.
2. Anderson, D. and Anderson, L. (2010). *The Change Leader's Roadmap: How to Navigate Your Organization's Transformation*. San Francisco: Pfeiffer.

FOREWORD

The concept of net zero has quickly evolved as the principal yardstick against which government policy ambitions and private sector activities on climate actions are proclaimed.

Propelled by the UN's Intergovernmental Panel on Climate Change (IPCC)'s conclusion from October 2018 that "*limiting temperature rise to 1.5°C and preventing the worst outcomes of climate change implies reaching net zero emission of CO$_2$ by mid-century*"—net zero has quickly moved from science to policy to mainstream in less than a decade.

Net zero pledges and commitments are everywhere—announced by two-thirds of the world's governments responsible for more than 90% of global GDP and 80% of the world's population. Concurrently, the private sector with about one-third of the largest publicly listed corporations representing annual revenues of more than US$25 trillion alongside the US$130 trillion Glasgow Financial Alliance for Net Zero (GFANZ) financial services coalition have announced net zero ambitions.

However, metrics and targets are not a plan, a commitment is not a long-term business strategy—without the implementation of a credible and bona fide strategic transition plan. While the airwaves have been flushed with net zero announcements, accompanying strategic actions have been amiss.

The Climate Action 100+ Net Zero Company Benchmark in October 2022 showed 75% of focus companies had announced at least a partial net zero target, but only 19% had produced quantified decarbonization strategies and related business plans including Innovation, R&D, and CAPEX plans. Thus, the real merits of net zero are in the understanding of the strategic decisions, operational actions, cashflows, returns on capital, and strategic leadership capacity required by corporations over the next three decades, and especially during the 2020s, that will enable an orderly transition to a net zero global economy.

Net Zero Business Models creates such a robust analytical framework that will help corporations and investors analyze the required strategic decisions of the transition. The **Five Core Eco-Efficiency Processes** outlines a set of the "must-have" minimum requirements that any net zero transition plan must include to be comprehensive and a credible plan. The **Four Pathways to Net Zero** discusses and outlines the critical strategic business model choices facing every corporation's executive management and board of directors—their banking and insurance providers, as well as their existing and potential debt and equity investors.

The **Three Domains of Systems Thinking** outlines the strategic leadership capacity of the C-Suite and Board required to transform business models, and in some cases, complete industry eco-systems to net zero, while achieving a return on capital greater than the cost of capital.

In short, *Net Zero Business Models* presents an invaluable analytical framework built on insightful contributions from leading business strategy and finance experts along with sustainability practitioners in the real economy. It provides a playbook for corporate boards, the C-Suite, and investors alike to evaluate and implement the optimal net zero transition strategies and plans that will create long-term sustainable and competitive business models and assess whether companies are on the path to thrive, survive, or die.

Henrik K Jeppesen, CFA
Director, ESG Implementation at Janus
Henderson Investors
Co-chair of the Sustainable Investing Group at
the CFA Society New York.

PREFACE

We wrote *Net Zero Business Models* to guide companies to transition successfully from an economy based on fossil fuels to a global net zero emissions economy. *Net Zero Business Models* is a primer, a toolkit for business model design, and a collection of best practices about how to conform a company's business model to a net zero emissions economy and achieve commercial success, including longer-term shareholder and societal value.

We assume readers have accepted the scientific consensus that greenhouse gases are contributing to global warming and we must act to reduce greenhouse gas emissions to limit global temperature rise to 1.5°C. Our overarching vision for *Net Zero Business Models* is to facilitate and accelerate the transition to a net zero emissions economy, and, ultimately, to a regenerative economy and civilization so our children and grandchildren can thrive on a healthy planet.

To better understand the rapidly emerging global conversation, we conducted primary research, including conversations with over 100 C-Suite executives, corporate directors, asset managers, asset owners, and other institutional investors representing over $50 trillion in assets under management. We also undertook secondary research, including reviews of key sustainability and climate-related disclosures from over 200 leading Global 2000 companies with declared net zero aspirations. *Net Zero Business Models* provides companies with a research-based framework to manage proactively and strategically the transformational forces facing every C-Suite and board of directors.

Our research identifies that many companies grossly underestimate these pressures and the enormity of the scale of transformation required for them to conform their business models to a net zero economy. Most companies do not recognize the need to fully integrate reducing their greenhouse gas emissions with their fundamental long-term business strategy.

Ultimately, we distilled a community of best practices for inventorying greenhouse emissions, setting science-based emissions-reduction targets, and creating credible and bona fide net zero transition plans that positively impact company valuation by effectively telling a company's long-term strategy and net zero business model story. We also identified the best practices of our subject companies, including those listed on Appendix P.1, for effectively telling a company's net zero story. *Net Zero Business Models* provides strategic insights for companies, their executive teams, and their boards of directors about what leading companies with declared net zero aspirations are planning, investing in, and doing to conform their business models to a global net zero economy.

Our research reveals that companies are under increasing transformational pressure. On the one hand, asset managers, asset owners, and other institutional investors demand companies conform their business models to a net zero emissions economy while simultaneously generating positive returns for shareholders. On the other hand, policy makers, legislators, and securities regulators increasingly are adopting policies and regulations to direct companies to reduce their greenhouse gas emissions and report on them. Within the next two years, the newly formed International Sustainability Accounting Standards Board, the U.S. Securities and Exchange Commission, and the UK's newly formed Net Zero Taskforce all will establish new mandatory disclosure standards for sustainability and climate reporting integrated with financial reporting. These pressures subject companies and their business models to material market and regulatory pressures and risks that will continue to increase.

We also wrote *Net Zero Business Models* to help frame and direct the global conversation about net zero emissions, net zero emission business models, the transition to a net zero emissions economy, and, ultimately, the transition to a net zero emissions civilization. The prevailing conversation is challenged not only by a lack of a common pattern language but also by an overly simplistic focus on regulating, measuring, monitoring, auditing, and reducing emissions of greenhouse gases. *Net Zero Business Models* provides a common pattern language and highlights the larger, strategic, and systems implications of reducing greenhouse gas emissions as part of a net zero business model transformation, the creation of a sustainable model for capitalism, and the transformation of civilization itself.

The transition to a net zero economy will compel companies to choose one of four strategic options to achieve a net zero business model. We call these four strategic options the "Pathways," which are discussed in Part III of this book (see Exhibit P.1). Pathway One allows a company to maintain its current business model and achieve net zero with the eco-efficiency processes and systems. Pathway Two requires companies to transform their core business models to achieve net zero. Pathway Three is about creating new net zero business models through new ventures, spinouts, and start-ups. Pathway Four challenges companies to lead the net zero transformations of their industries and related industry ecosystems. Of course, a company could continue with business as usual and do nothing to reduce its emissions, but risks getting left behind and becoming a casualty in the transition to a global net zero economy.

The appropriate strategic choice for a company depends largely on the magnitude of its greenhouse gas emissions. If a company has relatively low emissions, it may be able to preserve its existing business model with relatively minor adjustments. If a company has relatively high emissions, it may have to transform its business model to achieve net zero or risk ultimately having to wind down and liquidate because its competitors achieve net zero first, leaving it behind. *Net Zero Business Models* provides a comprehensive toolkit to guide companies to analyze their businesses to make the appropriate strategic choice to become a winner in the global net zero economy.

Transforming a business model to align with a net zero economy will be a larger transformation initiative than most companies realize. Successfully

EXHIBIT P.1 The four Pathways to success in the global net zero economy.

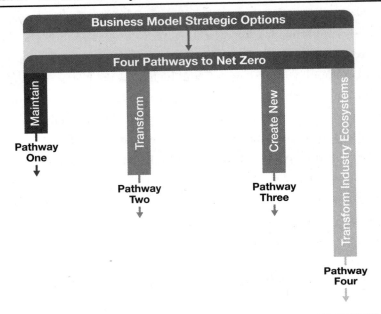

transforming a company's business model requires a team of talented executives with the appropriate strategic and systems-thinking capacities to handle the complexity of the transformation. Every company is unique, however, and there is no prescribed formula to develop its net zero transition plan. Boards of directors need sound board processes to transform their companies' business models and navigate the transition to a net zero emissions economy. *Net Zero Business Models* provides insights from quantitative and qualitative research into the required processes, benchmarks, and reporting that will empower boards of directors and executive management teams to lead their companies successfully into a net zero world.

Unfortunately, most corporate transformations fail because they focus on process without also addressing the underlying fundamental mindsets and cultural assumptions that propel the behaviors and systems necessary to drive the transformation. The leaders of a company's net zero transformation initiative need to understand the hidden dynamics of transformation so they can successfully lead it. *Net Zero Business Models* explores some of these dynamics, including some of the hidden determinants of corporate behavior such as the doctrine of shareholder primacy and neoliberal economics. These dynamics may impede a company's ability to conform its business model successfully to a net zero economy in time.

Finally, *Net Zero Business Models* provides a preliminary roadmap for the second leg of the transformational journey to a regenerative global economy and regenerative civilization. Achievement of a net zero emissions economy is only the first step in the journey to create a regenerative economy that reverses the global warming caused by the fossil fuel–based economy and restores the biosphere to lower levels of greenhouse gases. Climate change will only continue to accelerate, and its effects worsen, until we achieve net zero emissions. Temperatures will only stabilize if we can reverse the damage by achieving net zero and sequestering the carbon we have emitted into the atmosphere. The transition to a global net zero emissions economy paves the way for the further transition to a regenerative civilization based on care for each other and our planet that will provide a stable long-term basis for the global economy.

INTRODUCTION: HOW TO USE THIS BOOK

The primary purpose of *Net Zero Business Models* is to prepare companies, their executive teams, and their boards of directors to compete successfully and win in the net zero emissions economy. *Net Zero Business Models* outlines a process to conform a company's business model to a net zero emissions economy and be commercially successful.

In the context of the net zero economy and this book, a company that is commercially successful enjoys positive revenue growth, funds operations and capital expenditures internally, and produces an economic profit greater than the cost of capital over the timeframe needed to attain net zero emissions. (See Exhibit I.1.) *Net Zero Business Models* provides a framework for companies to use to develop their net zero transition plans to be among the winners in the transition from an economy based on fossil fuels to a zero-emission one, which we call the "Great Transformation."

Although we wrote *Net Zero Business Models* primarily for officers and directors of public companies, the book is useful for asset owners, asset managers, and other institutional investors who need to discern whether their portfolio companies have credible and bona fide net zero transition plans or are just greenwashing.

Net Zero Business Models provides asset owners, asset managers, and other institutional investors with useful frameworks to analyze how well their portfolio companies are progressing toward net zero and managing the related risks and opportunities so they can invest in the winners in the

EXHIBIT I.1 Winning business models: commercial and net zero success

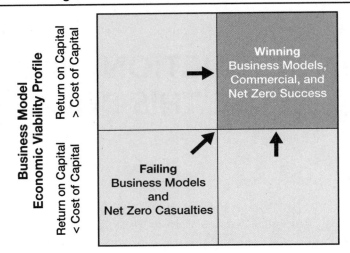

race to net zero. *Net Zero Business Models* will also assist commercial banks and other lenders in the risk and credit modeling of their lending and credit portfolios.

Net Zero Business Models is useful for regulators and policymakers trying to make sense of the conversation about net zero. The frameworks provided in the book can inform them about how to enact smart regulations, policies, and net zero disclosure standards to accelerate the transformation first to a net zero emissions economy and then to a regenerative economy.

Net Zero Business Models is useful for entrepreneurs and venture capitalists starting new companies in the net zero economy. New companies will have a competitive advantage in the net zero economy if they incorporate their companies with net zero, and circular, business models from the beginning. *Net Zero Business Models* provides entrepreneurs and venture capital investors with frameworks to design companies for success in the net zero economy and beyond.

Net Zero Business Models is useful for management consultants, accountants, lawyers, and other professional advisors counseling corporations about how to transition their business models to a net zero emissions economy. Finally, the book is useful for academics teaching courses about sustainable business in business schools and universities.

The book is organized into five parts. Part I sets the context for net zero business models. Part II lays the technical foundation for the four strategic pathways to achieve net zero described in Part III, which we call "Pathways." Part III introduces the heroes of the book, the four net zero Pathways. Part IV suggests how to put the four Pathways into action. Part V suggests how the creation of a net zero economy may be part of a larger transformation to stakeholder capitalism and a more just, inclusive, and regenerative civilization that takes care of the planet and the well-being of its citizens.

PART I: SETTING THE CONTEXT FOR NET ZERO

Part I sets the overall context of the Great Transformation and the business case for having net zero business models that achieve commercial success.

Chapter 1 identifies the key transformational forces driving the Great Transformation. These key forces include the changing expectations and demands of customers, institutional investors, and other stakeholders on the one hand and materially changing carbon policies and prices, legislation, and regulations on the other. These forces put business models under tremendous transformational pressure. This pressure will only intensify as the decade progresses to the critical 2030 milestone of reducing greenhouse gas (GHG) emissions by 50% and the effects of climate change continue to worsen.

Chapter 1 also introduces some of the key terminology relating to net zero and discusses the business opportunities inherent in the transition to a net zero economy.

PART II: THE TECHNICAL FOUNDATIONS OF NET ZERO BUSINESS MODELS

Part II provides the technical foundation to help companies critically assess business models in the context of the Great Transformation. The global conversation about GHGs and the transition to a global net zero economy is largely focused on the technical subject matter of Part II.

The material in Part II will be familiar to companies that already have inventoried their GHG emissions, determined their carbon shorts, and set near-term and long-term science-based emissions-reduction targets. Executives from these companies can use Part II as a reference and jump ahead to Part III to explore the Pathways.

The material in Part II will be particularly useful for the 71% of companies that have not inventoried their GHGs completely or have conducted only partial inventories of them.

Chapter 2 introduces the Greenhouse Gas Protocol and the GHG Corporate Accounting and Reporting Standard (GHG Protocol) and Scope 1, 2, and 3 emissions.[1] Scope 1 and 2 emissions generally are easier for companies to quantify because they fall under their immediate control. Scope 3 emissions are more challenging to quantify because they are emitted in companies' value chains and are not under a company's immediate control. Scope 3 emissions have 15 categories and require companies to collaborate with their value chains to quantify them.

It is important to acknowledge that the GHG Protocol is far from perfect and has some detractors, but it has emerged as the global standard for GHG corporate accounting, performance measurement, and reporting.

Chapter 2 is the most technical chapter of the book, but its content is critical to understanding greenhouse gas emissions. This understanding will provide a base of foundational knowledge that allows companies to inventory their emissions, develop targets to reduce them, and choose a Pathway to achieve net zero. To win in the net zero economy, a company's greenhouse gas inventory must include all Scope 1, 2 and 3 emissions.

Chapter 3 will help companies determine their carbon intensity and assess their vulnerability to a carbon shock in the form of a carbon tax or fee. Some jurisdictions, such as Canada, have already adopted an escalating carbon tax on CO_2 emissions. Other jurisdictions such as California and the European Union have adopted so called "cap-and-trade" regimes, which set yearly allowances on emissions that effectively create a carbon price through trading. Understanding the carbon intensity of a company's current business model and exposure to potential carbon shocks in the various jurisdiction in which it operates helps it set strategy and conduct effective scenario planning.

Companies need to understand not only their absolute GHG emissions profile but also the potential business risks that GHG emissions pose to future revenues and profits. Understanding a company's carbon intensity using the key performance indicator of metric tons of CO_2 equivalent (CO_2e) GHGs per \$1 million of revenue provides strategic insight to compare emissions performance across products and business units and with its competitors and industry sector. A company's business model, when stress-tested for a carbon fee of \$75 or \$100 per metric ton, may simply no longer be viable economically in its current design and at its current level of emissions.

Chapter 4 introduces the Science Based Targets Initiative (SBTi) and science-based emissions-reduction targets. This chapter will help companies set near-term and long-term emissions-reduction targets, which may be verified by the SBTi. These targets are complemented by their eco-efficiency targets discussed in Chapter 5 and their other emissions reduction–related goals. For example, an automobile manufacturer may set targets to have 5 electric vehicle models by 2025, 20 models by 2030, and an entirely electric vehicle product line by 2035.

It is important to acknowledge that the SBTi Corporate Net Zero Standard is far from perfect and has many detractors, but it is emerging as the global standard in setting science-based emissions-reduction targets.[2]

PART III: THE FOUR PATHWAYS TO NET ZERO

Part III presents the four strategic Pathways to conform a company's business model to a net zero economy and takes the global conversation beyond GHGs into strategies to design net zero business models. The Pathways provide a framework to analyze a company's current business model to identify the gap between its current state and the desired future net zero business model design. This analysis determines the magnitude of change required to conform its business model to a net zero economy and be commercially successful. This strategic analysis will also reveal whether its business model needs to be modified incrementally or completely redesigned and transformed.

The Pathways present integrated strategies that align a company's journey to net zero with commercial success and fully integrate the transition to net zero with a company's overall business strategy. The winners in the Great Transformation will focus on finding opportunities on the journey to net zero to innovate and create value. On the other hand, the losers and laggards, as casualties of the net zero economy, will focus on defending their existing business models and product portfolios. In other words, the journey to net zero provides a strategic opportunity for companies to create competitive advantage as measured by premium returns on capital after the cost of capital and the future cost of carbon.

The sooner a company analyzes its existing business model and carbon intensity and chooses the optimal strategic Pathway, the better. If a company is an early adopter of an effective net zero business model in its industry, it may garner a competitive advantage, earn a sustainability valuation premium in its enterprise value through better environmental, social, governance (ESG) performance, and become an industry leader.

Chapter 5 provides an overview of each of the four Pathways. The Pathways progress from low to high strategic planning complexity and from maintaining the current business model to leading an industry-wide transformation.

Chapter 6 provides an overview of Pathway One: Eco-Efficiency. Companies that choose Pathway One maintain their current business models and achieve net zero through eco-efficiency business processes and systems. Pathway One is best suited for companies that have low carbon intensity. Some companies with higher carbon intensity may choose Pathway One to defend their existing business models and try to achieve net zero through eco-efficiency business processes and systems and by using carbon offsets, carbon credits, and carbon capture.

Chapter 7 provides an overview of Pathway Two, Option One: Incremental Business Model Transformation—Zero-Carbon Products and Services. On this version of Pathway Two, companies create a portfolio of zero-emission products and services. Companies innovate to not only reduce the carbon footprint of their existing products and services but also to develop or acquire new breakthrough, zero-carbon businesses, products, and services.

This version of Pathway Two is transformational because it requires companies to reassess the fundamentals of their core business models and to restructure and transform their entire portfolio of products and services to achieve zero emissions.

Chapter 8 provides an overview of Pathway Two, Option Two: Complete Transformation of the Business Model. Companies that choose this version of Pathway Two innovate not only to create a portfolio of zero-carbon emission products and services but also to let go of their current business models, which are the basis of their success in the fossil fuel–based economy.

This version of Pathway Two increases the magnitude of transformational change required because it requires companies to transform their business models completely. Companies often reinvent the fundamental purposes of their businesses to reflect a brand-new business model.

Chapter 9 provides an overview of Pathway Three: Eco-Startups, New Ventures, Spinouts, and Industry Disrupters. Companies that choose Pathway Three create an entirely new net zero business. An established company on Pathway Three might spinout, create, or acquire an independent business with a net zero business model and low- or no-carbon footprint. New startups and new ventures on Pathway Three create new net zero business models with low or no GHG emissions.

Companies on Pathway Three have an advantage because there is no legacy businesses, assets, or processes to be modified or transformed. Pathway Three companies are built to succeed in the net zero economy from the start.

Chapter 10 provides an overview of Pathway Four: Industry Ecosystem(s) Transformers. Companies that choose Pathway Four face an even larger transformational change than those on Pathway Two, Option Two because they choose to lead the transformation of their entire industry and its related ecosystem(s). Any Pathway One, Pathway Two, or Pathway Three company could choose to lead the transformation of its industry to achieve net zero.

There are many industries, such as the energy, power utilities, transportation, materials, and manufacturing industries, that may be particularly ripe for industry level transformation and disruption because these industry sectors have relatively high carbon intensity in their current state design. This may create a historic opportunity for companies in high carbon industries not only to achieve net zero but also gain a competitive advantage by leading a multi-decade industry-wide transformation.

PART IV: IMPLEMENTING A PATHWAY TO NET ZERO

Part IV discusses how companies can implement their chosen Pathway and moves the global conversation beyond GHGs and strategies for designing net zero business models into action. Leading a company through the Great Transformation to a net zero business model is a major undertaking, especially if it has high carbon intensity. The good news is that by the time a company is ready to implement its chosen Pathway, most of the critical decisions have already been made. Those critical decisions include all the processes discussed in Parts II and III: inventorying greenhouse gases, determining carbon intensity, performing a carbon shock test, setting eco-efficiency targets, setting near-term and long-term science-based emissions-reduction targets, and selecting the appropriate Pathway.

Chapter 11 introduces Bartley Madden's Innovation and Return on Capital Life Cycle framework as a foundational strategic analytical process to help companies choose the appropriate Pathway.[3] This life-cycle framework provides an innovation and risk perspective that incorporates the implications of a potential carbon shock on a company's business model, its returns on capital, and its enterprise value that should be considered before a company chooses its optimal Pathway to net zero.

Chapter 12 discusses the challenges inherent in corporate transformations. Chapter 12 is immediately relevant for companies that choose Pathway Two or Pathway Four and may become relevant for Pathway One and Pathway Three companies that later decide to lead transformations of their industries. Chapter 12 helps companies optimize the probability they will transform their business models or industries successfully to have net zero emissions and be commercially successful.

Chapter 13 explores the three domains of systems thinking and related leadership capacity for complexity required for each Pathway to achieve net zero and commercial success. The sheer magnitude of change required to conform a business model to a net zero economy may overwhelm the current strategic and systems-thinking capacities of a board of directors and the executive management team, especially for Pathway Two, Option Two and Pathway Four companies which require strong strategic leadership and systems-thinking capacities in the C-Suite. Each Pathway represents a shift in the complexity of the challenges facing all levels of management and the level of systems-thinking and leadership capacity for complexity required in the C-Suite. Chapter 13 helps a company assess whether it has the right strategic leadership talent in the C-Suite and boardroom now, and a C-Suite talent pipeline for the next 5 to 20 years to succeed on its chosen Pathway.

Chapter 14 explores how companies can best tell their net zero transition stories to all their stakeholders. Chapter 14 explores the evolution of various ESG and climate-related reporting standards and reporting requirements so a company can tell its story with authority and credibility. Chapter 14 also prepares publicly listed companies for impending climate-related mandatory disclosure requirements under development by securities regulators worldwide.

Chapter 15 explores the many overt and hidden obstacles companies and the economy encounter on the journey to net zero. Chapter 15 explores the most common obstacles, including various forms of greenwashing, and suggests strategies for overcoming them.

PART V BEYOND NET ZERO: SYSTEMS CHANGE

Chapter 16 explores how a company's journey to net zero may be part of a larger transformation to a net zero civilization based on care for the planet and all its inhabitants. All sectors of the global economy recognize that now is the time for urgent, long-term-oriented action and investment to conform business models to a net zero economy. There is also a growing recognition that capitalism and the economic system need an upgrade to live within the limits of the biosphere and provide sustainable prosperity for all.

NOTES

1. Greenhouse Gas Protocol. (2021). CHG Protocol Corporate Accounting and Reporting Standard (October). https://ghgprotocol.org/corporate-standard.
2. Science Based Targets Initiative. (2021). SBTi corporate net-zero standard (October). https://sciencebasedtargets.org/resources/files/Net-Zero-Standard.pdf.
3. Holland, D. and Matthews, B. (2018). *Beyond Earnings: Applying the HOLT CFROI and Economic Profit Framework*. Hoboken, NJ: Wiley.

Part I

Setting the Context for Net Zero

1

THE NET ZERO OPPORTUNITY

"Every company and every industry will be transformed by the transition to a net zero world. The question is, will you lead, or will you be led?"[1]
—Larry Fink, Chairman and CEO, BlackRock

The shift from a fossil fuel–based economy to a net zero emission one is the biggest transformation project in human history (the Great Transformation). The global economy needs to achieve net zero emissions by 2050 to limit the rise in global temperature that began with the Industrial Age to a manageable 1.5°C. McKinsey & Company estimates that achieving a net zero emissions economy under the Net Zero 2050 scenario from the Network for Greening the Financial System will require $275 trillion of cumulative investments in physical assets alone by 2050.[2,3]

The Great Transformation is huge, but humanity has successfully transformed the basis of the economy before. The global economy previously transitioned its primary energy source from wood to coal and from coal to oil. Such transitions, however, were gradual and haphazard. The necessity to preserve a habitable planet for our children and grandchildren provides special urgency to the Great Transformation.

We have identified four strategic pathways companies can choose to achieve a net zero business model and commercial success in the Great Transformation, which we call the four "Pathways" and discuss at length in Part III, Chapters 5 through 10 (see Exhibit 1.1.). We briefly introduce the four Pathways here to emphasize the key point that a company's plans to eliminate the greenhouse gas (GHG) emissions from its business model must be integrated with its fundamental business and financial strategy.

EXHIBIT 1.1 The four Pathways to net zero and commercial success

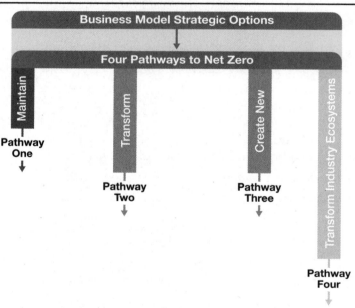

THE TRANSFORMATIONAL FORCES OF NET ZERO

Companies are under increasing transformational pressure to participate in the Great Transformation. Companies' stakeholders are pressuring them to join in the Great Transformation and will keep the pressure on until they have achieved net zero emissions. These transformational forces likely will get stronger as pressure builds to transition beyond net zero to a net negative or regenerative economy and one that also meets the UN Sustainable Development Goals (SDGs). Companies cannot escape these transformational forces, but they can proactively manage them to emerge as winners in the emergent net zero emissions economy.

Companies need to leverage these transformational forces to develop plans to conform their business models to a net zero emissions economy. One of the surest ways for companies to win in the emergent net zero emissions economy is to successfully strip the GHGs out of their business models. Companies must first conduct a complete inventory of their GHG emissions, as will be discussed in Chapter 2. This process is not merely a data collection exercise but an opportunity to identify a company's carbon dependencies—where and how much carbon enters the business process and business model, where and how much emissions are generated, and what processes and activities generate GHG emissions. This information-gathering process is time consuming but critical to determine which of the eco-efficiency and business transformation strategies discussed in Part III are appropriate.

Companies also need to use their GHG emissions data and information about their carbon dependencies to assess the financial impacts of this data and information on their business model in the event of the possible escalation in carbon prices, as will be discussed in Chapter 3. The purpose of these scenario-planning exercises is to identify the inputs and processes in the business model that have the greatest carbon dependencies to carbon emissions and their financial implications. If, for example, a core business process has high carbon intensity and there are no alternative solutions, then there is a high carbon dependency that may require a transformation of the business model.

There is also an opportunity for companies to use their GHG emissions data, information about their carbon intensities and results of testing for a carbon shock, also discussed in Chapter 3, to analyze their industries to identify the forces shaping them and to develop scenarios of what their net zero industries will look like in the future. This process will help companies identify what they need to do to compete successfully in their industries as they transition to net zero. It is challenging for companies to develop visions of the future net zero state of their industries, but the solution is to develop different scenarios and update them as the years progress and events unfold. To conduct this kind of scenario planning, however, companies must understand the transformational forces bearing down upon them:

Governments. After decades of talk, sovereign nations are getting serious about taking action to reduce GHG emissions. The European Union (EU) and 192 countries signed the Paris Agreement agreeing to reduce GHG emissions to limit the global temperature increase to 2°C while working to limit the increase to 1.5°C.[4] The EU and 33 countries have set net zero emissions targets and more than 100 countries have proposed, or are considering, net zero emissions targets.[5] The EU, for example, has adopted a 55% net emissions-reduction target from 1990 levels by 2030.[6]

These international commitments are resulting in carbon taxes and cap-and-trade trading systems aimed at reducing GHG emissions. Twenty European countries have adopted carbon taxes that range from less than €1 per metric ton of CO_2 equivalent (CO_2e) emissions in Poland and Ukraine to more than €100 per metric ton in Sweden, Lichtenstein, and Switzerland. The scope of the carbon taxes varies by country. Spain, for example, only taxes fluorinated gases. In addition, all member states in the European Union are part of the EU Emissions Trading System, a market designed to trade a capped number of GHG allowances. Switzerland and the United Kingdom have their own emission trading systems.[7]

Canada has also implemented carbon taxes on companies. The federal minimum price started at CD$20 per metric ton of CO_2e in 2019. In 2022, the tax is CD$50 per metric ton of CO_2e and will increase by CD$15 per year until it reaches CD$170 per metric ton in 2030. If Canadian provinces and territories do not accept the federal standard as the carbon tax default, they may set their own carbon taxes that meet or exceed the federal standard or adopt a cap-and-trade system to achieve the same result. Currently four provinces have accepted the federal standard, four have set their own carbon taxes, and two have adopted cap-and-trade systems.[8]

The United States has not adopted a carbon tax or cap-and-trade emissions trading system at the federal level, but 11 states are members of the Regional Greenhouse Gas Initiative designed to cap and reduce CO_2 emissions from the power sector and California has had a cap-and-trade system in place since 2013. China has also not adopted a carbon tax or cap-and-trade emission trading system at the national level, but several Chinese cities and provinces have implemented cap-and-trade programs.[9]

Publicly listed companies have become accustomed to disclosing and discussing how they address the climate-related risks to their businesses, but as will be discussed in Chapter 13, the EU and the United States have proposed securities regulations that would require companies to disclose their GHG inventories and other climate-related information starting with the 2023 fiscal year. The UK has already adopted regulations requiring public companies to make climate-related disclosures.

Institutional investors. BlackRock, the world's largest asset manager, has put public company CEOs and boards on notice that they must have strategies and transition plans to conform their business model designs to a net zero emissions economy.[10,11]

CPP Investments is a global investment management organization that invests the assets of the Canada Pension Plan (CPP) Fund in the best interests of the CPP's contributors and beneficiaries. Where climate change-related factors are material to the company, CPP Investments expects portfolio companies to have credible plans to reduce their GHG emissions. CPP Investments has proposed a three-step approach to GHG reporting and abatement that entails each company: 1) assessing its current baseline emissions, 2) identifying actions that can cost-effectively cut emissions now and 3) determining its projected abatement capacity under different carbon price assumptions.[12] CPP Investments seeks to take an active role in financing emissions reduction and supporting the decarbonization of assets.

The reallocation of capital by investors to sustainable asset classes puts pressure on companies to participate in the Great Transformation. The Glasgow Financial Alliance for Net Zero (GFANZ), for example, which includes over 450 institutional investors, banks, and insurance companies with a combined $130 trillion in assets under management, has committed to net zero and key milestones along the way.[13]

If companies fail to listen to their institutional shareholders, they may place shareholder proposals in the annual proxy statement to force companies into action. Costco's shareholders, for example, resoundingly approved a proposal without management support brought by Green Century Capital Management at the 2022 annual meeting requesting that "Costco adopt short, medium and long-term science-based [GHG] reduction targets, inclusive of emissions from its full value chain, in order to achieve net zero emissions by 2050 or sooner and to effectuate appropriate emissions reductions prior to 2030."[14,15]

If a company does not act quickly enough to align with a net zero emissions economy, its shareholders may replace its directors. Engine No. 1 led a coalition of institutional investors, for example, and was successful in replacing three directors at Exxon Mobil with its own nominated candidates who subsequently have acted as boardroom catalysts to inspire the company to develop a net zero transition plan, as will be discussed in Chapter 6.[16]

If a company has not developed a credible transition plan, it may end up in court like Shell plc (Shell). The Hague District Court in the Netherlands found that Shell owed a duty of care to Dutch citizens to prevent injury resulting from the carbon emissions associated with its operations and products.[17] Even though Shell's most recently published climate strategy contemplated reducing the carbon intensity of its products by 20% by 2030, 45% by 2035, and 100% by 2050, the court ordered Shell to reduce its overall emissions, including emissions from the use of its products, from 2019 levels on a net basis by 45% by 2030.

The value chain. Companies are under pressure to quantify and reduce their Scope 3 emissions, which are their indirect GHG emissions, such as those resulting from customers' downstream use of their products or those resulting from the upstream production of the raw materials used in their products. To be discussed further in Chapter 2, the intent behind the 15 categories of Scope 3 emissions is to encourage collaboration between companies to first gather the downstream and upstream emissions data from their value chains and then reduce emissions.

As a result, companies seeking to achieve net zero place increasingly stringent emissions-reduction requirements on their suppliers. Walmart, the world's largest retailer, for example, has enlisted over 4,500 companies in its supply chain network to eliminate a gigaton of GHG emissions from its value chain by 2030, as will be discussed in Chapter 6.[18]

Customers. Customers increasingly want companies to deliver sustainable and carbon-free products and services. A recent poll showed consumer sentiment toward electric vehicles may be reaching a tipping point in the United States, spurred, in part, by recent hikes in gasoline prices. In April 2022, 40% of consumers surveyed expected to own an electric vehicle within five years, up from only 18% in 2018.[19] As they become knowledgeable about the principles of circularity, consumers will likely also increasingly want carbon-free and circular products and services.

Climate change. Extreme weather events, heat waves, droughts, floods, and wildfires are turning up the pressure on companies to take action to reduce their GHG emissions. In 2022, India experienced its hottest March in the 122 years since weather records have been recorded there.[20] In July 2022, Europe experienced another heat wave with the UK experiencing its highest recorded temperatures in history and wildfires burned crops in France, Spain, Portugal, and Italy. At one point in July 2022, over 100 million Americans were under heat advisories. The American West is in a severe drought with the Great Salt Lake in Utah drying up and water levels of the major reservoirs on the Colorado River declining rapidly.[21] As extreme weather events, droughts, and wildfires increase around the globe, the pressure on companies to play their part in the transition to a net zero economy will only intensify.

MANAGING THE TRANSFORMATIONAL FORCES OF NET ZERO IN A VUCA WORLD

Managing in an increasingly VUCA world will make it more challenging for companies to manage the transformational forces of net zero. The acronym VUCA, which stands for volatile, uncertain, complex, and ambiguous, originated in the U.S. Army War College to describe the environment in which leaders of complex organizations operate.[22,23] In addition to managing the transformational forces of net zero, companies face an unstable operating environment with shifting economic, environmental, geopolitical, health, and technology risks. The Russia-Ukraine war, for example, has driven up the cost of fossil fuels and interrupted energy supplies, particularly in the EU. The conflict has also interrupted exports of grain and fertilizers, causing food insecurity around the world. The Covid-19 pandemic, in its third year as of this writing, has disrupted economies and wreaked havoc on global supply chains. Now, high inflation challenges global economies. Politics seem hopelessly polarized in many countries. This VUCA world is the new normal (see Exhibit 1.2).

Asset owners, asset managers, and other institutional investors also need to manage the transformational forces of net zero and the complexities of a VUCA world into their investment portfolio designs and how they engage with their portfolio companies. These investment professionals face the challenge of avoiding owning assets on the wrong side of the net zero transition while identifying those best placed to either navigate the transition successfully or provide solutions to support it.

Many investment professionals see government policy as the principal driver of the Great Transformation but CPP Investments with over $500 billion under management as of 30 September 2022 takes a more nuanced and strategic approach to long-term investment management. Richard Manley, Chief Sustainability Officer and Head of Sustainable Investing at CPP Investments, notes that CPP Investments uses five different

EXHIBIT 1.2 The transformational forces of net zero in a VUCA world

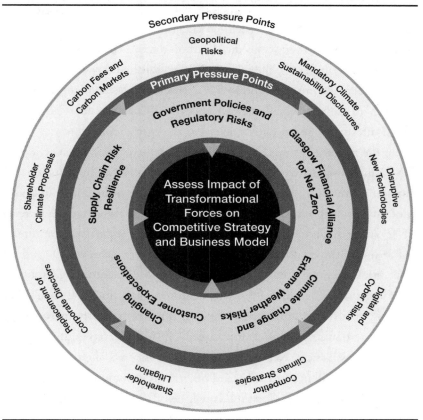

variables that echo the transformational forces that *impact* the transition to a net zero economy: government ambition and supporting regulations, development of global reporting standards and carbon markets, corporate progress toward net zero targets, development of new technologies and changing consumer and corporate behavior. Collectively, companies and investors need to adjust their approaches to net zero transition plans as these variables change to deliver the optimal net zero transition "that removes the most greenhouse gases from operations, while pursuing opportunities that create value for the business and its stakeholders."[24]

WHAT DOES "NET ZERO" MEAN?

Larry Fink, BlackRock's CEO, defined a net zero economy in his 2021 letter to CEOs as "one that emits no more carbon dioxide than it removes from the atmosphere by 2050, the scientifically-established threshold necessary to keep global warming well below 2°C." BlackRock's statement is limited, however, to carbon dioxide (CO_2) and the 2°C threshold is above the 1.5°C. threshold most scientists believe is the crucial one.

For the purposes of this book, the term "net zero" signifies an economy or a business model that produces no net GHG emissions by reducing and eliminating absolute emissions upstream and downstream across its entire value chain to support the target to limit the rise in global temperature to 1.5°C. Any remaining GHGs are offset with offsets and carbon capture.

For the purposes of this book, GHG emissions include CO_2 and all other GHGs enumerated in the *GHG Protocol*, discussed in Chapter 2, including methane, which is at least 25 times more potent than CO_2 at trapping heat in the atmosphere. Neither a net zero emissions economy nor a net zero business model eliminate all GHG emissions and, therefore, the use of fossil fuels. Net zero is not zero emissions. The economy and businesses will still produce CO_2 and other GHGs but any remaining production of hard-to-eliminate GHGs will be offset through carbon credits and carbon capture and negative emissions technologies and nature-based solutions for carbon capture.

The term net zero is not synonymous with the term "carbon neutral." People often conflate the terms, but they have very different meanings. A corporation may claim to be carbon neutral when it offsets its emissions by purchasing carbon credits or paying to remove carbon from the atmosphere without necessarily reducing or eliminating any of its own GHG emissions.

GOING BEYOND NET ZERO

Achieving a net zero economy by 2050 is a worthy goal but will probably not be enough to stabilize the climate. This is because the economy will continue to emit billions of metric tons of heat trapping GHGs into the atmosphere each year until it achieves net zero in 2050. Ultimately, the economy will need to transition from a net zero economy to a net negative one.

For the purposes of this book, a "carbon negative" economy or company is one that sequesters or eliminates more GHG emissions than it produces. Some companies, such as Microsoft, have begun to challenge net zero as the gold standard of corporate GHG emissions reduction. Microsoft has committed to be carbon negative by 2030 and to remove from the atmosphere all the carbon emitted from its operations since its incorporation in 1975, also discussed in Chapter 6.[25]

NextEra Energy, Inc., a Florida utility and one of the world's biggest renewable energy developers, is also moving beyond net zero. NextEra has committed to decarbonize its business to achieve "real zero" by 2045 by expanding its solar power generation capacity, converting its natural gas power plants to run on green hydrogen, and increasing its battery power storage capacity 100-fold. The company plans to use its expanded solar power capacity to generate green hydrogen. NextEra Energy expects to achieve real zero without using carbon capture, credits, or offsets.[26]

NextEra is engaged in three critical transformations over the next 5 to 30 years (see Appendix 1.1). The first is the transformation of its business model to real zero emissions. The second is its strategy and plan to work within the power sector to drive its transformation to real zero emissions through transformational investments, including green hydrogen gas turbines for carbon-free energy in the early 2040s and building out the power transmission, distribution, and battery storage backbone infrastructure for a smart, clean energy power grid. The third is to help lead the transformation of the U.S. economy to zero emissions by becoming the preferred partner for customers to transform their business models to net zero emissions and help customers and the United States achieve real zero emissions and the decarbonization of the economy. NextEra Energy intends that its strategy, plan, and blueprint will establish a new power industry standard for business model and power industry ecosystem transformation and decarbonization.[27]

Many businesses and industries will need to become carbon negative like Microsoft or achieve real zero emissions like NextEra because achieving a net zero economy is not the destination but a milestone on a longer journey, first to a carbon-negative global economy and then to a regenerative one that operates within the carrying capacity of the planet.

Johan Rockstrom from the Stockholm Resilience Centre identifies climate change caused by GHGs as one of nine human caused threats to components of the climate regulation system of the biosphere, including biodiversity loss, ocean acidification, ozone depletion, atmospheric aerosol pollution, freshwater use, biogeochemical flows of nitrogen and phosphorus, land-system change, and release of novel chemicals.[28,29] Each component has a maximum threshold, a planetary boundary that cannot be exceeded without putting life at risk. The race is on to achieve a net zero economy before the climate change threshold is breached (see Appendix 1.2).

Economist Kate Raworth, author of *Doughnut Economics*, calls these planetary boundaries "ecological ceilings" and combines them with the concept of "social foundations" to ensure everyone enjoys life's basic essentials, including food, water, housing, education, income and work, health, peace and justice, and gender equality (see Exhibit 16.1).[30,31] Ultimately, to be sustainable, the economy and the companies within it must operate within these planetary thresholds and ensure people's social foundations are met.

The United Nations recognizes a regenerative economy must not only be sustainable economically but also environmentally and socially. In 2015, the UN, with the support of 193 countries, adopted 17 Sustainable Development Goals (SDGs), including Goal 7, Affordable and Clean Energy; Goal 11, Sustainable Cities; and Goal 13, Climate Action, to achieve a better and more sustainable future by 2030 (see Appendix 1.3).

While each individual goal is important, all goals are interconnected and collectively provide a blueprint for a peaceful and prosperous future for people and the planet that transcends and includes a net zero economy. Many corporations, including Nestlé, ENI, and Vattenfall discussed in this book, have also incorporated the SDGs in their business strategies and net zero transition plans.

While the focus of this book is on net zero business models and the achievement of a net zero emissions global economy, there is a bigger opportunity for companies to think beyond net zero in crafting their long-term strategies to compete successfully in the net zero global economy and, more importantly, to lead the way to a sustainable and regenerative future.

WHAT DOES THE TRANSITION TO A NET ZERO ECONOMY LOOK LIKE?

Unfortunately, BlackRock's call to action contains little guidance about what a net zero economy looks like and what should be the core elements of a credible, bona fide, and even legally defensible net zero transition plan. The International Energy Agency (IEA) published a blueprint for the energy sector outlining how the global economy can achieve net zero emissions by 2050.[32] The IEA is careful to declare that its blueprint is not *the* blueprint but just one possible pathway to a net zero economy. Given recent disruptions in global energy markets caused by the Russia-Ukraine war, the IEA is in the process of updating its blueprint to better incorporate geopolitical risks.

Some countries have also promulgated country-specific roadmaps of how their national economies can achieve net zero emissions by 2050, such as the United Kingdom's UK Net Zero Strategy: Build Back Greener.[33] These roadmaps are useful in highlighting that achieving a net zero emissions economy will require a nonlinear, creative, iterative process that involves a variety of solutions to limit the rise in global temperatures to 1.5°C by 2050 and the domains of systems thinking, as will be discussed in Chapter 13.

The online En-ROADS Climate Solutions Simulator, a joint project of Climate Interactive and the MIT Management Sustainability Initiative, provides users with a better sense of how various combinations of these solutions will work in concert.[34] The simulator identifies the principal contributors to global warming, including GHG emissions, deforestation, and the relative contributions to GHG emissions of oil, natural gas, and coal. The simulator allows users to adjust the mix and intensity of solutions to quickly model strategies to mitigate emissions to limit global warming to 1.5°C by 2050. The simulator quickly shows which actions, such as eliminating methane emissions, will have the biggest positive impact on limiting global warming.

Using the simulator quickly confirms that fossil fuels—coal, petroleum, natural gas, and methane—are the largest contributors to global warming, generating about 70% of total GHGs. Using the simulator also confirms that achieving a net zero economy is simply not possible without reducing or eliminating GHG emissions from combusting fossil fuels. Spending time on the simulator brings to life models such as the IEA blueprint, the UK Net Zero Strategy, and the Net Zero 2050 scenario from the Network for Greening the Financial System discussed earlier because it allows users to quickly design and model many pathways that could achieve a net zero economy.

Collectively, the economy has a long journey ahead to net zero. According to a World Economic Forum and Boston Consulting Group analysis of Carbon Disclosure Project and Refinitiv data, only about 9% of companies have set net zero emissions targets and reduced their emissions. Most of the companies that have reduced their emissions, however, have not achieved a reduction of emissions at an annual rate sufficient to achieve a 50% overall reduction in emissions by 2030 (see Exhibit 1.3).[35]

Many companies have set some net zero emission targets, but most still do not know what this means at the operating level. Fewer companies have detailed transition plans of how they will get to net zero by 2050 or how to achieve 25 to 30% reductions in GHG emissions by 2025 and 50% reductions by 2030. Fortunately, many companies, including Microsoft, NextEra, Nestlé, Ørsted, Vattenfall, and other companies discussed in this book, have already promulgated comprehensive net zero transition plans that can help companies design their own. A few companies such as

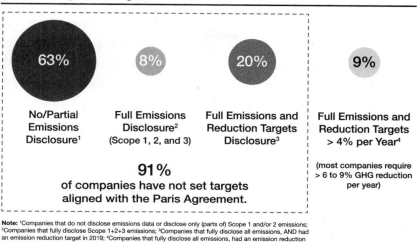

EXHIBIT 1.3 **91% of companies have yet to set targets aligned with Paris Agreement goals**

63%

8%

20%

9%

No/Partial Emissions Disclosure[1]

Full Emissions Disclosure[2] (Scope 1, 2, and 3)

Full Emissions and Reduction Targets Disclosure[3]

Full Emissions and Reduction Targets > 4% per Year[4]

(most companies require > 6 to 9% GHG reduction per year)

91% of companies have not set targets aligned with the Paris Agreement.

Note: [1]Companies that do not disclose emissions data or disclose only (parts of) Scope 1 and/or 2 emissions; [2]Companies that fully disclose Scope 1+2+3 emissions; [3]Companies that fully disclose all emissions, AND had an emission reduction target in 2019; [4]Companies that fully disclose all emissions, had an emission reduction target in 2019, AND reduced emissions 2018 vs. 2019 by > 4%.

Source: Boston Consulting Group based on Carbon Disclosure Project data and Refinitiv data from 2018 to 2020.

Ørsted can provide companies with additional guidance because they have largely completed their transformation to a net zero business model that is also commercially successful.

THE NET ZERO OPPORTUNITY

The real opportunity for companies lies in bridging the gap between their net zero transition plans and their implementation. The need to develop such a credible and bona fide transition plan invites companies to lead the transformation to a net zero economy. Leading the transformation might mean developing new carbon-free products and services, redesigning a business model to be carbon-free, creating an entirely new innovative business, or leading a complete transformation of an industry. These kinds of initiatives will naturally align a transition plan with a company's overall purpose, strategy, and vision, giving it pull to complement the push provided by the transformational forces of net zero. This will transform net zero transition plans from something being forced upon companies into something companies can enthusiastically stand behind because implementing them will make them better businesses.

Companies that treat creating a net zero transition plan as merely another item for their ESG checklists will miss the opportunity to align the plan with their overall purpose, strategy, and vision to create enterprise value by creating products and services aligned with a net zero, and circular, economy. Generally, if someone brings up a climate-related issue in the boardroom, the board will say, "Give it to the Chief Sustainability Officer," and the issue never comes back to the board. The transition to a net zero emission business model, however, is a business strategy issue that belongs in the boardroom because it may require a fundamental redesign of the business model and allocation of capital. Creating a net zero transition plan goes to the core of the fiduciary duties of corporate directors. Net zero is not only about reducing GHG emissions but also about core business strategy. Companies have also found that taking climate action delivers many benefits, finding it helps improve brand reputation, increases investor confidence, boosts resilience against regulations, and achieves cost reductions.

Having a credible net zero transition plan aligned and fully integrated with a company's current strategy and vision may not be enough to achieve a net zero business model. For many companies, especially those with high GHG emissions, achieving net zero will require a complete transformation of their business models and an overhaul of their strategies and visions. Companies need to get all their stakeholders behind their net zero transition plans to optimize the probability of success because it will be a long journey to achieve net zero by 2050.

SUMMARY: WHERE TO BEGIN

In many companies, climate-related programs get delegated to the sustainability or ESG function. To achieve a net zero business model, however, companies need to fully integrate their net zero transition plans into their overall business strategy and operations. To succeed, companies need to make the transition to a net zero business model integral to their core business strategy.

The biggest challenge, however, will not be how to come up with net zero transition plans but how to put them into action. Implementing a net zero transition plan may require change leadership and a transformation strategy, as will be discussed in Chapter 12. Companies need to assess the systems-thinking capacities of their current management teams to ensure they have the requisite strategic and systems-thinking capabilities to be able to implement a net zero transition plan, as will be discussed in Chapter 13.

For starters, however, companies need valid, accurate, and even third-party verified data about their total Scope 1, 2, and 3 GHG emissions to understand the gap between their current business models and their future net zero business models. The size of the gap varies from industry to industry depending on its carbon intensity. To address the gap, companies need to understand their carbon intensity in terms of metric tons of CO_2e per million dollars of revenue. Chapter 2 discusses the *GHG Protocol*, Scope 1, 2, and 3 emissions, and how companies can analyze their total GHG footprints.

Companies that have already inventoried their GHGs and set science-based emissions-reduction targets, to be discussed in Chapter 4, can use Part II (Chapters 2 through 4) as reference material and skip directly to Part III (Chapters 5 through 10).

Companies that have not inventoried their GHGs and set science-based emissions-reduction targets can use Part II as a primer on the *GHG Protocol*, carbon intensity, carbon shock stress testing, and setting science-based emissions-reduction targets.

NOTES

1. BlackRock, Inc. (2022). Larry Fink's 2021 letter to CEOs: the power of capitalism. https://www.blackrock.com/corporate/investor-relations/larry-fink-ceo-letter.
2. Network for Greening the Financial System. (n.d.). Scenarios Portal. https://www.ngfs.net/ngfs-scenarios-portal/explore/ (accessed 19 August 2022).

3. Krishnan, M., Samandari, H., Woetzel, J., et al. (2022). The economic transformation: what would change in the net-zero transition. McKinsey & Company blog (25 January). https://www.mckinsey.com/business-functions/ sustainability/our-insights/the-economic-transformation-what-would-change-in-the-net-zero-transition (accessed 19 August 2022).

4. The United Nations. The Paris Agreement. https://www.un.org/en/ climatechange/paris-agreement (accessed 19 August 2022).

5. Climate Action Tracker. (n.d.). Net zero targets. https://climateactiontracker .org/methodology/net-zero-targets/ (accessed 19 August 2022).

6. European Environment Agency. (n.d.). EU achieves 20-20-20 climate targets, 55% emissions cuts by 2030 reachable with more efforts and policies. https:// www.eea.europa.eu/highlights/eu-achieves-20-20-20 (accessed 19 August 2022).

7. Bray, S. (2022). Carbon taxes in Europe. Tax Foundation blog (14 June). https://taxfoundation.org/carbon-taxes-in-europe-2022/.

8. Globe Staff. (2021). Canada's carbon pricing: how much is it and how does it work? What you need to know. *The Toronto Globe and Mail* (25 March; updated 1 April 2022). https://www.theglobeandmail.com/canada/article-canada-carbon-tax-explained/.

9. The Regional Greenhouse Gas Initiative. www.rggi.org/ (accessed 19 August 2022).

10. BlackRock, Inc. (2021). Larry Fink's 2021 letter to CEOs: the power of capitalism.

11. BlackRock, Inc. (2022). Climate risk and the global energy transition (February). https://www.blackrock.com/corporate/literature/publication/blk-commentary-climate-risk-and-energy-transition.pdf.

12. CPP Investments. (2021). The future of climate change transition report-ing: decarbonizing the economy, molecule by molecule. CPP Investments Insights Institute (31 October). CPP Investments Insights Institute, 2 November 2022, The Decarbonization Imperative. *https://www.cppinvestments.com/insights-institute/the-decarbonization-imperative* (Accessed *15 November* 2022).

13. Glasgow Financial Alliance for Net Zero. www.gfanzero.com/ (accessed 19 August 2022).

14. Costco Wholesale Corporation. (2022). Schedule 14A for Costco Wholesale Corporation for 2021. U.S. Securities and Exchange Commission. https://

www.sec.gov/Archives/edgar/data/0000909832/000090983221000017/costproxy2021.htm.

15. Maiden, B. (2022). Costco shareholders back net-zero proposals including scope 3 emissions. Corporate Secretary (1 February). https://www corporatesecretary.com/articles/shareholders/32889/costco-shareholders-back-net-zero-proposal-including-scope-3-emissions.

16. Philips, M. (2021) Exxon's board defeat signals the rise of social good activists. *The New York Times* (9 June). https://www.nytimes.com/2021/06/09/business/exxon-mobil-engine-no1-activist (accessed 19 August 2022).

17. Bevan, A., Shorten, B., Ryan, C.M., et al. (2021). *Millieudefensie v. Shell*—a landmark court decision for energy and energy intensive companies. Shearman & Sterling Perspective (1 June). https://www.shearman.com/en/perspectives/2021/06/milieudefensie-v-shell--landmark-court-decision-for-energy-companies (accessed 19 August 2022).

18. Walmart Sustainability Hub. (n.d.) Project Gigaton. https://walmartsustainabilityhub.com/climate/project-gigaton (accessed 19 August 2022).

19. Popli, N. (2022). High gas prices are pushing electric car sales to a tipping point. *Time* (3 May). https://time.com/6173178/high-gas-prices-electric-vehicles/.

20. Fickling, D. and Pollard, R. (2022). India's deadly heatwave will soon be a global reality. *The Washington Post* (7 July). https://www.washingtonpost.com/business/energy/indias-deadly-heatwave-will-soon-be-a-global-reality/2022/07/07/.

21. The Editorial Board. (2022). Climate change is not negotiable. *The New York Times* (22 July). https://www.nytimes.com/2022/07/23/opinion/biden-climate-change.html.

22. Indigo Anchor. (n.d.). On the origins of VUCA and how it affects decision making. https://www.indigoanchor.com/blog/2019/10/31/on-the-origins-of-vuca-and-how-it-affects-decision-making.

23. Bennett, N. and Lemoine, G.J. (2014). What VUCA really means for you. *Harvard Business Review* (January/February). https://hbr.org/2014/01/what-vuca-really-means-for-you.

24. CPP Investments, 10 February 2022, https://www.cppinvestments.com/insights/investing-in-the-path-to-net-zero (Accessed November 15, 2022).

Manley, R. (2022). From a transcript of his remarks on a panel at the Credit Suisse Global Energy Conference (1 March).

25. Smith, B. (2020). Microsoft will be carbon negative by 2030. Official Microsoft Blog (20 June). https://blogs.microsoft.com/blog/2020/01/16/microsoft-will-be-carbon-negative-by-2030/.

26. Blunt, K. (2022). Power company NextEra plans to cut carbon emissions to close to nothing by 2045. *The Wall Street Journal* (14 June). https://www.wsj.com/articles/power-company-nextera-plans-to-cut-carbon-emissions-to-close-to-nothing-by-2045-11655207881.

27. NextEra Energy, Inc. (2022). A real plan for real zero. https://www.nexteraenergy.com/real-zero.html (accessed 19 August 2022).

28. Asher, C. (2021). The nine boundaries humanity must respect to keep the planet habitable. Mongabay (30 March). https://news.mongabay.com/2021/03/the-nine-boundaries-humanity-must-respect-to-keep-the-planet-habitable.

29. Stockholm Resilience Centre. (2022). Stockholm University. https://www.stockholmresilience.org/research/planetary-boundaries.html (accessed 19 August 2022).

30. Doughnut Economics Action Lab. (n.d.). About Doughnut Economics. https://doughnuteconomics.org/about-doughnut-economics (accessed 19 August 2022).

31. Raworth, K. (2017). *Doughnut Economics: 7 Ways to Think Like a 21st Century Economist*. White River Junction, VT: Chelsea Green Publishing.

32. International Energy Agency. (2021). Net zero by 2050. IEA, Paris (May). https://www.iea.org/reports/net-zero-by-2050.

33. UK Department for Business, Energy & Industrial Strategy (2021). Net zero strategy: build back greener. https://www.gov.uk/government/publications/net-zero-strategy (19 October; updated 5 April 2022).

34. En-ROADS. (n.d.). Scenario. https://en-roads.climateinteractive.org/scenario.html (accessed 19 August 2022).

35. World Economic Forum in collaboration with the Boston Consulting Group. (2022). Winning the race to net zero: the CEO guide to climate advantage (January). https://www3.weforum.org/docs/WEF_Winning_the_Race_to_Net_Zero_2022.pdf.

Part II

The Technical Foundations of Net Zero Business Models

NOTE: Readers who are already familiar with GHGs and the GHG Protocol Corporate Accounting and Reporting Standard, carbon intensity, and science-based emissions reduction targets or who first wish to understand the four Pathways to net zero and commercial success in the net zero economy can skip directly to Part III (Chapters 5 through 10) and use Part II (Chapters 2 through 4) as reference material or return to these chapters after learning about the Pathways.

2

AN OVERVIEW OF GREENHOUSE GAS EMISSIONS

"Collect as much primary transactional information as possible."
—Christopher Librie, Director, ESG, Applied Materials

The global economy has an enormous GHG emissions challenge. Collectively, we emit about 50 billion metric tons of CO_2 and other greenhouse gasses into the atmosphere every year.[1] To limit global warming to an average of 1.5°C, scientists estimate we have a budget of approximately 500 billion tons of CO_2e we can emit before global warming exceeds this threshold.[2] This means to get to a net zero economy by 2050, we need to cut carbon dioxide emissions by at least 50% by 2030 from 2018 levels and eliminate and offset the remainder by 2050. We also need to eliminate as many methane emissions as possible by 2030 in alignment with the COP26 pledge of a 30% reduction from 2020 levels by 2030.

Getting to net zero by 2050 will be a challenge, especially when the world's known crude oil reserves, not including known reserves of natural gas and coal, will produce an estimated 750 billion metric tons of CO_2e.[3] There is dynamic tension between the need to achieve a net zero emissions economy and the desire of petrostates, oil and gas companies, and coal producers to monetize their fossil fuel reserves that presages a titanic conflict.

WHAT ARE SCOPE 1, 2, AND 3 EMISSIONS?

To determine a company's contribution to our GHG emissions problem, it needs to inventory its Scope 1, 2, and 3 GHG emissions, as such emissions are defined in the *GHG Protocol Corporate Accounting and Reporting Standard (GHG Protocol)*. The *GHG Protocol* covers the accounting and reporting of seven GHGs covered by the Kyoto Protocol, including carbon dioxide (CO_2), methane (CH_4), nitrous oxide (N_2O), hydrofluorocarbons (HFCs), perfluorocarbons (PCFs), sulfur hexafluoride (SF_6), and nitrogen trifluoride (NF_3). The *GHG Protocol* was jointly convened in 1998 by the World Business Counsel for Sustainable Development and the World Resources Institute and has become the de facto global standard for GHG accounting. Almost every corporate GHG reporting program uses the *GHG Protocol* as its GHG accounting platform.[4]

Briefly, Scope 1 emissions are a company's direct GHG emissions, Scope 2 emissions are its indirect emissions from the generation of electricity heating and cooling it consumes, and Scope 3 emissions are all other emissions that occur in its value chain, including its supply chain and customers' use of its products. Inventorying a company's Scope 1, 2, and 3 GHG emissions requires a basic understanding of these categories of emissions.

It is relatively straightforward to inventory a company's Scope 1 and Scope 2 emissions because it should have access to primary data about these emissions from the operations of its business. It is more challenging to inventory a company's Scope 3 emissions because it is harder to gather the data, much of which comes from third parties in its supply chain who

EXHIBIT 2.1 Overview of GHG Protocol scopes and emissions across the value chain

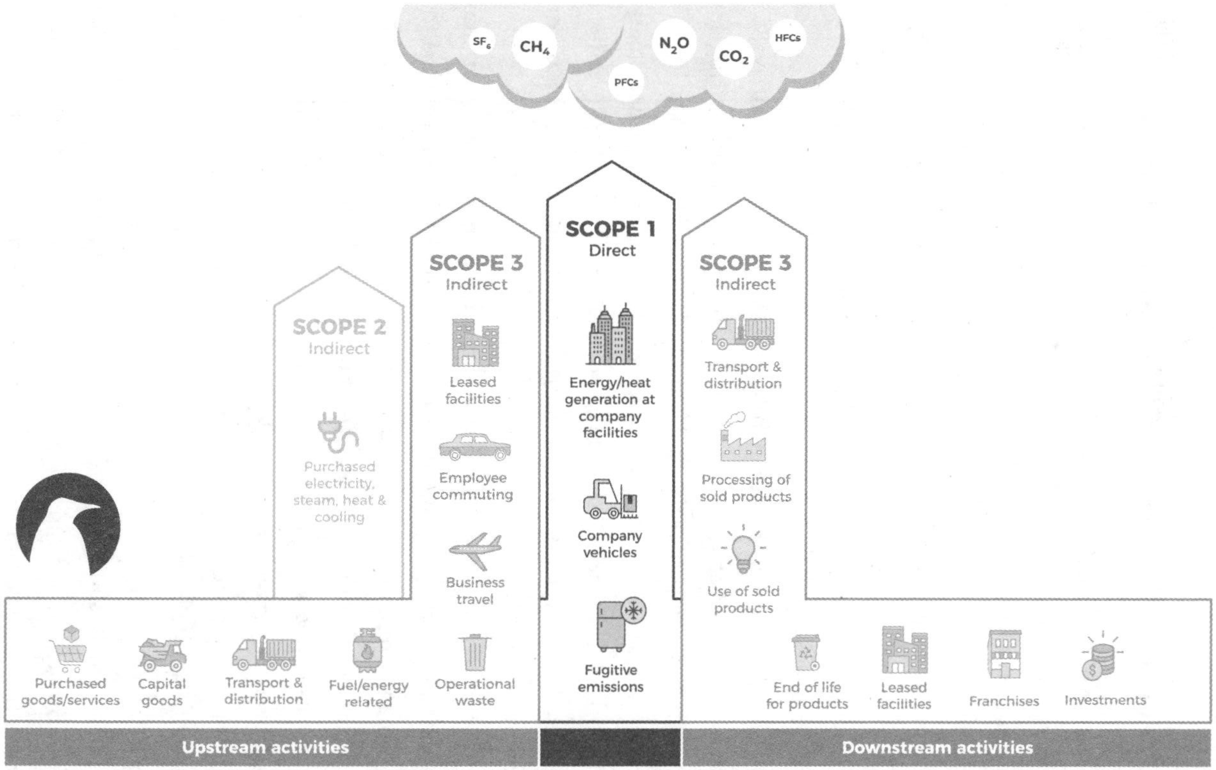

Source: South Pole.

often do not want to gather and provide the data. Scope 3 emissions are also more complicated because there are 15 distinct categories of them.

DEVELOPING A GHG EMISSIONS DATA STRATEGY

The task of accurately and comprehensively inventorying, analyzing, and reporting a company's GHG emissions is a big job. The enormity and complexity of the task increases with the enormity and complexity of the business. Inventorying GHGs presents an enormous big data problem. It will be easier for a company to achieve a net zero emissions business model if it has a comprehensive GHG data analytics strategy. Achieving a net zero emissions economy requires GHG data analytics technology and capacities that can rapidly scale.

According to the Boston Consulting Group, approximately 86% of companies still record and report their emissions manually using spreadsheets.[5] For companies that still do so, Thomas Davenport's DELTTAA model provides a framework to improve their use of GHG data analytics.[6] DELTTAA is an acronym with D for data, E for enterprise, L for leadership, T for target, T for technology, A for analysts, and A for analytic techniques.[7]

Inventorying Scope 1, 2, and 3 emissions generates massive amounts of data from across an enterprise that need to be tracked for years to help a company reach its emissions-reduction targets. A company's top leadership, especially the CEO and Chairman of the Board, needs to support an enterprise-wide approach to GHG data that has the necessary resources and data analysts to process and organize it. Companies need to invest in appropriate technology and deploy appropriate analytic techniques such as artificial intelligence to help them automatically update and track their overall GHG emissions in real time.

Companies should aspire to become what Davenport calls "analytical competitors" as quickly as possible. Analytical competitors have an enterprise-wide commitment to data analytics to help them achieve their GHG emissions-reduction targets and achieve a sustainable competitive advantage. Analytical competitors have GHG analytics–based cultures, routinely reap benefits from their GHG analytics strategy, and constantly work to refine and improve their GHG analytics capabilities. Google, for example, is an analytical competitor with 24/7 monitoring of its energy use, which matters to Google and its cloud customers because it runs large data centers that consume huge amounts of electricity. Being a GHG analytical competitor enabled Google to become a carbon neutral enterprise in 2007, offset all its megawatts of energy consumption with renewable energy in 2017, and track the sources of the energy it uses in its operations (see Appendix 2.1).[8]

The Boston Consulting Group offers a four-stage model to measure companies' maturity in reporting their GHG emissions, with "expert" being the most mature stage. Companies should aspire to become experts, which corresponds to analytical competitors in Davenport's model. An expert company generally has comprehensive and accurate emissions data, has systematically set targets for all emissions, and has achieved significant reductions in emissions. According to the Boston Consulting Group, however, 71% of companies have not fully inventoried their GHG emissions and may be considered "analytically impaired" under Davenport's model.[9,10]

WHAT ARE SCOPE 1 EMISSIONS?

Generally, a company's Scope 1 emissions come from the combustion of fuels in stationary combustion and mobile sources. According to the U.S. Environmental Protection Agency (EPA), the most common sources of emissions from stationary combustion sources include boilers, dryers, flares, furnaces, heaters, kilns, ovens, thermal oxidizers, and any other equipment or machinery that combusts carbon-bearing fuels or waste stream materials. Stationary combustion sources result in the emission of carbon dioxide, methane, and nitrous oxide, with the vast majority being carbon dioxide.[11]

A company's Scope 1 emissions also include those produced by its owned or leased mobile sources as their fuels are burned. Mobile sources are conveyances with internal combustion engines, including aircraft, boats, cars, construction equipment, forklifts, trains, and trucks. Mobile combustion sources result in the emission of carbon dioxide, methane, and nitrous oxide, with approximately 99% being carbon dioxide.[12] Mobile air conditioning and transport refrigeration leaks also result in Scope 1 emissions of hydrofluorocarbons and perfluorocarbons.[13]

Companies should account for all carbon dioxide, methane, nitrous oxide emissions, and other GHGs resulting from their stationary combustion and mobile sources. Many companies, however, exclude methane and nitrous oxide emissions from their GHG emissions because they assume they are not material relative to the magnitude of their CO_2 emissions. Under the *GHG Protocol*, however, companies need to measure all sources of GHGs to determine their materiality. While the amount of methane produced will usually be less than 1% of a company's total GHG emissions, such amounts will probably be material because methane is at least 25 times more effective in trapping greenhouse gases than CO_2.

Quantifying Scope 1 GHG emissions is surprisingly tricky. On the one hand, it is relatively easy to quantify CO_2, methane, and nitrous oxide emissions by applying established combustion factors based on the amount of a particular fuel consumed. On the other hand, it is more difficult to quantify emissions of methane and nitrous oxide because these gases are subject to additional variable factors, including the age of the equipment, what kind of emission controls it uses, and how well it is maintained.

Quantifying Scope 1 GHG emissions gets even trickier because not all stationary combustion and mobile sources burn fossil fuels exclusively. Some burn biomass fuels such as ethanol and biodiesel, which may be combusted alone or in combination with fossil fuels. Companies can calculate the emissions of these biofuels using the same calculation methods they use to calculate emissions from fossil fuels, but the *GHG Protocol* requires companies report such emissions as biomass CO_2 and track them separately from fossil fuel CO_2 emissions.

Companies do not have to include their biomass CO_2 emissions in their overall CO_2e emissions inventory if they track them separately. They must, however, include their methane and nitrous oxide emissions from biofuels in their overall CO_2e emissions inventory. This sounds relatively straight-forward until one realizes that biofuels, such as ethanol, are commonly blended with fossil fuels in a variety of different formulas with varying proportions of each type of fuel. It is very complicated to produce accurate GHG emissions data because the sheer quantity of data to track and analyze is massive and changing constantly. This is another illustration of why it is essential for companies to have a GHG data analytics strategy.

WHAT ARE SCOPE 2 EMISSIONS?

Generally, a company's Scope 2 emissions are indirect GHG emissions associated with its purchase of electricity, steam, heat, or cooling.[14] Although Scope 2 emissions physically occur at the facility where they are generated, companies need to account for them because they result from their electricity use. For the purposes of this book, the term "electricity" refers to purchased electricity, steam, heat, or cooling.

Combusting fossil fuels to produce electricity emits CO_2, methane, and nitrous oxide into the atmosphere. A company's use of purchased electricity indirectly causes GHG emissions. The amount of its Scope 2 emissions depends on the quantity of megawatt hours of energy generated and the mix of fuel and power sources that produced it.

To understand the mix of power generated today by electric utilities around the world, it helps to understand the difference between "carbon-free" energy and "green and renewable" energy. Essentially, carbon-free energy emits no GHG emissions and would include a broad portfolio of clean and zero-emission power generation sources including hydro, nuclear, geothermal, wind, and solar, regardless of whether the resource is renewable or can potentially harm the environment. Green and renewable electrical power is primarily wind- and solar-generated power, which emits no GHG emissions, is renewable, and does not pollute the atmosphere or harm the environment. The key challenge with wind and solar electrical power generation is that they are intermittent power sources and classified in the power industry as "variable energy resources" because the wind does not always blow or the sun always shine. Electrical power systems around the world are all measured on power reliability and power quality with an expectation in the developed world for greater than 98% power reliability and security from the grid.

The best way to reduce Scope 2 emissions is to choose energy sources that are carbon free and renewable with high electrical system reliability. Geothermal, low-impact hydropower, solar, and wind are sources of energy that are both clean and green. Nuclear energy and large hydropower are reliable sources of carbon-free energy used for base load power for the grid but have a greater environmental impact depending on how they are developed, operated, or decommissioned. Biomass, such as biofuels made from organic matter like ethanol, is a renewable energy source that is neither clean nor green. Electricity and the electrons produced from fossil fuel power generation—coal, natural gas, and oil—are "dirty" or "gray" electrons because their generation sources are not renewable, clean, or green and are one of the biggest contributors to GHG emissions around the world.

As with Scope 1 emissions, quantifying Scope 2 GHG emissions is tricky. A company that has operations in Northern California, for example, and purchases its electricity from Pacific Gas & Electric (PG&E) has relatively low Scope 2 emissions per kilowatt because approximately 85% of this utility's electricity is produced from clean and green sources.[15] A company that has operations in Florida and is a customer of Duke Energy will have higher Scope 2 emissions per kilowatt because approximately 50% of Duke Energy's electricity is produced from combusting natural gas and coal.[16] The situation gets more complicated because both PG&E and Duke Energy technically contribute their power to the North American power grid, which distributes 52% of its power from fossil fuel sources as discussed in Chapter 13.

Quantifying Scope 2 emissions gets trickier because there are two methods for quantifying them: one is location-based and the other is market-based. The location-based method considers average emission factors for the electricity grids that provide electricity to a company's facilities. The market-based method considers contractual arrangements under which a company purchases clean and green electricity.

Many companies purchase a differentiated energy option from their utilities, which offer clean or green electricity product options or enter into power purchase agreements (PPAs) to purchase clean or green energy. This is often possible in North America and Europe, where there are many developed sources of clean and green energy, but harder to do in Asia or Africa, which have fewer available sources of clean, green, and carbon-free energy. Applied Materials, for example, is a member of a group PPA that purchases green and clean renewable power from NextEra's White Mesa Texas wind project.[17]

Companies are now competing for limited sources of green and clean energy and the cost of green and clean energy available under PPAs is rising.[18] Competition for clean and green electricity is intense in places such as Silicon Valley with high concentrations of companies. Ultimately, however, the electrons that companies purchase from their utility or under a PPA have the same mix of green, clean, and fossil fuel–sourced electrons as the overall grid, regardless of their source, as will be discussed in Chapter 12. Clean or renewable power purchased in a differentiated program or through a PPA is technically a form of offset. This highlights the looming problem to be discussed in Chapter 13—the need for a clean and carbon-free North American power grid and for similar clean and carbon-free grids around the world. A net zero emissions economy is not achievable without having clean and carbon-free energy power grids.

If a company purchases a combination of traditional electricity from the grid and differentiated or PPA-sourced electricity, it should calculate and report its emissions using both methods and include subtotals derived from each in the calculation of its total emissions as Google does (see Appendix 2.1). As with Scope 1 emissions, a company should account for all carbon dioxide, methane, nitrous oxide emissions, and other GHGs resulting indirectly from its consumption of electricity. As discussed in the section on Scope 1 emissions, although the amount of methane produced usually will be less than 1% of total Scope 2 GHG emissions, such amounts probably will be material because methane is far more effective in trapping greenhouse gases than CO_2.

WHAT ARE SCOPE 3 EMISSIONS?

A company's Scope 3 emissions consist of indirect GHG emissions that occur both upstream and downstream in its value chain. Scope 3 emissions come from a variety of activities, including business travel, customers' use of a company's products and services, employee commuting, and purchased goods and services. Although Scope 3 emissions probably account for the majority of most companies' overall GHG emissions, they are hard to quantify because tracking them is outside of their direct control. Many companies overlook their Scope 3 emissions. To achieve a net zero emissions business model, however, companies need to take responsibility for inventorying, tracking, and eliminating their Scope 3 emissions. As discussed in Chapter 1, a company is under tremendous transformational pressure to conform its business model to a net zero emissions economy, including inventorying, tracking, and eliminating its Scope 3 emissions.

Best practices for measuring Scope 3 emissions are emergent. Measuring works best when companies have access to primary data for each of the 15 categories relevant to their businesses. Most companies can get their suppliers and vendors to provide them with relevant data. Salesforce, a cloud-based software company, for example, attaches a sustainability exhibit to its procurement contracts requiring suppliers to provide it with their Scope 1, 2, and 3 emissions data and commit to setting science-based emissions-reduction targets. If companies' suppliers are reluctant to provide them with data, they can turn to third parties such as BSR, a sustainable business network and consultancy, that can help collect Scope 3 data.

Many companies are critical of the apparent "double accounting" of Scope 3 emissions because one company's Scope 3 emissions are comprised of another company's Scope 1 and 2 emissions. Other companies complain that Scope 3 data is not available. This was a conscious design element in the *GHG Protocol* with respect to Scope 3 emissions; it was created with the intent to encourage collaboration between companies to make substantive reductions in emissions.

Many companies are critical of Scope 3 emissions because of their imprecision. The point of Scope 3 emissions is not to measure a company's carbon footprint to precision, but rather to measure it accurately enough for diagnostic purposes. Using the data, companies can target the emissions categories most relevant to their businesses—the hot spots—and create projects that will result in emissions reductions. By documenting Scope 3 assumptions, the measurement can be replicated over time, thereby tracking these reduction targets.

Determining a company's Scope 3 emissions will be an iterative process. To make calculations of Scope 3 emissions as accurate as possible, it helps to obtain as much primary information as possible and continually refine the estimates as more primary data becomes available. As we will see, interpreting the data can be tricky because there are many choices in how to account for the emissions in many of the Scope 3 categories. It is worth

EXHIBIT 2.2 Scope 3 emissions represent between 75% and 98% of all GHG emissions in 10 out of 12 sectors of the economy

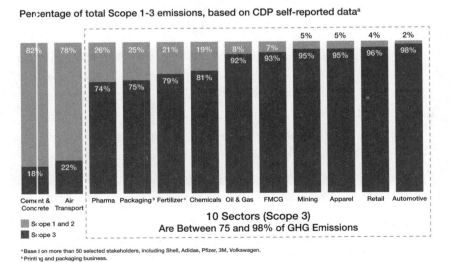

Percentage of total Scope 1-3 emissions, based on CDP self-reported data[a]

[a] Based on more than 50 selected stakeholders, including Shell, Adidas, Pfizer, 3M, Volkswagen.
[b] Printing and packaging business.
[c] Includes agricultural chemicals.

Source: GreenGauge, Carbon Disclosure Project, and McKinsey & Company.

the effort for a company to quantify all its Scope 3 emissions as accurately as possible to have a better understanding of its overall CO_2e footprint and to proactively manage its climate-related risks.

For example, approximately 80% of Applied Materials' Scope 3 emission are in category 11 (use of sold products). These emissions largely stem from the energy its customers use to power its tools in their manufacturing facilities. Another 15% of Applied Materials' Scope 3 emissions are in category 1 (purchased goods and services). These emissions largely stem from third-party production and manufacture of the materials that comprise its tools. The remaining 5% of its Scope 3 emissions are spread over the other Scope 3 categories relevant to its business. Applied Materials can make its products more efficient in their energy use by customers (category 11) and in the materials and processes they require to be manufactured (category 1), but without collaborating directly with its suppliers and customers to get their GHG emissions data, it will be difficult for it to set science-based emissions-reduction targets.[19]

Quantifying Scope 3 emissions is complex. The *GHG Protocol* has produced a series of useful guides for calculating each category of Scope 3 emissions, which are listed on Appendix 2.2 and in the endnotes. What follows is a brief description of each of the 15 categories of Scope 3 emissions. Calculating Scope 3 emissions is complicated because most of the 15 categories have multiple methods of calculating their emissions. We have only enumerated the calculation methods for a few of the 15 categories to illustrate the complexity of calculating Scope 3 emissions. We direct readers to the *GHG Protocol* guides for each of the Scope 3 categories for full descriptions of the applicable methodologies. Many of the *GHG Protocol* guides have helpful decision trees to help companies select the methodologies most appropriate for them.

Category 1: Purchased Goods and Services. Every year, companies purchase a variety of goods and services. Category 1 emissions are emitted in the production or provision of such goods and services.[20] There are four methods of calculating these emissions. To use the first two methods—supplier-specific and hybrid—companies need to collect primary data from their suppliers. To use the second two methods—average product method and average spend method—companies need to use secondary data, such as industry average emission factor data, to calculate these emissions.

These four methodologies are covered in detail in the CHG Protocol guides referenced in the endnotes and on Appendix 2.2. Generally, the amount of primary data available from a company's suppliers will determine which is the appropriate quantification methodology. The CHG Protocol guide provides a useful decision tree to help companies choose the appropriate methodology.

Category 2: Capital Goods. Companies purchase capital goods with an extended life to manufacture products, provide services, or sell, store, and deliver merchandise.[21] It may not be clear whether a company should report the Scope 3 emissions from the production of a particular product it has purchased in category 1 or in category 2. Companies should make this allocation consistent with their financial accounting practices and avoid double counting emissions in categories 1 and 2.

Quantifying emissions from purchases of capital goods is challenging because the category not only includes emissions from the production of equipment, machines, and other traditional capital goods but also new facilities and buildings. Unlike under traditional accounting practices where capital goods are amortized or depreciated over the useful life of an asset, all CO_2e emissions related to the production of a capital good is recognized in the year of its acquisition. With a new facility or building, this means a company must recognize all CO_2 emissions resulting from its construction and materials in the year it is finished. This may cause spikes in a company's Class 3 emissions as its new facilities and laboratories come online.

As with category 1 emissions, things get even more complicated because category 2 emissions are calculated using the same four methodologies discussed in category 1, which are covered in detail in the CHG Protocol guide referenced in the endnotes and on Appendix 2.2 (see Appendix 2.2). The amount of primary data available from a company's suppliers will determine which is the right quantification methodology. Again, the CHG

Protocol guide provides a useful decision tree to help companies choose the appropriate methodology.

The most accurate approach to quantify category 1 and 2 emissions uses the supplier-specific method relying on primary information from suppliers. Ideally, a company's suppliers have done life cycle assessments of their products and services. A complete life cycle assessment quantifies CO_2e emissions at all stages of a product's life cycle, including sourcing raw materials, manufacturing, transport, use, and end of life. It can be challenging to conduct a comprehensive life cycle assessment for a complex product with many components such as an automobile. It helps to start with a fully developed bill of materials and break it down by its individual components. Who made it? Where? How?

Some companies, such as Walmart, have used their market position to inspire their suppliers to reduce the CO_2e footprint of their products. Walmart's Project Gigaton has engaged 4,500 of its suppliers to avoid 1 billion metric tons of CO_2 emissions by 2030.[22] This initiative shares best practices to help suppliers get started on their emissions-reduction journey by targeting emissions reduction in energy, nature, packaging, transportation, product use and design, and waste.

Product designers will have a huge impact on reducing carbon footprints and helping companies achieve net zero business models. It is far easier to make a sustainable product that is decarbonized from the beginning, and designed for a circular economy, than to retrofit an existing product.

Category 3: Fuel- and Energy-Related Activities Not Included in Scope 1 or Scope 2. This category includes emissions related to the extraction, production, and transportation of fuels and energy purchased and consumed by a company that are not included in Scope 1 or Scope 2.[23]

Category 4: Upstream Transportation and Distribution. This category includes emissions from the transportation and distribution of products from companies' tier 1 suppliers in vehicles they do not own or operate. This category also includes purchases of third-party transportation and distribution services, including inbound logistics, outbound logistics, and third-party transportation and distribution between company facilities. Emissions may arise from air, marine, rail, and road transport and from storage of purchased products in warehouses, distribution centers, and retail facilities.[24]

Categories 4 and 9 are relatively easy to calculate because companies have invoices, purchase orders, and other readily available information about how much it paid third parties for transportation and distribution and by what means.

Category 5: Waste Generated in Operations. This category includes emissions from third-party disposal and treatment of waste generated in a company's owned or controlled operations. This category includes emissions from disposal of both solid waste and wastewater.[25]

Category 6: Business Travel. This category includes emissions from the transportation of employees for business-related activities in vehicles owned or operated by third parties, such as aircraft, trains, buses, and passenger cars. This category is relatively easy to monitor because companies generally have their employees' travel data from their expense reports.[26]

Category 7: Employee Commuting. This category includes emissions from the transportation of employees between their homes and a company's facilities. Emissions from employee commuting may arise from air, automobile, bus, rail, and other modes of transportation such as subways. Employee computing is generally not a huge contributor to Scope 3 emissions and is relatively easy to calculate.[27]

Category 8: Upstream Leased Assets. This category includes emissions from the operation of assets companies lease that are not already included in their Scope 1 or Scope 2 emissions. This category is applicable only to lessees of leased assets.[28]

Category 9: Downstream Transportation and Distribution. This category includes emissions from transportation and distribution of sold products in vehicles and facilities a company does not own or control.[29]

Category 10: Processing of Sold Products. This category includes emissions from processing of companies' intermediate products by manufacturers after their sale. Intermediate products are those that require further processing, transformation, or inclusion in another product before use, and therefore result in emissions from processing after their sale and before use by the end consumer. Emissions from processing generally are allocated to the intermediate product.[30]

Category 11: Use of Sold Products. This category includes emissions from the use of goods and services sold by a company. Category 11 emissions products include the Scope 1 and Scope 2 emissions of end users, including both consumers and business customers who use final products. Generally, the total of emissions of sold products over their useful life is accounted for in the year they are sold. This gets tricky. Applied Materials, for example, may sell a semiconductor manufacturing machine that has a 10-year useful life but may commonly be refurbished for an additional 5 years of use. This illustrates how challenging it is sometimes to determine a product's reasonable life.[31]

Category 12: End-of-Life Treatment of Sold Products. This category includes emissions from the waste disposal and treatment of products sold by a company at the end of their life.[32]

Category 13: Downstream Leased Assets. This category includes emissions from the operation of assets a company owns as lessor and leases to other parties not already included in its Scope 1 or Scope 2 emissions.[33]

Category 14: Franchises. This category includes emissions from the operation of franchises not included in a company's Scope 1 or Scope 2 emissions. This category is applicable to franchisors that grant licenses to other entities to sell or distribute their goods or services in return for payments, such as royalties for the use of trademarks and other services. Franchisors should account for the Scope 1 and Scope 2 emissions of their franchisees that occur from the operation of franchises in this category.[34]

Category 15: Investments. This category includes Scope 3 emissions associated with a company's investments in the reporting year not already included in its Scope 1 or Scope 2 emissions. This category is applicable to investors and companies that provide financial services. This category also applies to investors that are not profit-driven (e.g., multilateral development banks), and the same calculation methods should be used. A company's investments are categorized as a downstream Scope 3 category because providing capital or financing is a service.

This category is subject to increasing scrutiny because financial institutions often provide financing for fossil fuel projects or own interests in fossil fuel companies. Many financial institutions have committed to eliminate their CO_2e emissions and to achieve net zero business models by 2050 but continue to finance new fossil fuel projects, as will be discussed in Chapter 15. According to the International Energy Agency blueprint, a net zero emissions economy is impossible unless funding stops now for new fossil fuel developments.[35]

Shareholders of financial institutions are increasingly taking matters into their own hands. For example, shareholders of Citigroup, Bank of America, Credit Suisse, Royal Bank of Canada, Morgan Stanley, and JP Morgan Chase voted on proposals to stop financing new fossil fuel projects at their 2022 annual meetings. None of the proposals passed but many shareholder proposals get enacted without majority approval. Significant support for a proposal may cause a bank to change its policy. Although a shareholder proposal for JP Morgan to disclose how it intended to align its lending practices with the Paris Agreement was narrowly defeated at the 2020 annual meeting, the bank made a commitment to align its lending practices with the Paris Agreement in 2021.[36] In short, shareholders are pressuring financial institutions to reduce or eliminate their Scope 3, category 15 emissions.

Shareholder scrutiny also extends to financial institutions' practice of facilitating the transfer of fossil fuel assets. Some oil and gas and energy companies have sold their dirtiest operations to reduce their emissions. Puget Sound Electric, for example, recently tried to sell two of its coal-fired power plants.[37] Often these discarded operations are taken over by private companies with no climate policies or little accountability.

Private equity and venture capital investors, most of which are private, are beginning to pay close attention to the Scope 3 emissions of their portfolios and the Scope 1, 2, and 3 emissions of their portfolio companies. Due diligence in financing and exit transactions increasingly requires comprehensive disclosure about emissions data. Lack of such data or high emissions can negatively impact the value of such transactions. For venture capital investors, it is a lot less expensive to design a startup with a net zero and circular business model from incorporation than to retrofit it later. Some venture capital investors have begun to include requirements to be carbon neutral in their financing term sheets for startups.

SUMMARY: GETTING STARTED

Most companies are concerned about reducing their GHG emissions but may have trouble converting such concerns into action without a comprehensive data analytics strategy to help them measure their emissions comprehensively, accurately, frequently, and automatically. Measuring a company's Scope 1, 2, and 3 emissions will generate massive amounts of data. Companies need an enterprise-wide approach to track their GHG data that is supported fully by top management and involves many disciplines, including sustainability officers and data analysts. The better a company measures and analyzes its GHG emissions, the better able it will be to achieve its emissions-reduction targets and a net zero emissions business model.

Having a comprehensive GHG data analytics strategy is critical because information about a company's Scope 1, 2, and 3 emissions is material to an investor's understanding of its climate-related risk exposure and likely will soon become mandatory disclosure data, to be discussed in Chapter 14.

NOTES

1. Ritchie, H. and Roser, M., and Rosado, P. (2020). CO_2 and greenhouse gas emissions. Our World in Data. https://ourworldindata.org/greenhouse-gas-emissions (accessed 19 August 2022).

2. The Intergovernmental Panel on Climate Change (IPCC). (2018). Summary for policymakers. In: *Global Warming of 1.5°C. An IPCC Special Report on the impacts of global warming of 1.5°C above pre-industrial levels and related global greenhouse gas emission pathways, in the context of strengthening the global response to the threat of climate change, sustainable development, and efforts to eradicate poverty* 3–24. Cambridge UK and New York: Cambridge University Press. https://www.ipcc.ch/sr15/chapter/spm/.

3. World Population Review. (2022). Oil reserves by country 2022. https://worldpopulationreview.com/country-rankings/oil-reserves-by-country (accessed 19 August 2022).

4. Greenhouse Gas Protocol. (2021). CHG Protocol Corporate Accounting and Reporting Standard (October). https://ghgprotocol.org/corporate-standard.

5. Boston Consulting Group. (2021). PowerPoint presentation: Use AI to measure emissions exhaustively, accurately and frequently.

6. Davenport, T. (2006). Competing on analytics. *Harvard Business Review* (January). https://hbr.org/2006/01/competing-on-analytics.

7. Davenport, T. (2018). Research brief: Delta Plus model and five stages of analytics maturity: a primer. International Institute for Analytics. https://iianalytics.com/resources/delta-plus-model-and-five-stages-of-analytics-maturity-a-primer.

8. Hözle, U. (2020). Announcing 'round-the-clock clean energy for cloud. Inside Google Cloud Blog (14 September). https://cloud.google.com/blog/topics/inside-google-cloud/announcing-round-the-clock-clean-energy-for-cloud.

9. Boston Consulting Group (2021). PowerPoint presentation: Use AI to measure emissions exhaustively, accurately and frequently.

10. Davenport, T. (2018). Research brief: Delta Plus model and five stages of analytics maturity: a primer. International Institute for Analytics. https://iianalytics.com/resources/delta-plus-model-and-five-stages-of-analytics-maturity-a-primer.

11. EPA Center for Corporate Climate Leadership. (2020). *Greenhouse Gas Inventory Guidance: Direct Emissions from Stationary Combustion Sources.* U.S. Environmental Protection Agency. https://www.epa.gov/sites/default/files/2020-12/documents/stationaryemissions.pdf.

12. EPA Center for Corporate Climate Leadership. (2020). *Greenhouse Gas Inventory Guidance: Direct Emissions from Mobile Combustion Sources.* U.S. Environmental Protection Agency. https://www.epa.gov/sites/default/files/2020-12/documents/mobileemissions.pdf.

13. EPA Center for Corporate Climate Leadership. (2020). *Greenhouse Gas Inventory Guidance Direct Fugitive Emissions from Refrigeration, Air Conditioning, Fire Suppression, and Industrial Gases.* U.S. Environmental Protection Agency. https://www.epa.gov/sites/default/files/2020-12/documents/fugitiveemissions.pdf.

14. EPA Center for Corporate Climate Leadership. (2020). *Greenhouse Gas Inventory Guidance: Indirect Emissions from Purchased Energy.* U.S. Environmental Protection Agency. https://www.epa.gov/sites/default/files/2020-12/documents/electricityemissions.pdf.

15. PG&E. (n.d.). Renewable energy and storage. https://pgecorp.com/corp_responsibility/reports/2021/pf04_renewable_energy.html (accessed 19 August 2022).

16. Alves, B. (2022). Duke Energy's electricity generation share 2021, by source. Statista (21 June). https://www.statista.com/statistics/1154960/duke-energy-s-power-production-share-by-source.

17. Applied Materials. (2020). Applied materials commits to 100 percent renewable energy sourcing worldwide. Press release (21 July). https://investors.appliedmaterials.com/news-releases/news-release-details/applied-materials-commits-100-percent-renewable-energy-sourcing.

18. Penrod, E. (2022). PPA prices rise 28.5% as supply and regulatory challenges pile up: report. UtilityDive (13 April). https://www.utilitydive.com/news/ppa-prices-rise-285-as-supply-and-regulatory-challenges-pile-up-report/621859/.

19. Applied Materials. (2022). Sustainability Report 2021. https://www.appliedmaterials.com/content/dam/site/company/csr/doc/2021_Sustainability_F.pdf.coredownload.inline.pdf.

20. Greenhouse Gas Protocol. (n.d.). Chapter 1: Category 1: purchased goods and services. In: *Technical Guidance for Calculation Scope 3 Emissions* 20–35. https://ghgprotocol.org/sites/default/files/standards_supporting/Chapter1.pdf.

21. Greenhouse Gas Protocol. (n.d.). Chapter 2: Category 2: capital goods. In: *Technical Guidance for Calculation Scope 3 Emissions* 36–37. https://ghgprotocol.org/sites/default/files/standards_supporting/Chapter2.pdf.

22. Walmart Sustainability Hub. (n.d.). Project Gigaton. https://www.walmartsustainabilityhub.com/climate/project-gigaton (accessed 19 August 2022).

23. Greenhouse Gas Protocol. (n.d.). Chapter 3: Category 3: fuel and energy related activities not included in Scope 1 or Scope 2. In: *Technical Guidance for Calculation Scope 3 Emissions* 38–48. https://ghgprotocol.org/sites/default/files/standards_supporting/Chapter3.pdf.

24. Greenhouse Gas Protocol. (n.d.). Chapter 4: Category 4: upstream transportation and distribution. In: *Technical Guidance for Calculation Scope 3 Emissions* 49–71. https://ghgprotocol.org/sites/default/files/standards_supporting/Chapter4.pdf.

25. Greenhouse Gas Protocol. (n.d.). Chapter 5: Category 5: Waste generated in operations. *Technical Guidance for Calculation Scope 3 Emissions* 72–80. https://ghgprotocol.org/sites/default/files/standards_supporting/Ch5_GHGP_Tech.pdf.

26. Greenhouse Gas Protocol. (n.d.). Chapter 6: Category 6: Business travel. *Technical Guidance for Calculation Scope 3 Emissions* 81–86. https://ghgprotocol.org/sites/default/files/standards_supporting/Chapter6.pdf.

27. Greenhouse Gas Protocol. (n.d.). Chapter 7: Category 7: Employee commuting. *Technical Guidance for Calculation Scope 3 Emissions* 87–93. https://ghgprotocol.org/sites/default/files/standards_supporting/Chapter7.pdf.

28. Greenhouse Gas Protocol. (n.d.). Chapter 8: Category 8: Upstream leased assets. *Technical Guidance for Calculation Scope 3 Emissions* 94–101. https://ghgprotocol.org/sites/default/files/standards_supporting/Chapter8.pdf.

29. Greenhouse Gas Protocol. (n.d.). Chapter 9: Category 9: Downstream transportation and distribution. *Technical Guidance for Calculation Scope 3 Emissions* 102–105. https://ghgprotocol.org/sites/default/files/standards_supporting/Chapter9.pdf.

30. Greenhouse Gas Protocol. (n.d.). Chapter 10: Category 10: Processing of sold products. *Technical Guidance for Calculation Scope 3 Emissions* 106–112. https://ghgprotocol.org/sites/default/files/standards_supporting/Chapter10.pdf.

31. Greenhouse Gas Protocol. (n.d.). Chapter 11: Category 11: Use of sold products. *Technical Guidance for Calculation Scope 3 Emissions* 113–124. https://ghgprotocol.org/sites/default/files/standards_supporting/Chapter11.pdf.

32. Greenhouse Gas Protocol. (n.d.). Chapter 12: Category 12: End-of-life treatment of sold products. *Technical Guidance for Calculation Scope 3 Emissions* 125–127. https://ghgprotocol.org/sites/default/files/standards_supporting/Chapter12.pdf.

33. Greenhouse Gas Protocol. (n.d.). Chapter 13: Category 13: Downstream leased assets. *Technical Guidance for Calculation Scope 3 Emissions* 128–129. https://ghgprotocol.org/sites/default/files/standards_supporting/Chapter13.pdf.

34. Greenhouse Gas Protocol. (n.d.). Chapter 14: Category 14: Franchises. *Technical Guidance for Calculation Scope 3 Emissions* 130–135. https://ghgprotocol.org/sites/default/files/standards_supporting/Chapter14.pdf.

35. International Energy Agency. (2021). Net Zero by 2050. IEA (May). https://www.iea.org/reports/net-zero-by-2050.

36. JPMorganChase. (2022). Annual meeting of shareholders proxy statement (4 April). https://www.jpmorganchase.com/content/dam/jpmc/jpmorgan-chase-and-co/investor-relations/documents/proxy-statement2022.pdf.

37. Berton, H. (2020). Deal falls through to sell Puget Sound Energy's stake in Montana's Colstrip coal plant. *The Seattle Times* (30 October). https://www.seattletimes.com/seattle-news/deal-falls-through-to-sell-puget-sound-energys-stake-in-montanas-colstrip-coal-plant/.

3

APPLYING A CARBON SHOCK TEST

"We need carbon pricing."[1]

—Anne Simpson, Global Head of Sustainability,
Franklin Templeton

Companies with higher carbon intensity are more vulnerable to potential carbon shocks from a prospective carbon tax and have greater climate risk exposure than companies with lower carbon intensity. Once a company has performed a comprehensive analysis of its overall GHG emissions, it can determine its carbon intensity with a relatively straightforward metric: metric tons of CO_2e emissions per million dollars of revenue. Knowing a company's overall GHG emissions enables it to estimate the magnitude of its potential liability exposure resulting from hypothetical carbon taxes.

The general rule is that the complexity and cost of conforming a company's current business model to a net zero emissions economy increases with its carbon intensity. Companies with higher carbon intensity generally will have a higher transition burden to achieve a net zero business model than companies with lower emissions.

For example, Duke Energy, which produces approximately 4,022 metric tons of Scope 1 and 2 GHG emissions per million dollars of revenue, has a higher transition burden than Ontario Hydro (Hydro One), which produces 69 metric tons of Scope 1 and 2 GHG emissions per million dollars of revenue.[2] Knowing its carbon intensity helps a company determine the appropriate business strategy, the four Pathways discussed in Chapters 5 through 10, needed to conform its business model to a net zero emissions economy and compare its carbon intensity to those of its competitors and industry sector.

THE $20 TRILLION PROBLEM

Most companies underestimate the risk to their businesses posed by a potential carbon tax. For example, FutureZero, in collaboration with Credit Suisse HOLT[3] applied a carbon shock stress test based on a hypothetical carbon tax of $75 per metric ton of CO_2e emissions to over 11,100 global securities based on their reported Scope 1 and 2 GHG emissions (see Exhibit 3.1). The stress test revealed over $20.4 trillion of enterprise value is at risk because such a carbon tax or fee would impact materially and negatively many companies' current business models and economic performance.

Many companies' business models, when stress tested for a hypothetical carbon tax of $75 or $100 per metric ton, may no longer be viable economically. Exxon Mobil, for example, reported 111 million metric tons of Scope 1 and Scope 2 CO_2e emissions in 2020.[4] With a hypothetical carbon tax of $75 per metric ton of Scope 1 and 2 emissions, Exxon Mobil would face a carbon tax of approximately $8.325 billion. With a hypothetical carbon tax of $10 per ton on its approximately 600 million metric tons of Scope 3 emissions, Exxon Mobil would face an additional carbon tax of about $6 billion. Such combined carbon taxes would exceed Exxon Mobil's average annual profits for its last five fiscal years.[5,6]

EXHIBIT 3.1 **Percentage of companies in various sectors with a greater than 5% reduction in return on capital resulting from a $75 per ton carbon tax**

		GLOBAL				
	Companies	Carbon Data (Scope 1 and 2)		> 5% Return on Capital Negative Impact (CFROI)		Enterprise Value at Risk ($m)
Materials	962	854	89%	723	75%	$ 4,041,014
Utilities	259	234	96%	165	64%	$ 3,698,549
Energy	480	451	97%	350	73%	$ 3,416,406
Industrials	2,475	2,236	95%	870	35%	$ 3,504,753
Consumer Staples	741	693	90%	466	63%	$ 2,228,310
Consumer Discretionary	1,997	1,693	85%	484	24%	$ 1,516,140
Financials	1,417	1,264	91%	8	1%	$ 722,296
Information Technology	1,703	1,397	87%	258	15%	$ 722,423
Healthcare	1,308	1,052	82%	73	6%	$ 197,264
Real Estate	796	725	98%	37	5%	$ 194,073
Communication Services	740	564	89%	36	5%	$ 133,197
	12,883	11,163	87%	3,470	27%	$ 20,374,424

Source: Credit Suisse HOLT.

Most companies do not address adequately the potential risk of a carbon tax to their business models. Most companies assume their emissions will not be subject to a carbon tax in the future because their emissions are not subject to a carbon tax in most jurisdictions today. Companies need to be sensitive to these risks, however, because the world appears to be moving toward a carbon price. As discussed in Chapter 1, more than 20 countries already have carbon taxes and many others have adopted cap-and-trade systems that set prices on carbon. The International Energy Agency projects carbon prices in advanced economies will have risen to $250 per metric ton of CO_2e emissions by 2050.[7] Through some combination of carbon taxes and carbon trading markets, it seems likely the world will set prices on CO_2e emissions.

Companies need to be prepared for carbon taxes. If companies fail to address this risk, shareholders may replace their directors. As discussed in Chapter 1, for example, a climate activist investor, Engine No.1, was successful in nominating four directors to Exxon Mobil's board of directors and having three of them elected. Unfortunately, many companies are focused on how to measure and report on their CO_2e emissions and have not recognized the potential liability exposure of a carbon tax.

In addition, companies have underestimated the scale of the transformation necessary to achieve a global net zero emissions economy. We prepared a further analysis of the effect of a carbon tax of $100 per ton on over 18,000 publicly traded companies that confirmed the enormity of the transformation because every industry sector had a negative return on capital after the cost of capital and the cost of carbon (see Appendix 3.1).

SOME CONTEXT FOR A CARBON TAX

To comprehend fully the context of a hypothetical carbon tax of $75 per metric ton of CO_2e, it helps to understand the combustion factors of various fossil fuels to provide a sense of the quantities of various fossil fuels that need to be combusted to generate 1 metric ton (1,000 kg) of CO_2e.

According to the EPA's published combustion factors, a gallon of combusted gasoline generates approximately 8.78 kg of CO_2, a gallon of combusted diesel generates approximately 10.21 kg of CO_2, and a gallon of crude oil generates approximately 10.29 kg of CO_2. A barrel of crude oil contains 42 gallons and generates approximately 432.18 kg of CO_2 per barrel from the fuels refined from it. Using the EPA's combustion factors, to generate 1 metric ton of CO_2 requires combusting approximately 113.89 gallons of gasoline and approximately 97.94 gallons of diesel. The fuels refined from approximately 2.31 barrels of crude oil, approximately 97.18 gallons, will generate 1 metric ton of CO_2e when combusted.[8]

At 3.785 liters per gallon, combusting approximately 431.07 liters of gasoline or approximately 370.7 liters of diesel will generate 1 metric ton of CO_2. The approximately 367.2 liters in 2.31 barrels of crude oil will generate 1 metric ton of CO_2.

A hypothetical carbon tax of $75 per metric ton of CO_2e would yield a carbon tax of approximately $32.46 per barrel of crude oil, a carbon tax of approximately $0.65 per gallon or $0.17 per liter of gasoline, and a carbon tax of approximately $0.76 per gallon or approximately $0.20 per liter of diesel. Based on a dollar to Euro exchange rate of 0.98, this translates to a carbon tax of approximately € 31.81 per barrel of crude oil, € 0.166 per liter of gasoline, and € 0.196 per liter of diesel. These hypothetical carbon taxes are less per gallon or liter than recent price increases in these fuels in North America, Europe, and the rest of the world following Russia's invasion of Ukraine, which, as discussed in Chapter 1, increased consumer interest in electric vehicles.

SCENARIO PLANNING FOR CARBON TAXES

Once a company has calculated its carbon intensity and understands the implications of hypothetical carbon taxes on its business, it needs to quantify its financial risk from a potential carbon shock. Companies need to model their projected future emissions to determine whether their carbon intensity and emissions will increase or decrease as revenues rise. Most companies in North America, for example, are not aligned with the Paris COP21/26 goals for the world, with only approximately 9% having reduced their GHG emissions.[9] Some companies, such as Amazon, have celebrated a decrease in their carbon intensity while their overall CO_2e emissions increased as their revenues increased.[10]

Once a company has modeled its future emissions, it then can conduct scenario planning using its projected future GHG emissions with a variety of carbon tax prices and phase-in dates. This gets complicated very quickly, especially if a company has worldwide operations in a variety of countries at varying stages of development. The International Energy Agency roadmap to net zero 2050 lays out a variety of projected carbon tax prices and phase-in dates that could provide a useful baseline for scenario planning purposes.[11] The general expectations is that developed countries will adopt carbon taxes sooner than developing countries and that their carbon taxes will be higher.

If a company has worldwide operations, such as Amazon, its scenario planning should include projected carbon tax prices and phase-in dates for every country in which it does business. This scenario planning quickly generates a lot of data that needs to be integrated with a company's financial data and becomes another data analytics issue. For companies unsure about how to conduct scenario planning for future carbon taxes, the Carbon Disclosure Project's (CDP) free online database is a good source for models.[12] Many companies, such as Nestlé, provide detailed disclosure about how they conduct scenario planning for carbon taxes and other climate-related risks in their submissions to the CDP.

Based on a company's models of projected carbon taxes and phase-in dates and its projected GHG emissions per year, it can quantify its potential carbon shock risk in future fiscal years. Many companies ignore their carbon short positions—the potential liability exposure due to potential carbon taxes—because carbon emissions have no cost today and they assume that GHG emissions will have no cost tomorrow. Under the doctrine of shareholder primacy, which encourages them to maximize profits, companies have normalized externalizing many of the negative costs of doing business onto society and the environment. Thus, these externalized costs, such as GHG emissions, are often invisible or ignored.

Asset managers also tend to ignore their portfolio companies' carbon shorts because they do not believe the world's largest nations are serious about transforming the world's fossil fuel economy into a net zero one. Since accountants do not yet book the cost of carbon in the financial statements, it is not yet a real cost. There is no immediate hit to the financial statements or risk for companies. When a carbon shock does hit with real costs, it could be as disruptive to financial statements as the Covid-19 pandemic or the downturn of 2008.

Although relatively few national governments have yet mustered the political will to implement carbon taxes, the political winds can shift rapidly, as we have seen, for example, with the swift reinvigoration of the NATO alliance in the aftermath of Russia's invasion of Ukraine. If, for example, Europe experienced another heat wave like the one that killed an estimated 70,000 people in 2003, it is easy to imagine carbon taxes being imposed across the European Union in response. Nestlé recognizes this risk in its CDP disclosure: "Countries may rapidly implement legislation to reduce greenhouse gas emissions. Such a response may be forceful, abrupt, and disorderly."[13]

Scenario planning for carbon taxes helps companies identify and prioritize emissions-reduction projects. By identifying and prioritizing these projects, companies are better able to design transition plans to conform their business models to a net zero emissions economy.

Some projects, such as acquiring a clean fleet or carbon-free electricity, are relatively cheap and can be phased in now. Some projects, such as removing the carbon from product offerings, may be more expensive because they require significant research and development and capital expenditures. Some projects, such as removing the carbon from an entire business model, may require enormous capital expenditures. The point is that companies need to be prepared for carbon taxes. The general rule is that a company's carbon shock risk increases with its carbon intensity.

SUMMARY: HAVE GOOD PROCESSES

Climate change is more than just a carbon-centric issue. At the core, it is a business model design, business strategy, and long-horizon risk management issue that belongs in the boardroom and C-Suite. The transition to a net zero business model is not another component of ESG that can be delegated to the head of sustainability because it is core to a company's fundamental business strategy and its capital allocations. Although the *GHG Protocol* reflects an understanding that achieving a net zero economy requires change to a highly complex system, companies tend to focus on reducing Scope 1, 2, and 3 GHG emissions at the exclusion of an analysis of their fundamental business strategies.

Quantifying a company's potential carbon short position will get the attention of its board of directors and management, especially if it has a high carbon intensity. The prevailing conversation, however, has also greatly underestimated not only the complexity and enormity of the carbon fee and cross-border carbon adjustment risk but also the scale of change and transformation required to address these risks properly. The price of carbon may be zero in most jurisdictions today, but it is unlikely to be zero in the future. Every company needs to be prepared for a carbon shock.

Courts will generally respect board decisions supported by sound board processes. A company's board of directors needs to have a sound process for documenting its emissions, carbon intensity, and carbon short position.

NOTES

1. Simpson, A. (2022). What are the implications of net zero? 8th Annual Sustainable Investing Conference (24 January). https://cfany.gallery.video/cfasaltlake/detail/video/6293999947001/what-are-the-implications-of-net-zero-:-8th-annual-sustainable-investing-conference:-are-you-ready-for-net-zero.
2. Credit Suisse HOLT® database.
3. Credit Suisse HOLT® is a risk and value consultancy group within Credit Suisse Group, AG, a global investment bank and financial services firm. https://www.credit-suisse.com/microsites/holt/en.html.
4. Exxon Mobil Corporation. (2022). Advancing Climate Solutions 2022 Progress Report (July update). https://corporate.exxonmobil.com/-/media/Global/Files/Advancing-Climate-Solutions-Progress-Report/2022/ExxonMobil-Advancing-Climate-Solutions-2022-Progress-Report.pdf.
5. Exxon Mobile Corporation. (2021). Form 10-K for the fiscal year ended 31 December. U.S. Securities and Exchange Commission. https://www.sec.gov/ix?doc=/Archives/edgar/data/34088/000003408822000011/xom-20211231.htm.
6. Exxon Mobile Corporation. (2018). Form 10-K for the fiscal year ended 31 December. U.S. Securities and Exchange Commission. https://www.sec.gov/Archives/edgar/data/0000034088/000003408819000010/xom10k2018.htm.
7. International Energy Agency. (2021). World energy outlook 2021 (October). https://www.iea.org/reports/world-energy-outlook-2021.
8. EPA Center for Corporate Climate Leadership. Emission factors for greenhouse gas inventories. U.S. Environmental Protection Agency (1 April).

https://www.epa.gov/system/files/documents/2022-04/ghg_emission_factors_hub.pdf.

9. World Economic Forum in collaboration with the Boston Consulting Group. (2022). Winning the race to net zero: the CEO guide to climate advantage (January). https://www3.weforum.org/docs/WEF_Winning_the_Race_to_Net_Zero_2022.pdf.

10. Amazon. (2021). Amazon sustainability report 2020: further and faster, together (June). https://sustainability.aboutamazon.com/amazon-sustainability-2020-report.pdf.

11. International Energy Agency. (2021). Net zero by 2050: a roadmap for the global energy sector. IEA (May). https://www.iea.org/reports/net-zero-by-2050.

12. Carbon Disclosure Project. www.cdp.net/en (accessed 19 August 2022).

13. Carbon Disclosure Project. (2021). Nestlé Climate Change 2021. https://www.cdp.net/en.

4

SCIENCE-BASED EMISSIONS-REDUCTION TARGETS

'Decarbonizing the Power Sector is key to the energy system transition."[1]

—SBTi Power Sector Guidance

Science-based CO_2e emissions-reduction targets can help companies succeed in the net zero emissions economy. Once a company has an inventory of its Scope 1, 2, and 3 emissions and knows its carbon intensity and the size of its carbon short, it can set scienced-based CO_2e emissions-reduction targets. Science-based targets are designed to enable businesses to set ambitious emissions reductions in line with the latest climate science. Such targets' overarching goal is to limit the global rise in temperatures since the beginning of the Industrial Age to 1.5°C. The goal is to achieve a 50% reduction in CO_2e emissions by 2030 and achieve net zero on or before 2050.

The Science Based Targets Initiative (SBTi) is a global partnership between the United Nations Global Compact, the Carbon Disclosure Project, the World Resources Institute, and the World Wide Fund for Nature. In 2021, the SBTi promulgated the *Corporate Net Zero Standard* (*Net Zero Standard*) to complement the *GHG Protocol* and provide the guidance and tools companies need to set science-based net zero targets.[2] Such targets provide companies with a clearly defined path to reduce their emissions in line with Paris Agreement goals. The methodologies set forth resulted from a highly collaborative process and were stress tested by 80 companies before their release.

The *Net Zero Standard* was largely inspired by the *Special Report on Global Warming of 1.5°C* delivered by the Intergovernmental Panel on Climate Change (IPPC), the UN body for assessing the science related to climate change.[3] In the report, the IPCC warned that limiting global temperature rise to 1.5°C and achieving net zero CO_2e emissions by 2050 is humanity's best approach to avoid a catastrophic breakdown of our climate systems. The IPCC's *Sixth Assessment Report* confirmed climate change is already adversely affecting every region on Earth.[4] In the United States alone, extreme weather events caused more than $145 billion in damages in 2021.[5]

The SBTi not only defines and promotes best practices for companies to reduce their CO_2e emissions and set net zero targets but also provides technical assistance and expert resources to help companies set their targets. The SBTi also provides independent assessment and validation of companies' targets. As of 10 August 2022, 1,605 companies have used the *Net Zero Standard* to set and validate science-based targets, 1,225 companies have made net zero commitments, and 3,526 businesses have used it to set their CO_2e emissions targets.

The *Net Zero Standard* is a work in progress. The SBTi, for example, is currently developing Net Zero Standards for the oil and gas and automotive industries. It is also developing guidelines for the financial industry and the forestry, land use, and agriculture sectors.

Setting science-based targets has numerous benefits. Having its targets approved by a global initiative gave Sony Group Corporation, a Japanese multinational manufacturer of consumer electronic products with interests in the entertainment business, "more confidence and greater authority."[6] Using an accepted international standard helps companies demonstrate they have used a sound process to arrive at their targets. Having science-based targets helps Dell Technologies, a global technology company, "attract and retain the right staff," particularly Millennials who "care how responsible a company is and will use that as the basis of a decision around who to work for."[7] Setting science-based targets can help companies save money. Pfizer Inc., a pharmaceutical and biotechnology company, for example, has achieved over $150 million in annualized savings by implementing over 3,000 energy efficiency measures.[8]

THE FOUR OBJECTIVES OF THE NET ZERO STANDARD

The *Net Zero Standard* has four key objectives. The first is to achieve rapid, deep cuts in companies' CO_2e emissions. This is the most effective and scientifically sound way of limiting the global rise in temperatures to 1.5°C., which is the focus of the *Net Zero Standard*. The *Net Zero Standard* addresses a company's Scope 1, 2, and 3 emissions. Most companies will need to eliminate 90 to 95% of their CO_2e emissions to achieve net zero under the *Net Zero Standard*.

The second objective is for companies to set near-term and long-term CO_2e emissions-reduction targets. This means making rapid reductions in emissions now to achieve a 50% reduction in CO_2e emissions by 2030. By 2050, companies need to produce almost no CO_2e emissions and use carbon offsets and carbon capture to neutralize any remaining emissions.

The third objective is to require companies to achieve their long-term science-based targets before they can claim net zero status. This objective ensures a consistent approach and reduces potential greenwashing. To claim net zero status, a company must have reduced its Scope 1, 2, and 3 emissions to a residual level consistent with reaching net zero emissions at the global or sector level in eligible 1.5°C aligned pathways. In addition, a company must have neutralized any residual emissions as of its net zero target year and any GHGs released into the atmosphere thereafter.

The fourth objective is to encourage companies not to limit their efforts to eliminating their own Scope 1, 2, and 3 emissions by making investments beyond their value chains to help mitigate climate change across the economy. A company's investments in carbon sequestration, for example, should be in addition to, not instead of, deep emission cuts. In addition, companies are encouraged to follow the SBTi's mitigation hierarchy, committing first to reduce their own emissions before investing to mitigate emissions outside their immediate value chains.

GENERALLY ACCEPTED GHG ACCOUNTING AND REPORTING PRINCIPLES

Another objective of the *Net Zero Standard* is to create a universal pattern language by standardizing principles for accounting for, and reporting on, GHG emissions. The SBTi's objective is to create generally accepted GHG accounting and reporting principles like generally accepted accounting principles (GAAP) in the world of accounting. The five principles are:

1. **Relevance.** Ensure the GHG inventory appropriately reflects the GHG emissions of the company and serves the decision-making needs of users—both internal and external to the company.
2. **Completeness.** Account for and report on all GHG emission sources and activities within the inventory boundary. Disclose and justify any specific exclusion.
3. **Consistency.** Use consistent methodologies to allow for meaningful performance tracking of emissions over time. Transparently document any changes to the data, inventory boundary, methods, or any other relevant factors in the time series.

4. **Transparency.** Address all relevant issues in a factual and coherent manner based on a clear audit trail. Disclose any relevant assumptions and make appropriate references to the accounting and calculation methodologies and data sources used.

5. **Accuracy.** Ensure the quantification of GHG emissions is systematically neither over nor under actual emissions, as far as can be judged, and uncertainties are reduced as far as practicable. Achieve sufficient accuracy to enable users to make decisions with reasonable confidence as to the integrity of the reported information.

These five principles also provide a useful approach for companies to use to guide the implementation of their net zero transition plans.[9]

FIVE STEPS TO SET SCIENCE-BASED TARGETS

The SBTi provides a straightforward, five-step process to help all companies set science-based CO_2e emissions-reduction targets regardless of whether they work with the SBTi to set and validate them (see Exhibit 4.1).

The first step is to select a base year to track a company's emissions-reduction performance over the target period. The base year emissions should be representative of a company's typical emissions and should not be earlier than 2015. Companies are required to use the same base year for their near-term and long-term science-based targets.

The second step is to develop a full GHG inventory that includes at least 95% of a company's Scope 1 and 2 emissions and a complete screening of its Scope 3 emissions. A complete screening of Scope 3 emissions

EXHIBIT 4.1 The five steps to set science-based targets

SELECT A BASE YEAR — CALCULATE COMPANY'S EMISSIONS — SET TARGET BOUNDARIES — CHOOSE A TARGET YEAR — CALCULATE TARGETS

is necessary to identify emissions hotspots, reduction opportunities, and areas of risk upstream and downstream in the value chain. The *GHG Protocol Corporate Value Chain (Scope 3) Accounting and Reporting Standard* and SBTi's *Scope 3 Calculation Guidance* provide guidance on how to conduct the inventory.[10,11] As discussed in Chapter 2, a useful approach is to conduct a high-level screening inventory of a company's Scope 3 emissions and improve data quality by increasing the amount of primary data over time.

To be in alignment with the *GHG Protocol* and *SBTi Criteria*,[12] companies must select a single method—operational control, financial control, or equity share—to determine their organizational boundary. Under the operational control method, a company has the authority to introduce and implement the operating policies of an entity. Under the financial control method, a company has the authority to direct the financial and operating policies of an entity with a view toward gaining economic benefit. Under the equity share method, a company accounts for GHG emissions from an entity's operations according to its share of equity in the entity.

For consistency and transparency, a company should use the same method to calculate its CO_2e emissions inventory and to define its science-based target boundaries. Both the emissions inventory and target boundary should include all seven GHGs or classes of GHGs covered by the Kyoto Protocol previously discussed in Chapter 2.

Companies also need to set science-based targets for their subsidiaries consistent with their chosen boundary-setting methodology. Subsidiaries may set their own science-based targets, but, generally, their emissions should be included in the parent company's GHG inventory.

Under *SBTi Criteria*, carbon credits do not count as emissions reductions toward meeting science-based targets. Generally, companies cannot include reductions in emissions that occur outside of their operations and value chains.

The SBTi publishes several sector-specific guides to support companies in setting their targets and suggest best practices for inventory and target boundary setting. Guides for additional sectors are planned.

The third step is to set target boundaries for near-term and long-term emissions targets. Comprehensive target boundaries are necessary to substantiate a company's net zero status at the end of its decarbonization journey.

A company's near-term and long-term targets must include at least 95% of its Scope 1 and 2 emissions. If its Scope 3 emissions are at least 40% of its total emissions, its near-term targets must include at least 67% of such Scope 3 emissions. If a company is in a sector with particularly high Scope 3 emissions, it may be required under the *SBTi Corporate Manual* to include particular sources or categories of emissions in its science-based targets.[13] A company's long-term science-based targets must also include at least 90% of its Scope 3 emissions.

In recognition of the challenge that companies face in reducing their Scope 3 emissions, the SBTi *Net Zero Standard* takes an expansive approach to setting target boundaries (see Exhibit 4.2).

The intention behind this expansive approach is to encourage companies to collaborate to decarbonize their value chains. The approach seems to be working. PepsiCo, a multinational food, snack, and beverage corporation,

EXHIBIT 4.2 The SBTi's expansive approach to setting target boundaries

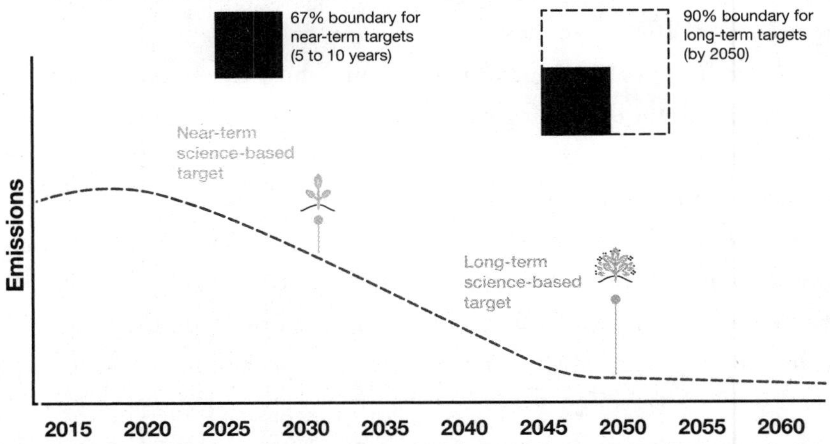

Source: Science Based Targets Initiative.

for example, collaborated with fellow food companies Mars, Incorporated and McCormick & Company, and Guidehouse, a management consultancy, to form the Supplier Leadership on Climate Transition coalition to mobilize suppliers on climate action and inspire them to develop their own climate plans to reduce their impact on the planet. Already, over 200 suppliers are participating in the coalition.[14]

The expansive approach encourages companies to tackle their most material emission sources across Scopes 1, 2, and 3 now while giving them time to work through the complexity of reducing their Scope 3 emissions. The SBTi *Net Zero Standard* has special boundary coverage requirements for use of phase emissions from sold or distributed fossil fuels and emissions from biomass combustion, processing, and distribution.

The SBTi *Net Zero Standard* allows companies to set several targets that collectively meet the overall near-term or long-term boundary requirements. A company may, for example, set targets that cover emissions from different sectors in which its subsidiaries operate or cover different Scope 3 categories.

The fourth step is to choose a target year for near-term and long-term targets. Near-term targets should be 5 to 10 years out or from the date of submission with the SBTi. Long-term targets must have a target year of 2050 or sooner. Companies in the power sector need to have a long-term target year of 2040 or sooner.

The fifth step is to calculate long-term and short-term targets. There are three methods for calculating near-term and long-term Scope 1 and 2 targets: absolute contraction, physical intensity convergence, and, for Scope 2 only, renewable electricity.

With the absolute contraction method, companies reduce their overall Scope 1 and 2 emissions by an amount consistent with a mitigation pathway. For near-term targets, this means expressing the minimum reduction as a linear reduction rate such as 4.2% per annum. For long-term targets, this means expressing the minimum reduction as an overall amount such as 95%.

With the physical intensity method, all companies in a sector converge on a shared emissions intensity for Scope 1 and 2 emissions in 2050, or 2040 for the power sector. For near-term targets, companies use a prescribed formula that adjusts their targets based on their starting points, their target years, and projected output growth. For long-term targets, the target year's emissions intensity equals the sector's target emission intensity in 2050.

With the renewable energy method, which is only applicable to Scope 2 emissions, companies set targets to procure at least 80% renewable energy by 2025 and 100% renewable energy by 2030. Ultimately, however, the grids from which companies obtain their energy need to be renewable themselves, as will be discussed in Chapter 13. Companies like Ørsted,[15] the first energy company to have its net zero targets validated by the SBTi, and Iberdrola,[16] the Spanish utility that has been working to decarbonize its business model for over 20 years, have an opportunity to provide industry-wide leadership to create power grids that generate clean and renewable energy.

There are two methods for calculating near-term and long-term Scope 3 targets: the physical intensity contraction method and the economic intensity method. With the physical intensity contraction method, a company defines its own emissions intensity metric, such as tons of CO_2e per $1 million of revenue, and sets targets to reduce emissions by an amount consistent with limiting warming to at least well below 2°C for near-term targets and 1.5°C for long-term targets. With the economic intensity method, companies reduce economic emissions intensity, such as tons of CO_2e per unit of value added, by an amount consistent with limiting warming to at least well below 2°C for near-term targets and 1.5°C for long-term targets. Under both methods, the minimum reduction for near-term targets is calculated as a 7% year on year reduction and the minimum reduction for long-term targets is 97% overall.

There is also a method for setting near-term targets for suppliers and customers that represent a certain percentage of a company's Scope 3 emissions.

Once a company has calculated its long-term target, the SBTi provides guidance for how to communicate its net zero targets.

SCIENCE-BASED TARGETS UNIQUE TO THE POWER SECTOR

The SBTi recognizes the energy sector will play a central and key role in the transformation to a net zero emissions economy. Approximately three-quarters of global CO_2e emissions are energy related, mostly from the combustion of fossil fuels. The SBTi is blunt in its assessment of the critical role the energy sector will play: "decarbonizing the power sector will require the sustained rapid growth of renewable electricity and significant reductions in coal-fired and gas-fired generation at a global level over the next ten years"[17] (see Exhibit 4.3).

In the United States, almost two-thirds of emissions come from electricity, transportation, and buildings (see Exhibit 4.4).

EXHIBIT 4.3 Percentages of global GHG emissions by sector

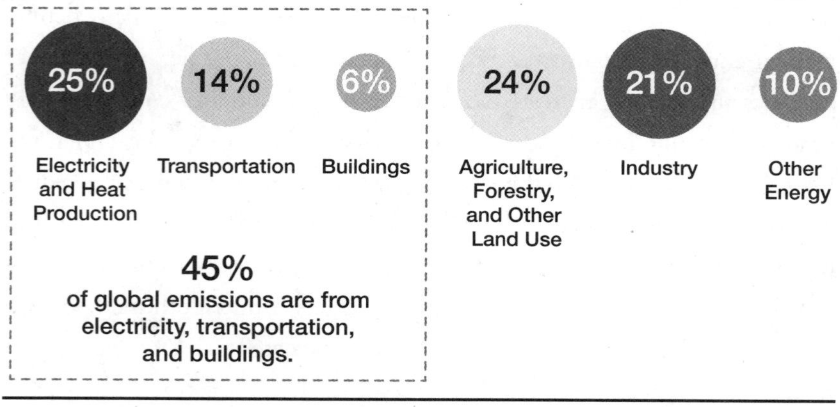

25%	14%	6%	24%	21%	10%
Electricity and Heat Production	Transportation	Buildings	Agriculture, Forestry, and Other Land Use	Industry	Other Energy

45%
of global emissions are from electricity, transportation, and buildings.

Source: Intergovernmental Panel on Climate Change.

The SBTi believes the power sector is well-poised to establish steep reductions in its CO_2e emissions due to innovation and rapid cost reductions

EXHIBIT 4.4 Percentages of U.S. GHG emissions by sector

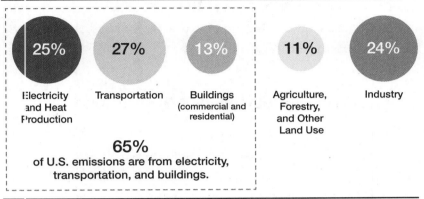

25%	27%	13%	11%	24%
Electricity and Heat Production	Transportation	Buildings (commercial and residential)	Agriculture, Forestry, and Other Land Use	Industry

65%
of U.S. emissions are from electricity, transportation, and buildings.

Source: U.S. Environmental Protection Agency.

in technology for solar, wind, and battery storage, favorable policy conditions, and growing demand for renewable energy. "Nonetheless, electric utilities also need to establish innovative business models around smart grids, demand management, and energy storage to be consistent with a net zero economy."[18] In short, we cannot create a net zero emissions economy unless we decarbonize the power sector.

Because of the critical role the power sector must play in the transition, the SBTi's science-based targets for the power sector contemplate that its long-term targets achieve net zero by 2040 and an 85% reduction in emissions intensity between 2020 and 2035. Because carbon removal technologies are nascent and subject to considerable risks and uncertainties, the SBTi currently does not recognize their use in setting near-term and long-term targets.

Currently, 52% of electricity from the North American grid comes from the combustion of fossil fuels. Although the SBTi guidance encourages power companies to be innovative and contribute to a smart grid and encourages companies to purchase renewable energy to create pressure on the power industry to accelerate its use of renewables, it falls short of naming the big issue. As will be discussed in Chapter 13, we will never achieve a net zero economy without clean power grids. There are approximately 3,000 utilities in North America contributing power to the grid, but there is no comprehensive transition plan for the North American grid to become a clean grid.

SCIENCE-BASED TARGETS UNIQUE TO THE FOREST, LAND, AND AGRICULTURE (FLAG) SECTOR

The SBTi recognizes the forest, land, and agriculture sector (FLAG) will also play a key role in the transformation to a net zero emissions economy. The FLAG sector contributes approximately 20% of global CO_2e emissions, with half from agriculture and half from land use, land use change, and forestry. This sector's emissions are unique to it. CO_2e emissions associated with land use change include biomass and soil carbon losses from deforestation, forest degradation, conversion of coastal wetlands, and peatland burning. FLAG sector emissions arise from land management (nitrous oxide and methane from enteric fermentation, biomass combustion, nutrient management, fertilizer use, and manure management) and CO_2 emissions from machinery and fertilizer manufacture.

The FLAG sector needs to not only reduce its CO_2e emissions by at least half by 2050 but also enhance carbon sinks. Mitigation in the land sector requires accounting for GHG removals due to the potential of forests and soils to sequester carbon. GHG sequestration can be achieved by restoring natural ecosystems, improving forest management practices, and enhancing carbon sequestration in soils. The SBTi is still developing its guidance for the FLAG sector but its *Forest, Land and Agriculture Science Based Target Setting Guidance* provides preliminary guidance on setting science-based targets for this sector with *GHG Protocol Land Sector and*

Removals Guidance expected to be released in 2023 before this book is published.[19,20]

The SBTi contemplates companies in other sectors that have more than 20% of their revenues coming from forests, land, or agriculture or companies whose FLAG emissions total more than 20% of their emissions across all scopes must set a FLAG-specific target separate from its targets for other emissions. Any company with FLAG emissions is encouraged to set FLAG targets in addition to its other targets. Removals and emission reductions must be accounted for separately and removals cannot be used to meet any non-FLAG targets. Companies should only include CO_2 removals with ongoing storage and monitoring.

Companies setting FLAG targets are also required to publicly commit to zero deforestation covering all scopes of emissions. The SBTi also recommends companies make commitments to stop converting undeveloped land and burning peat.

UPDATING AND COMMUNICATING TARGETS

The SBTi has recently tightened its ambition requirements for near-term and long-term science-based targets. SBTi will only validate targets with a minimum level of ambition of 1.5°C for Scope 1 and 2 CO_2e emissions and well below 2°C for Scope 3. In addition, the SBTi reduced the minimum time frame for near-term targets from 15 years to 10 years.

If a company has not set near-term and long-term science-based emissions-reduction targets, the SBTi encourages it to model long-term science-based targets. Validating targets through the SBTi signals a company's commitment to aligning its net zero ambitions with science. Having a third-party validation of a company's targets will also help demonstrate that its board of directors has exercised its duty of care. This creates an audit trail that prepares companies for the pending mandatory disclosure of climate related data discussed in Chapter 14 or a books and records request under Delaware law or equivalent statute.

If a company has set long-term emission targets that are not as ambitious as those promulgated by the SBTi in terms of limiting warming to 1.5°C, the SBTi recommends that it model long-term science-based targets, revisit its implementation strategy, and seriously consider increasing the ambition of its targets to align with the science. As investors and stakeholders become more knowledgeable about science-based targets and demand companies have them, companies will be prepared.

If a company has set long-term emission targets but is worried it will be unable to achieve them, the SBTi recommends it review its implementation strategy to identify other ways of eliminating emissions from its business model. If a company is still worried that it cannot meet its targets, it can consider moving the net zero target date into the future. The SBTi has provided additional guidance for how to communicate changes to targets with stakeholders.

THE VALIDATION PROCESS

The SBTi provides a process to help companies validate their science-based emissions-reduction targets. Companies going through the process benefit from detailed feedback and support from SBTi technical experts. Setting science-based targets future-proofs growth, saves money, provides resilience from prospective regulation, carbon fees, and carbon taxes, encourages innovation and competitiveness, and boosts investor confidence. It also demonstrates a company's commitment to sustainability to its increasingly climate-conscious stakeholders.

The SBTi has a five-step process to validate near-term and long-term emissions-reduction targets (see Exhibit 4.5).

The first step is to register online and submit a commitment letter to set science-based targets. Companies then have 24 months to submit their targets to the SBTi.

By committing to net zero, companies automatically join the SBTi's Business Ambition for 1.5°C and the UN Race to Zero, provided, however, that oil and gas companies, airports, or companies that receive more

EXHIBIT 4.5 **The Science Based Targets Initiative's five-step process to validate near-term and long-term emissions-reduction targets**

than 50% of their revenues from coal are precluded currently from joining the Race to Zero.[21,22] The Race to Zero is the world's largest alliance committed to achieving net zero carbon emissions by 2050 at the latest. Its members represent almost 25% of global CO_2 emissions.[23]

The second step is to develop near-term and long-term science-based targets in line with the *GHG Protocol*, the *SBTi Criteria,* and the *SBTi Target Validation Protocol*.[24] Even if a company chooses not to have its targets validated by the SBTi, these resources provide excellent guidance to help it set its targets.

The third step is to submit the targets for validation along with the applicable fees. Although the *Net Zero Standard* is designed for businesses with more than 500 employees, the SBTi has a streamlined and less expensive validation process for small- to medium-sized enterprises. The SBTi may waive fees for companies from less developed countries.

The fourth step occurs after the SBTi has validated the targets. Once verified, the SBTi adds a company's name to the list of companies with commitments to science-based targets on its and its partners' websites. The SBTi publishes validated targets within a month of approval and companies have six months to announce them.

The fifth step requires companies to disclose their emissions at least annually and monitor their progress in reaching their targets. The SBTi also provides recommendations on how to disclose targets through the Carbon Disclosure Project, annual reports, sustainability reports, and on company websites.

SUMMARY: SCIENCE-BASED TARGETS ARE NOT A TRANSITION PLAN

Setting science-based emissions-reduction targets provide structure to a company's plan to conform its business model to a net zero emissions economy. Such targets lay a solid foundation upon which to build a net zero transition plan and provide other benefits. EDP, the largest generator, distributor, and supplier of energy in Portugal, also discovered that having such targets "differentiated us from other companies in the sector, clarifies our position as a leader and allows fruitful dialog with customers."[25]

Science-based targets do not, however, show how companies will achieve them. Just as a company's annual budget is not its strategic plan, science-based emissions-reduction targets are not its plan to transition to a net zero business model. The Pathways, the strategic options available to companies to achieve net zero business models and design net zero transition plans, are discussed next in Part III.

(See Appendix 4.1 for resources about setting science-based emissions-reduction targets.)

NOTES

1. Science Based Targets Initiative. (2020). Setting 1.5°C-aligned science-based targets: quick start guide for electric utilities. SBTi (June). https://sciencebasedtargets.org/resources/legacy/2020/06/SBTi-Power-Sector-15C-guide-FINAL.pdf.
2. Science Based Targets Initiative. (2021). SBTi corporate net-zero standard. SBTi (October). https://sciencebasedtargets.org/resources/files/Net-Zero-Standard.pdf.
3. The Intergovernmental Panel on Climate Change. (2018). Summary for policymakers. In: *Global Warming of 1.5°C. An IPCC Special Report on the impacts of global warming of 1.5°C above pre-industrial levels and related global greenhouse gas emission pathways, in the context of strengthening the global response to the threat of climate change, sustainable development, and efforts to*

eradicate poverty 3–24. Cambridge, UK and New York: Cambridge University Press. https://www.ipcc.ch/sr15/chapter/spm/.

4. The Intergovernmental Panel on Climate Change. (2021, 2022). Sixth Assessment Report. IPCC (9 August 2021, 28 February 2022, and 4 April 2022). https://www.ipcc.ch/assessment-report/ar6/.

5. Neuman, S. (2022). Extreme weather in the U.S. cost 688 lives and $145 billion last year, NOAA says. NPR (11 January). https://www.npr.org/2022/01/11/1072077479/extreme-weather-in-u-s-cost-688-lives-and-145-billion-noaa.

6. Science Based Targets Initiative. (n.d.). Case study – Sony [transcript of interview with Keiko Shiga of Sony's Quality and Environmental Department]. https://sciencebasedtargets.org/companies-taking-action/case-studies/sony (accessed 19 August 2022).

7. Science Based Targets Initiative. (n.d.). Case study – Dell [transcript of interview with John Phlueger, Dell's Principal Environmental Strategist]. https://sciencebasedtargets.org/companies-taking-action/case-studies/dell (accessed 19 August 2022).

8. Science Based Targets Initiative. (n.d.). Case study – Pfizer [transcript of interview with Sally Fisk, Pfizer's senior corporate counsel and environmental sustainability advisor]. https://sciencebasedtargets.org/companies-taking-action/case-studies/pfizer (accessed 19 August 2022).

9. Science Based Targets Initiative. (2021). *The Net-Zero Standard*. https://sciencebasedtargets.org/net-zero.

10. Greenhouse Gas Protocol. (n.d.). Corporate value chain (Scope 3) accounting and reporting standard. https://ghgprotocol.org/sites/default/files/standards/Corporate-Value-Chain-Accounting-Reporing-Standard_041613_2.pdf.

11. Greenhouse Gas Protocol. (n.d.). Technical guidance for calculating Scope 3 emissions. https://ghgprotocol.org/sites/default/files/standards/Scope3_Calculation_Guidance_0.pdf.

12. Science Based Targets Initiative. (2021). SBTi criteria and recommendations. SBTi (October). https://sciencebasedtargets.org/resources/files/SBTi-criteria.pdf.

13. Science Based Targets Initiative. (2021). SBTi Corporate Manual. SBTi (December). https://sciencebasedtargets.org/resources/files/SBTi-Corporate-Manual.pdf.

14. Science Based Targets Initiative. (n.d.). Case Study – PepsiCo [transcript of interview with Noora Singh, Pepsi's Senior Director of Sustainability]. https://sciencebasedtargets.org/companies-taking-action/case-studies/pepsico (accessed 19 August 2022).

15. Science Based Targets Initiative. (n.d.). Case Study – Ørsted [transcript of interview with Filip Engel, Ørsted's Senior Director of Group Sustainability]. https://sciencebasedtargets.org/companies-taking-action/case-studies/orsted (accessed 19 August 2022).

16. Science Based Targets Initiative. (n.d.). Iberdrola: leading the energy revolution with science-based targets [transcript of interview with Roberto Fernández de Albendea, Iberdrola's Director of Responsibility and Corporate Social Responsibility]. https://sciencebasedtargets.org/companies-taking-action/case-studies/iberdrola (accessed 19 August 2022).

17. Science Based Targets Initiative. (2020). Setting 1.5°C-aligned science based-targets: quick start guide for electric utilities. SBTi (June). https://sciencebasedtargets.org/resources/files/SBTi-Power-Sector-15C-guide-FINAL.pdf.

18. Ibid.

19. Science Based Targets Initiative. (2022). Forest, land, and agriculture science based target setting guidance. SBTi (January). https://sciencebasedtargets.org/resources/files/FLAG-Guidance-Public-Consultation.pdf.

20. Greenhouse Gas Protocol. (n.d.). Land sector and removals guidance. https://ghgprotocol.org/land-sector-and-removals-guidance (accessed 19 August 2022).

21. Science Based Targets Initiative. (n.d.). Business ambition for 1.5°C. https://sciencebasedtargets.org/business-ambition-for-1-5c (accessed 19 August 2022).

22. UN Framework Convention on Climate Change. (n.d.). Race to zero. https://unfccc.int/climate-action/race-to-zero-campaign (accessed 19 August 2022).

23. Ibid.

24. Science Based Targets Initiative. (2020). Target validation protocol. SBTi (April). https://sciencebasedtargets.org/resources/legacy/2019/04/target-validation-protocol.pdf.

25. Science Based Targets Initiative. (n.d.). Case Study – EDP [transcript of interview with Sara Goulartt, EDP's deputy director of Climate & Environment from the Corporate Sustainability Office]. https://sciencebasedtargets.org/companies-taking-action/case-studies/edp (accessed 19 August 2022).

Part III

The Four Pathways
to Net Zero

5

THE FOUR PATHWAYS TO NET ZERO: AN INTRODUCTION

"The world has never done anything quite this big."[1]

—Bill Gates

Transforming a company's business model to achieve commercial success in a net zero world is a complex process. A company must address many issues, including the risks related to climate change and managing the transition to a net zero economy. Larry Fink, CEO of BlackRock, points out in his 2022 letter to CEOs that "delivering on the competing interests of a company's many divergent stakeholders is not easy."[2]

The six chapters in Part II outline four strategic options, which we call "Pathways," to achieve a net zero business model. These strategic options should help executive management and boards determine their net zero strategies, emissions-reduction targets, and net zero transition plans required to achieve a net zero business model. Although all four strategic options share the common goal of achieving net zero emissions, the role the company's business model plays in achieving the overarching objectives of net zero emissions and commercial success is the differentiating feature between them.

Since the transition to net zero will require significant capital investments, the minimum threshold for commercial success for each Pathway is that the company's financial returns on invested capital exceed its cost of capital, and thus generate a positive economic profit.

The Pathway to net zero is different for established companies that have existing products, services, business models, and assets with high carbon intensity than for startup companies with innovative carbon-free products and services in search of markets and investors. Established companies have business processes and embedded cultures that need to be transformed while startup companies can build net zero, and circularity, into their business models from the start.

Startup companies and other companies that have already developed, or are developing, carbon-free products and services face a different set of challenges. These include whether they can develop a multiyear business plan and narrative that will win investor support for getting started, attracting talent, building a business, and developing a net zero business model that will also enable them to be commercially successful in the future. Some of these companies may become Pathway Four industry disruptors and could pose serious threats to established companies.

For established companies, choosing a Pathway forward to net zero requires a company's CEO and board of directors to answer two fundamental questions:

1. Can our existing business model achieve our net zero emissions-reduction targets and be successful commercially through eco-efficiency process improvements and other actions like purchasing carbon credits or carbon offsets?

2. Will achieving our net zero emissions-reduction targets and commercial success require us to fundamentally redesign our business model, strategies, and organization?

If a company answers "yes" to either question, it needs to determine the appropriate Pathway to achieve a net zero business model. A company's GHG emissions inventory, its carbon intensity, the results of a carbon shock stress test, and its near-term and long-term science-based emissions-reduction targets put its management and board in a position to choose a Pathway, set strategies and targets, and develop a transition plan to confirm its business model to a net zero emissions economy.

If a company answers "no" to both questions, then it may need to develop a plan to sell or wind up its business and return capital to shareholders. (See Exhibit 5.1 for a decision tree to illustrate the four Pathways and help companies choose the most appropriate option.)

Pathway One companies believe that if they maintain their existing business models together with eco-efficiency process improvements, carbon offsets, and carbon capture, they will achieve their net zero emission

EXHIBIT 5.1 The four Pathways to a net zero business model

| Established Companies | Startup or Spinout and Industry Disrupter Companies |

Pathway One
Maintain

Pathway Two
Transform

Pathway Three
Create New

Pathway Four
Transform Industry Ecosystem(s)

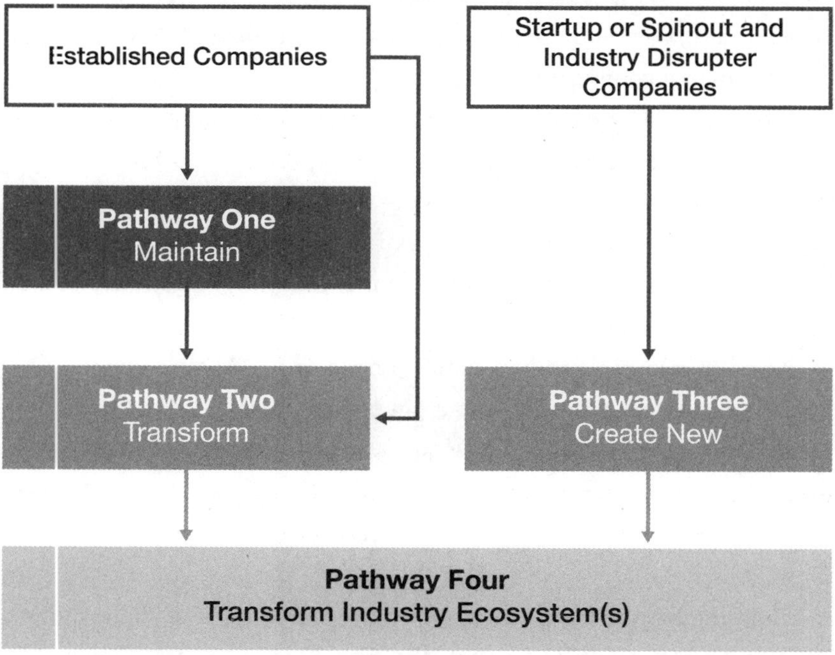

targets and comply with climate regulations. Pathway One is best suited for companies whose existing business models have low carbon intensity. Microsoft's low carbon intensity, for example, allows it to set an aggressive target to become carbon negative by 2030 and to sequester the equivalent of all the CO_2 it has emitted since incorporation by 2050.

Pathway Two companies have moved beyond compliance and fundamentally will need to transform their strategies and business models in their transition to net zero. Honeywell invests 50% of its research and development budget on developing products and technologies that benefit the environment. Honeywell's Solstice line of low global warming potential refrigerants, propellants, and solvents, for example, has avoided over 250 million metric tons of CO_2e emissions.[3]

Pathway Three companies create new net zero business models through new ventures that have developed carbon-free products and services. Such companies do not have legacy business models to transform but they lack the markets, organization, and resources of established companies. Tesla, for example, was first a Pathway Three company that pioneered the electric vehicle market without the legacy infrastructure of vehicles with high carbon internal combustion engines.

The transition to net zero for Pathway Four companies involves an industry-wide transformation and the opportunity to take a leadership role in working with governments, industry associations, and other organizations to shape and guide this transformation. Energy providers such as Iberdrola and Ørsted, for example, that have already eliminated most of the fossil fuel power plants from their operations are in excellent positions to become Pathway Four companies to lead the power sector industry ecosystem transition to a clean power grid in Europe.[4,5] Similarly, energy provider Hydro One in Ontario, Canada, whose electricity is 94% from carbon-free energy sources, is in an excellent position to become a Pathway Four company to lead the transition to a clean power grid in North America.[6]

Choosing among the four options is a dynamic process. For example, a company that initially chooses Pathway One, may conclude in the future that its business model is no longer economically viable because of changed circumstances. As a result, the company may have no choice but to shift to a Pathway Two transformation to achieve net zero emissions and commercial success. In addition, Pathway One, Pathway Two, and Pathway Three companies may sooner or later decide that their industry also needs to be transformed and Pathway Four will become their optimal strategy to achieve net zero (see Exhibit 5.2).

The Pathways differ in their degrees of strategic planning complexity for net zero business model design and leadership capacity for complexity, as will be discussed in Chapter 13. In general, Pathway Four has a higher degree of strategic planning complexity for industry ecosystem(s) and requires greater leadership capacity for complexity than Pathway Two and Pathway Three, which in turn have a higher degree of strategic planning

EXHIBIT 5.2 The four Pathways to net zero and commercial success

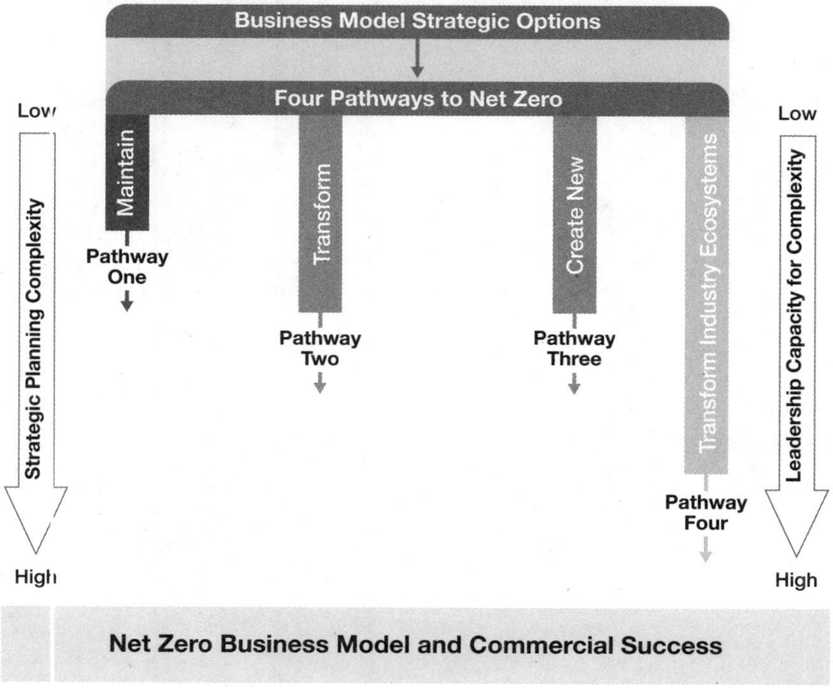

complexity and require greater leadership capacity for complexity than Pathway One.

ECO-EFFICIENCY PROCESSES AND SYSTEMS

Our research has identified that all four Pathways share a commitment to eco-efficiency with net zero transition plans built on a set of five core eco-efficiency processes (see Exhibit 5.3). In addition, all four Pathways use some combination of carbon credits, carbon offsets, carbon capture, and storage and similar mitigation strategies.

Carbon-free energy. A rapid transition to carbon-free energy is fundamental to eco-efficiency. The SBTi expects companies to use 80%

EXHIBIT 5.3 The five core eco-efficiency processes and systems

Zero-Emission Virtual Travel Policy

Zero-Emission SMART Transportation Fleet

Zero-Emission SMART Buildings

Energy Efficiency and Energy Conservation

24/7
Carbon-Free
Energy
(SMART Grid)

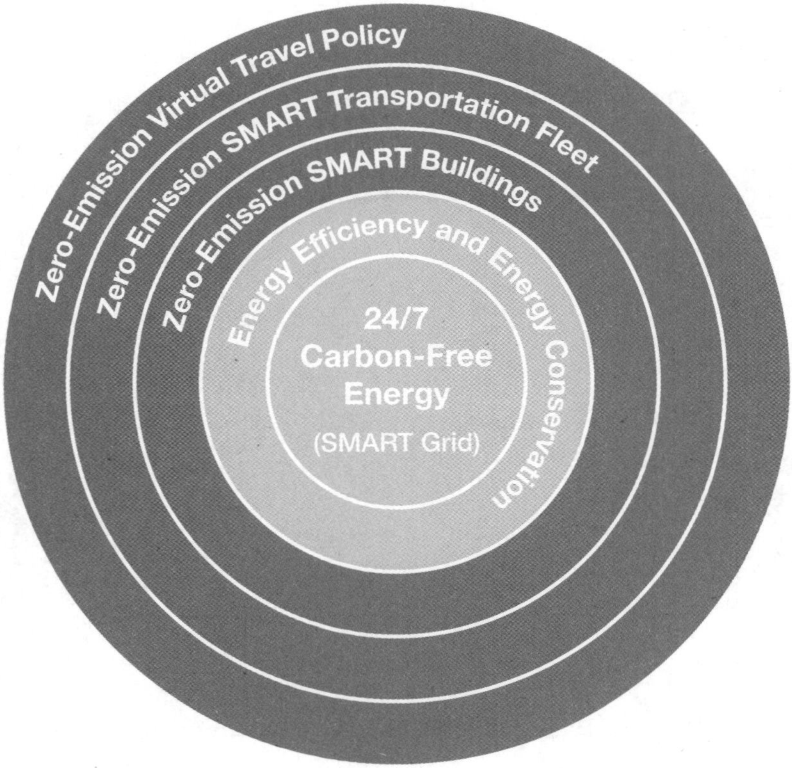

renewable energy by 2025 and 100% renewable energy by 2030. Companies can do this by building their own renewable energy resources such as on-site wind and solar and by purchasing renewable energy through PPAs and similar arrangements. PepsiCo, for example, is working toward 100% renewable energy across its operations by installing wind and solar systems at many of its facilities and procuring renewable energy through PPAs.[7]

Renewable energy and the electrons delivered through existing power grid systems is "gray" because it is blended from electrons from various power generation sources that are generated by fossil fuel power plants. Creating strong demand for carbon-free energy, however, is essential to drive innovation in the energy and electrical power systems and their transformation to ultimately create clean, carbon-free, and zero-emission power grids and sub-systems or microgrids.

This problem is particularly acute in developing countries where renewable energy or carbon-free energy may not even be available. Wipro, a multinational provider of information technology, consulting, and business process services based in India, has committed to use 100% renewable energy by 2030 but renewable energy is scarce in the seven Indian states in which it primarily operates. Wipro is actively engaged in advocacy with different state governments to facilitate access to supply and remove tariff barriers that discourage the development of renewable energy sources.[8]

Energy efficiency and conservation. Using less energy is fundamental to eco-efficiency and provides immediate financial benefit in the form of cost savings. Many energy saving measures are simple, including substituting low wattage LED lighting for incandescent bulbs, installing insulation and double-paned windows, purchasing low energy appliances and equipment, and turning down the thermostat in winter and turning it up in summer.

Procter & Gamble, a multinational consumer goods corporation, saved over $500 million over four years through energy efficiency initiatives.[9] Colgate-Palmolive, another multinational consumer products company, has reduced the amount of energy used to manufacture its products by 37% since 2002.[10]

Energy efficiency and conservation are fundamental to Landsec Securities Group plc, a commercial property company based in the UK, in achieving its science-based emissions-reduction targets. Landsec balances the need to make its buildings more energy efficient with the need to provide cost effective rents to its tenants. Landsec's strategy includes replacing or upgrading equipment with more energy-efficient substitutes as it needs to be replaced rather than replacing everything at once.[11]

Zero-emission SMART buildings. Having zero-emission buildings is a key component of eco-efficiency because the built environment and real estate infrastructure are among the world's largest emitters of GHGs. New buildings can be designed to be free of GHG emissions not only in how they are operated but also in how they are built. Zero-emission buildings are also smart in that they use the latest digital technologies to monitor and control their energy use, energy conservation, and security. Johnson Controls, a producer of fire, HVAC, and security equipment for buildings, for example, provides its customers with smart, sustainable, secure, and digitally enabled net zero emission building solutions through its Open Blue Net Zero Buildings technology platform.[12] Zero-emission smart buildings and homes will be a core component of the digital transformation and semiconductor enabled infrastructure that will create smart cities and a smart planet (see Exhibit 5.4). Intel Corporation, a multinational semiconductor and technology company, aspires to contribute to a smart planet by leading the technology industry ecosystem to "Carbon Neutral Computing," and developing breakthrough semiconductor, computing, and artificial intelligence technologies to address the world's biggest global challenges such as climate change.[13] (See Appendix 5.1.)

As discussed in Chapter 2, new buildings are considered capital goods under the *GHG Protocol* (Scope 3, category 2) and the emissions resulting from their construction are recognized when they become operational. This encourages companies to reduce the emissions in the construction process, including the manufacture and distribution of the building materials used. Designing a new building, or retrofitting an existing building, with on-site renewable power generation can help a building achieve net zero emissions.

EXHIBIT 5.4 The digital transformation into a SMART planet

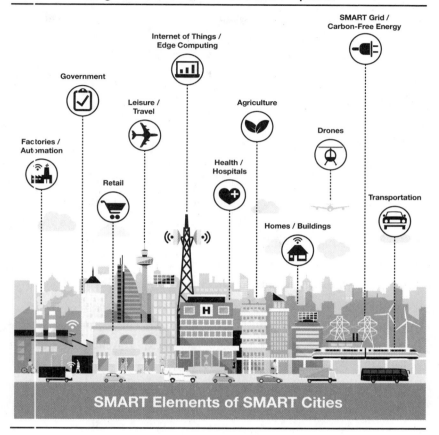

SMART Grid / Carbon-Free Energy

Internet of Things / Edge Computing

Government

Leisure / Travel

Agriculture

Drones

Factories / Automation

Health / Hospitals

Retail

Transportation

Homes / Buildings

SMART Elements of SMART Cities

In addition to making energy and refrigeration efficiency improvements, Tesco, a multinational retailer of groceries and general merchandise based in the UK, has invested heavily in on-site energy generation. Its plans to achieve 100% renewable energy consumption by 2030 include a commitment to provide at least half of its renewable energy from on-site generation.[14]

Zero-emission SMART transportation fleets. Companies need to eliminate GHG emissions from their owned and leased vehicles to achieve net zero emissions. Zero-emission fleets are also smart in that they use the latest digital technologies to find the most efficient routes, track vehicles, and monitor and control energy use.

For companies with large vehicle fleets, this can be a significant challenge. Amazon is engaged in a massive electrification program for its delivery fleet. In 2019, Amazon ordered 100,000 custom electric delivery vehicles from Rivian and plans to deploy all these vehicles in the United States by 2030. In 2020, Amazon ordered 1,800 electric vans from Mercedes for its European operations. Amazon also plans to add 10,000 two-, three-, and four-wheeled electric vehicles to its delivery fleet in India by 2025.[15]

In 2020, Amazon partnered with other fleet operators and Ceres to launch the Corporate Electric Vehicle Alliance to accelerate the transition to electric vehicles.[16] Amazon is building the infrastructure to support electric vehicles by adding hundreds of charging stations across its facilities in North America and Europe and partnering with publicly accessible charging networks to provide charging outside of its own network.[17]

Zero-emission virtual travel policy. Companies can reduce their Scope 3, category 6 emissions (employee travel) and their Scope 3, category 7 emissions (employee commuting) by adopting policies that encourage employees to use video conferencing instead of traveling to meetings and to use public transportation, car-pooling, bicycling, and other lower carbon means of getting to work. JLL, a commercial real estate services company based in the United States, for example, has reduced unnecessary business travel and provided incentives for its 98,000 employees to use public transportation.[18] Dentsu International, one of the largest global marketing and advertising agency networks, has committed to reduce emissions from flights 65% by 2030 by using collaboration technologies in lieu of traveling to meetings. When flying to meetings is required, Dentsu uses data analytics to choose more environmentally friendly modes, airlines, and routes.[19]

Carbon offsets. Carbon offsets are reductions or removals of GHG emissions to compensate for emissions that occur elsewhere. Carbon offsets are important because they allow companies to make a positive contribution to the environment, but they do not eliminate or reduce a company's existing emissions. With humanity generating approximately

54 billion metric tons of CO_2e emissions per year, companies will not be able to offset their way to a net zero business model. There simply are not enough carbon offsets to go around.

As discussed in Chapter 4, the SBTi prioritizes eliminating GHG emissions from a company's operations over carbon offsets and does not count carbon offsets toward meeting a company's science-based emissions-reduction targets. The SBTi's goal is to eliminate GHG emissions and use carbon offsets and carbon capture and storage to offset any hard-to-eliminate emissions that remain after a company has reached its long-term science-based targets. Companies should prioritize decarbonizing their operations over using carbon offsets, including using nature-based solutions such as preserving forests, reforesting land, developing carbon sinks, or sequestering carbon in soil.

Many companies that have set GHG emissions-reduction targets may over-rely on carbon credits to offset their emissions. GreenBiz estimates that carbon offset prices will increase tenfold by 2030. The surplus of available carbon credits likely will disappear, and it will become less expensive to remove emissions than to offset them.[20]

Carbon-elimination processes. Companies can use various approaches to reduce CO_2e emissions in their manufacturing processes. Concrete, for example, has a large carbon footprint due to CO_2 emitted during cement production and contributes significantly to the CO_2e emissions of the built environment, which is responsible for 40% of global carbon emissions.

CarbonCure Technologies, a manufacturer of carbon removal and utilization technologies based in Canada, for example, has developed an easy-to-adopt technology that enables concrete producers to use captured carbon dioxide to produce lower-carbon concrete mixes. The technology introduces recycled CO_2 into fresh concrete to reduce emissions without compromising performance. Once injected, the CO_2 undergoes a mineralization process and becomes permanently embedded in concrete. This results in economic and climate benefits for concrete producers. Carbon-Cure's carbon capture technology has been installed in more than 400 concrete plants around the world.

Carbon capture and storage. Carbon capture and storage (CCS) is the process of capturing CO_2 formed during power generation and industrial processes and storing it to avoid emitting it into the atmosphere. Such technologies have the potential to reduce CO_2 emissions in energy systems. In addition, captured CO_2 can be used to produce manufactured goods and in industrial and other processes, such as making CarbonCure's concrete curing technology.

Another use for captured CO_2 is for enhanced oil recovery, which injects water and CO_2 into oil wells to drive oil up the well. Such use falls under the acronym CCUS—carbon capture, utilization, and storage. Globally, as of 2021, there were 31 carbon capture facilities in operation or under construction that have the capacity to capture up to 40 million metric tons of CO_2 per year.[21] This represents less than one-tenth of 1% of all emissions and illustrates that carbon capture and storage is not yet a viable strategy to reduce emissions at scale. Some suggest that carbon capture and storage will never be a viable solution to reduce GHG emissions at scale.[22]

There are three categories of carbon capture: post-combustion carbon capture, which is largely used by power plants; pre-combustion carbon capture; and oxy-fuel combustion systems. All three approaches pose significant challenges. With post-combustion carbon capture, the CO_2 is separated from the exhaust of the combustion process. This approach is only feasible with new fossil fuel power plants because it is currently prohibitively expensive to retrofit an existing fossil fuel power plant. Oxy-fuel combustion systems are also post-combustion systems. Oxy-fuel combustion combusts the fossil fuel with pure oxygen and results in purer CO_2 emissions that are easier to capture. Once the CO_2 is captured, it is chilled into a liquid and compressed. The liquified CO_2 is then transported to a storage site where it is stored underground in former oil and gas reserves, coal mines, and saline formations.

CCS technologies are currently expensive and require energy for the capture and compression stages. Capturing CO_2 can reduce the efficiency of a power or industrial plant and require more water use. There are also significant challenges related to transporting the captured CO_2. Pipelines are expensive and existing pipelines often cannot be used because of the high pressure of the liquified CO_2e. Underground storage may be problematic because the stored CO_2 is subject to leakage.[23]

While the oil and gas and energy sectors are optimistic that CCS technologies will be able to help them eliminate their GHG emissions, such technologies currently are not viable at scale. It is for these reasons that the SBTi has not included their use in setting science-based targets. Such technologies are promising and should be closely monitored as they develop.

The net zero casualties. Some companies may have such high carbon intensity that their business models may not be viable in a net zero economy. Such companies may not be able to achieve net zero emission business models. As a result, they may choose to sell or wind up their businesses and return capital to shareholders or dispose of the commercially and environmentally unsustainable businesses and develop new ones.

SUMMARY

Chapters 6 through 10 describe in more detail each of these four Pathways, including the factors critical for success and risks that need to be managed. All four Pathways rely on the five core eco-efficiency processes and systems discussed in this chapter: carbon-free energy, energy efficiency and conservation, zero-emission smart buildings, zero-emission smart transportation fleets, and zero-emission virtual travel policies.

NOTES

1. Gates, B. (2021). How to Avoid a Climate Disaster: The Solutions We Have and the Breakthroughs We Need. New York: Alfred A. Knopf.
2. BlackRock, Inc. (2022). Larry Fink's 2022 letter to CEOs: the power of capitalism. https://www.blackrock.com/corporate/investor-relations/larry-fink-ceo-letter.
3. Honeywell International Inc. (2021). Honeywell solstice low-global-warming-potential technology reduces global greenhouse gas emissions. Press release (28 October). https://www.honeywell.com/us/en/press/2021/10/

honeywell-solstice-low-global-warming-potential-technology-reduces-global-greenhouse-gas-emissions.

4. Science Based Targets Initiative. (n.d.). Iberdrola: leading the energy revolution with science-based targets [transcript of interview with Roberto Fernández de Albendea, Iberdrola's Director of Responsibility and Corporate Social Responsibility]. https://sciencebasedtargets.org/companies-taking-action/case-studies/iberdrola (accessed 19 August 2022).

5. Science Based Targets Initiative. (n.d.). Case study – Ørsted. https://sciencebasedtargets.org/companies-taking-action/case-studies/orsted (accessed 19 August 2022).

6. Hydro One. (n.d.). Ontario's system-wide electricity supply mix: 2020 data. https://www.hydroone.com/about/regulatory/supply-mix (accessed 19 August 2022).

7. Science Based Targets Initiative. (n.d.). Case study – PepsiCo [transcript of interview with Noora Singh, Pepsi's Senior Director of Sustainability]. https://sciencebasedtargets.org/companies-taking-action/case-studies/pepsico (accessed 19 August 2022).

8. Science Based Targets Initiative. (n.d.). Case study – Wipro. https://sciencebasedtargets.org/companies-taking-action/case-studies/wipro (accessed 19 August 2022).

9. Science Based Targets Initiative. (n.d.). Case study – Procter & Gamble. https://sciencebasedtargets.org/companies-taking-action/case-studies/procter-gamble (accessed 19 August 2022).

10. Science Based Targets Initiative. (n.d.). Case study – Colgate-Palmolive. https://sciencebasedtargets.org/companies-taking-action/case-studies/colgate-palmolive (accessed 19 August 2022).

11. Science Based Targets Initiative. (n.d.). Case study – Landsec [transcript of interview with Tom Byrne, Landsec's Energy Manager]. https://sciencebasedtargets.org/companies-taking-action/case-studies/landsec (accessed 19 August 2022).

12. Johnson Controls, Inc. (n.d.). OpenBlue Net Zero Buildings. https://www.johnsoncontrols.com/openblue/net-zero-buildings (accessed 28 August 2022).

13. Intel Corporation. (n.d.). Our 2030 RISE strategy and goals. https://www .intel.com/content/www/us/en/corporate-responsibility/2030-goals.html (accessed 28 August 2022).

14. Science Based Targets Initiative. (n.d.). Case study – Tesco. https:// sciencebasedtargets.org/companies-taking-action/case-studies/tesco (accessed 19 August 2022).

15. Amazon. (n.d.). Sustainability. https://sustainability.aboutamazon.com/ environment/sustainable-operations/transportation (accessed 19 August 2022).

16. Ceres. (n.d.). Corporate Electric Vehicle Alliance. https://www.ceres.org/ climate/transportation/corporate-electric-vehicle-alliance (accessed 19 August 2022).

17. Amazon. (n.d.). Sustainability.

18. Science Based Targets Initiative. (n.d.). Net-zero case study – JLL. https:// sciencebasedtargets.org/companies-taking-action/case-studies/net-zero-case-study-jll (accessed 19 August 2022).

19. Science Based Targets Initiative. (n.d.). Net-zero case study – Dentsu. https:// sciencebasedtargets.org/companies-taking-action/case-studies/net-zero-case-study-dentsu (accessed 19 August 2022).

20. Holder, M. (2021). Carbon offset prices set to increase tenfold by 2030. GreenBiz (14 June). https://www.greenbiz.com/article/carbon-offset-prices-set-increase-tenfold-2030.

21. Gonzales, V., Krupnick, A., and Dunlop, L. (2020). Carbon capture and storage 101. Resources for the Future (6 May). https://www.rff.org/ publications/explainers/carbon-capture-and-storage-101/.

22. Harvey, C. and House, K. (2022). Every dollar spent on this climate technology is a waste. *The New York Times* (16 August). https://www.nytimes .com/2022/08/16/opinion/climate-inflation-reduction-act.html.

23. Gonzales, V., Krupnick, A., and Dunlop, L. (2020). Carbon capture and storage 101. Resources for the Future (6 May). https://www.rff.org/publications/ explainers/carbon-capture-and-storage-101/.

6

PATHWAY ONE: ECO-EFFICIENCY

"Contributing to climate solutions is a key part of our sustainability strategy."[1]

—Ara Erickson, Vice President of Corporate Sustainability,
Weyerhaeuser

Companies that choose Pathway One are defenders of their current business models. They believe that combining their existing business models with eco-efficiency processes and systems and regulatory compliance will enable them to be successful commercially while meeting their net zero emissions-reduction targets. Companies in Pathway One engage an eco-efficiency, risk mitigation, and compliance-oriented approach to conforming their business models to a net zero emissions economy.

With Pathway One, companies pursue an adaptation and cost containment strategy in which their core business models remain intact. The increased cost of reducing their Scope 1, 2, and 3 emissions and compliance with changing climate regulations is offset by efficiency improvements or passed on to customers. Some companies also mitigate their emissions with carbon credits and offsets and carbon capture.

Fundamentally, companies that choose Pathway One are not trying to transform their business models. Their objective is to find substitutes for carbon inputs and mitigate the impact of carbon price escalation and climate regulations. They view climate change as an exercise in management and mitigation, and their strategic planning focuses on regulatory compliance, cost containment, and carbon risk identification and mitigation. Pathway One companies have a relatively low degree of net zero transition planning complexity and require leaders with leadership capacity in the operational systems-thinking domain, to be discussed in Chapter 13 (see Exhibit 6.1).

For companies with low carbon intensity, the eco-efficiency business processes and systems risk mitigation and compliance approach of Pathway One may be very effective. For companies with high carbon intensity, Pathway One may be more costly and difficult. Many companies in Pathway One rely on unproven technology, such as carbon capture and storage, and double down on their existing strategies and business models.

EXHIBIT 6.1 Pathway One

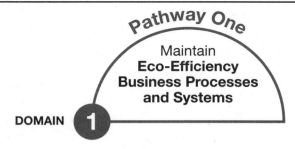

Pathway: Strategic Option for Net Zero Business Model Design
DOMAIN: Degree of Strategic Planning Complexity

PATHWAY ONE: COMPANIES WITH LOW CARBON INTENSITY BUSINESS MODELS

Weyerhaeuser

Pathway One is an obvious choice for Weyerhaeuser, a timberland company that owns or controls 10.6 million acres of timberlands in the United States and manages an additional 14.1 million acres of timberlands under long-term licenses in Canada, because it is already a carbon-neutral company. Weyerhaeuser has a low carbon intensity business model that is net negative when factoring in the carbon sequestered by its forests.

Weyerhaeuser has completed a comprehensive inventory of its Scope 1, 2, and 3 emissions to determine that it emits approximately 930,000 metric tons per year across its Scope 1 and 2 emissions and approximately 6.5 million metric tons per year across its Scope 3 emissions.[2] In 2021, Weyerhaeuser's carbon intensity was approximately 9 metric tons per $1 million of revenue across its Scope 1 and 2 emissions and approximately 72 metric tons per $1 million of revenue across its Scope 1, 2, and 3 emissions.[3]

Weyerhaeuser emits an additional 2.5 million metric tons of CO_2e from the combustion of biomass fuels, such as wood and waste, which it uses to power its facilities.[4] Under the *GHG Protocol*, biomass fuels are considered carbon neutral and Weyerhaeuser accounts for its biomass emissions separately.

Weyerhaeuser is carbon neutral because its forests remove and store approximately 35 million metric tons of CO_2e per year.[5] Its business sequesters approximately 343 metric tons of CO_2e per $1 million of revenue. Net of its estimated Scope 1, 2, and 3 emissions and excluding its biomass emissions, Weyerhaeuser sequesters approximately 271 metric tons of CO_2e per $1 million of revenue.[6]

Weyerhaeuser estimates that its forests store between 2.3 and 3.6 billion metric tons of CO_2e, with approximately 1 billion metric tons in its trees and roots and 1.3 to 2.6 billion metric tons in soil and biomass.[7] Under the *GHG Protocol* and the *Net Zero Standard*, the company is in the FLAG (forestry, land use, and agriculture) sector and sets FLAG specific emissions-reductions targets that offset emissions by the carbon sequestered in operations. As discussed in Chapter 4, the SBTi is still developing its guidance for the FLAG sector but Weyerhaeuser has used the *SBTi Forest, Land and Agriculture Science Based Target Setting Guidance* to set its science-based targets.

Having already achieved carbon-neutral status enables Weyerhaeuser to focus on making incremental improvements to its business model. The company was one of the first to establish science-based emissions-reduction targets and have them validated by the SBTi. Its near-term targets contemplate reducing its Scope 1 and 2 emissions and its Scope 3 emissions by 42% and 25%, respectively, by 2030. From 2000 to 2020, Weyerhaeuser reduced its Scope 1 and 2 emissions by 57% primarily by consolidating operations to higher efficiency mills, replacing fossil fuels with biomass fuels, and reducing fertilizer use.[8] The company meets 70% of its energy needs in its manufacturing facilities by using residual wood waste to generate energy.[9] The company is on the path to net zero emissions by 2050 and its targets are in line with the SBTi's highest level of ambition: limiting global warming to 1.5°C. Weyerhaeuser also embodies the principles of a circular economy: reduce, reuse, and recycle.[10]

Weyerhaeuser employs sustainable forestry practices in compliance with internationally recognized forestry standards. It never cuts more trees than it grows. It plants 130 to 150 million trees per year and only harvests about 2% of its trees.[11] The company turns approximately 95% of each log it mills into a useful product.[12] Weyerhaeuser actively participates in independent certification programs for forest management, fiber sourcing, and chain of custody. For example, its entire timberland portfolio is certified to the Sustainable Forestry Initiative Forest Management Standard.

Weyerhaeuser uses its carbon-neutral status to play a leadership role in the transition to a net zero emissions economy. One of its key objectives is to lead the forestry industry in positioning forests and wood products as climate solutions. The company supported the American Wood Council and the Carbon Leadership Forum to host the Wood Carbon Seminars in 2020 to address the carbon impacts of wood from the building industry.[13] The company supports the development of Environmental Product Declarations (EPDs) for wood products and developed and implemented an action plan with the American Wood Council to improve the quality of data collected from manufacturing companies.[14] In 2021, Weyerhaeuser was one of the founding members of the Net Zero Business Alliance, a group of leading companies from key sectors working with industry and policymakers to achieve net zero emissions by 2050.[15]

Microsoft Corporation

Microsoft, a multinational information technology and software corporation, is another company for whom Pathway One is an obvious choice. Like many companies in the information technology sector, Microsoft has a low carbon intensity business model. In 2021, Microsoft's carbon intensity was approximately 1.4 metric tons per $1 million of revenue across Scope 1 and 2 emissions and approximately 71 metric tons per $1 million of revenue across Scope 1, 2, and 3 emissions.[16]

Microsoft has been carbon neutral since 2012 by investing in offsets that primarily avoid emissions, but it recently committed to become carbon negative by 2030 across Scope 1, 2, and 3 emissions. The company concluded, however, that "neutral is not enough to address the world's needs."[17] Microsoft remains committed to avoiding emissions but has accelerated its activities to remove carbon from the atmosphere.

Microsoft's Scope 3 emissions are approximately 98% of its overall emissions. In 2021, Microsoft had approximately 124,000 metric tons of Scope 1 emissions, approximately 164,000 metric tons of Scope 2 emissions, and approximately 13.8 million tons of Scope 3 emissions.[18] Prior to 2020, Microsoft had mostly focused on reducing its Scope 1 and 2 emissions and paid less attention to reducing its Scope 3 emissions, except for employee travel. To achieve net negative status by 2030, the company aims to reduce its Scope 1 and 2 emissions by shifting to 100% renewable energy by 2025 and electrifying its internal vehicle fleet by 2030. It is remodeling its Silicon Valley and Puget Sound campuses to International Living Future Institute Zero Carbon Certification standards.

To accelerate the reduction of its emissions, Microsoft initiated an internal carbon tax of $15 per metric ton of CO_2e to cover its Scope 1 and 2 emissions plus its Scope 3 employee travel emissions. The fee is paid by each Microsoft division and used to fund sustainability improvements.[19] Microsoft recently applied a smaller internal carbon tax to its Scope 3 emissions. Microsoft recognizes that financial incentives such as an internal carbon tax need to be aligned to encourage reductions in its emissions. The company also works proactively with its suppliers to incentivize them to reduce emissions and has signed a commitment letter with the SBTi to set science-based emissions-reduction targets.

By 2030, Microsoft aims to be carbon negative and firmly on a path to remove by 2050 all CO_2 emitted either directly or by electrical consumption since its incorporation in 1975.

It will achieve this by employing a variety of negative emission technologies, which may include afforestation and reforestation, soil carbon sequestration, bioenergy with carbon capture and storage, and direct air capture. In fiscal 2020, for example, Microsoft purchased the removal of 1.3 million metric tons of carbon from 26 projects around the world.[20] Microsoft recognizes that technology-based carbon capture solutions are not yet viable commercially at scale and will focus initially on using nature-based solutions. To this end, it created the Climate Innovation Fund to invest $1 billion in new technologies to accelerate the development of carbon-capture technology.

Microsoft recognizes that becoming carbon negative is a "moonshot."[21] The company also recognizes that the complexity of achieving a net zero emissions economy will need to become a moonshot for the world. Microsoft believes its most important contribution to carbon reduction will come from helping its customers reduce their carbon footprints by sharing its knowledge and through data science, artificial intelligence, and digital technology.

Canada Goose Holdings, Inc.

Canada Goose, a maker of performance luxury apparel based in Canada, is representative of companies electing to choose Pathway One. Canada Goose's core business is particularly at risk due to global warming because a significant portion of its business comes from manufacturing and selling cold-season outerwear.[22] The company is driven by a commitment to "keep the planet cold and the people on it warm."[23]

Canada Goose has completed an inventory of its Scope 1 and 2 emissions and is in the process of conducting an inventory of its Scope 3 emissions. Like Weyerhaeuser and Microsoft, Canada Goose's core business has relatively low carbon intensity and the company is well-positioned to choose Pathway One. In fiscal year 2020, the company's Scope 1 emissions were 2,760 metric tons and its Scope 2 emissions were 1,318 metric tons, giving it a carbon intensity across its Scope 1 and 2 emissions of approximately 4 metric tons per $1 million of revenue.[24] The company's combined Scope 1 and 2 emissions increased more than 20% over their 2019 levels primarily because the company added 11 retail locations and added space at some of its manufacturing facilities.[25]

The company has committed to achieve net zero emissions across its Scope 1 and 2 emissions by the end of 2025. It has achieved carbon neutrality by investing in projects that reduce, avoid, or sequester the equivalent of 200% of each year's Scope 1 and 2 emissions and intends to maintain carbon neutrality until achieving net zero emissions across Scope 1 and 2 emissions by 2025. With respect to Scope 3 emissions, the company is in the process of conducting life-cycle assessments to identify the carbon footprint of its top selling products.

Although Canada Goose has not set science-based emissions-reduction targets, it is a founding member of the Climate Action Corps of the Outdoor Industry Association, which aims to become the world's first climate positive industry by 2030 and create "a bold example for others around the world to follow." To be climate positive, Climate Action Corp members must reduce GHG emissions in line with a science-based target across their Scope 1, 2, and 3 emissions, remove even more carbon from the atmosphere than they emit, and advocate for broader systemic change.[26]

Canada Goose is relying on key eco-efficiency processes and systems to meet its emissions-reduction goals. It is adopting renewable energy commitments, purchasing renewable energy, and investing in renewable energy credits. It is conducting energy audits of its facilities and stores to identify energy-saving opportunities and retrofitting its facilities to improve energy efficiency. It has replaced traditional incandescent lighting with LED lights in all its manufacturing facilities and is using motion-controlled lighting systems to reduce power usage.

Canada Goose's commitment to become climate positive is part of a larger sustainability strategy that aligns with four of the UN's Sustainable Development Goals. Its emissions-reduction efforts are in alignment with SDG 13 (Take Urgent Action to Combat Climate Change and Its Impacts), but the company is also committed to fulfilling SDG 8 (Promote Inclusive and Sustainable Economic Growth, Employment and Decent Work for All), SDG 9 (Build Resilient Infrastructure, Promote Sustainable Industrialization and Foster Innovation), and SDG 12 (Ensure Sustainable Consumption and Production Patterns).

With respect to corporate governance, Canada Goose is committed to being a good corporate citizen.[27] It has adopted the multiple stakeholder approach to doing business advocated by organizations such as the Business Roundtable.[28] The company looks to the future when making decisions and considers what is best for the people it impacts, including its customers, employees, business partners, investors, suppliers, and the communities it calls home. The company's commitments to become climate positive by 2030 and operate in alignment with several of the UN SDGs have the apparent support of Bain Capital Private Equity, LP, a private equity firm whose affiliates control enough super voting shares to give it voting control of the company. Two of Canada Goose's directors are managing directors of Bain Capital.

JAB

JAB is an investment partnership between JAB Holding Company, an evergreen investor based in Luxembourg, and JCP, a regulated investment fund also based in Luxembourg that co-invests with JAB Holding Company in the consumer goods and services sector. JAB has more than $50 billion of invested capital. JAB was one of the first investment firms to set science-based targets and was in the first cohort of financial institutions to set emissions-reduction targets with the SBTi.

JAB has completed an inventory of its Scope 1, 2, and 3 emissions. Like most financial institutions, JAB's core business has relatively low carbon intensity and the company is well-positioned to choose Pathway One. In fiscal year 2020, the company's Scope 1 and 2 emissions were approximately 56 metric tons.[29] More than 99% of JAB's emissions are Scope 3, category 15, stemming from its investment portfolio.[30]

JAB has committed to achieve a 46.2% reduction across its Scope 1 and 2 emissions by the end of 2025.[31] To reduce its Scope 3 emissions, JAB has committed that at least 80% of its portfolio companies will have SBTi-validated science-based targets in place by 2025 and at least 95% of them will have set science-based targets by 2030.[32] To accelerate reducing its Scope 3 emissions, JAB has established a quarterly ESG Collaboration Forum that enables the leadership teams of its public and private portfolio companies to share best practices.[33] JAB provides a model for other financial institutions, including asset managers, investment banks, banks, and private equity and venture capital firms to take a comprehensive, portfolio-wide approach to reducing GHG emissions. JAB believes its portfolio companies benefit from enhanced long-term performance and reduced risk by setting science-based targets.

Its approach to setting portfolio-wide targets is already having an accelerating effect. JAB's portfolio company Keurig Dr. Pepper, the eighth largest food and beverage company in the United States, has already adopted science-based targets that have been validated by the SBTi. Because more than 95% of its emissions are Scope 3, to meet its near-term 2030 targets it needs at least 50% of its suppliers to have set their own science-based targets. At the end of 2020, 38% of its suppliers had already set their own science-based targets.[34]

JAB's portfolio company Panera Bread, an American chain of bakery-café restaurants, also has committed to set science-based targets with the SBTi. The company completed a comprehensive inventory of its Scope 1, 2, and 3 emissions and set its first emissions-reduction goals in 2017.[35] Panera has set a target to be climate positive—removing more carbon from the atmosphere than it emits—by 2050. This goal means removing approximately 2.4 million metric tons of CO_2 per year compared to Panera's 2019 baseline.[36] Like Keurig Dr. Pepper, the vast majority—87%—of its emissions are Scope 3. It has set short-term targets to use green, renewable energy for at least 50% of its company-owned operations by 2025 and transition to 100% circular—reusable, recyclable, and compostable—packaging.

JAB is also a pioneer in sustainability-linked financing. Sustainability-linked securities have attributes that are linked to an issuer's achievement of key performance indicators and sustainability performance targets. JAB floated a note offering with several sustainability performance targets. If JAB fails to achieve its 2030 Scope 1 and 2 science-based emissions-reduction targets, if 95% of its portfolio companies have not set SBTi validated targets by 31 December 2030, and if all portfolio companies fail to have boards of directors with women in at least 30% of all non-executive director positions by 31 December 2025, then the interest payable on the notes will increase at the beginning of 2031.[37]

PATHWAY ONE: COMPANIES WITH HIGH CARBON INTENSITY BUSINESS MODELS

Exxon Mobil Corporation

Exxon Mobil, one of the world's largest oil and gas producers, has a high carbon intensity business. In fiscal 2021, the company's reported Scope 1 and 2 emissions were a combined 112 million metric tons of CO_2e and its reported Scope 3 emissions from petroleum product sales were an estimated 690 million metric tons.[38] In fiscal 2021, the company's carbon intensity across its Scope 1 and 2 emissions was approximately 404 metric tons per $1 million of revenue. Its carbon intensity across its estimated Scope 3 emission was approximately 2,493 metric tons per $1 million of revenue. Exxon Mobil's carbon intensity across all estimated Scope 1, 2, and 3 emissions was approximately 2,897 metric tons per $1 million of revenue.[39] To put the magnitude of Exxon Mobil's emissions in perspective, in 2021, its Scope 3 emissions were equivalent to the GHG emissions for the entire country of Canada.[40]

Exxon Mobil has announced its ambition to achieve net zero greenhouse gas emissions across Scopes 1 and 2 for its operated assets by 2050. Eco-efficiency processes and systems will play a key role in helping Exxon Mobil reach its goal. It has identified 150 potential eco-efficiency actions that can be applied to its operations. It is already implementing energy efficiency, methane mitigation, equipment upgrades, and elimination of venting and routine flaring. The company has identified additional eco-efficiency opportunities, including power and steam co-generation, electrification of operations, and using renewable or lower emission power.[41]

Exxon Mobil has not set scienced-based emissions-reduction targets across its Scope 1, 2, and 3 emissions but has established emissions-reduction targets from 2016 levels across its Scope 1 and 2 emissions for 2030. Such targets include a 20 to 30% reduction in corporate-wide GHG intensity and an absolute reduction in annual CO_2e emissions of 20%, or approximately 23 million metric tons. In addition, the company aims to achieve a 40 to 50% reduction in upstream GHG intensity and an absolute reduction of approximately 30% per year, or approximately 15 million metric tons. Exxon Mobil also aims to achieve a 70 to 80% reduction in corporate-wide methane intensity and a 60 to 70% reduction in corporate-wide flaring intensity. The company intends to work with its equity partners to achieve similar emissions reductions by 2030 in its non-operated assets.[42]

As of this writing, Exxon Mobil is developing a detailed roadmap to address approximately 90% of its operations-related GHG emissions with the remainder to be addressed in 2023. Exxon Mobil has no apparent plans to address its Scope 3 emissions and "due to lack of third-party data" has no data for its Scope 3 emissions in any of the 15 categories, except category 11. The company believes "Scope 3 emissions do not provide meaningful insight into the Company's emissions-reduction performance and could be misleading in some respects."[43] If, for example, Exxon Mobil sells more natural gas to the power industry as a substitute for coal, which produces more GHG emissions per kilowatt than natural gas, overall GHG emissions may decline while its Scope 3 emissions increase.

The company is not addressing its own Scope 3 emissions directly and is not yet working collaboratively with its value chains to gather data and reduce Scope 3 emissions. It believes "changes in society's energy use coupled with the development and deployment of affordable lower-emission technologies will be required to drive meaningful Scope 3 emissions reductions."[44]

Exxon Mobil is maintaining its existing business model despite its high carbon intensity. The company is the industry leader in carbon capture and storage with an equity share of about 20% of the global carbon capture and storage capacity of approximately 40 million metric tons of CO_2 per year.[45] The company currently has the capacity to capture and store 8.5 million metric tons of CO_2e per year or approximately 1.1% of its overall Scope 1, 2, and 3 emissions.

The company is leveraging its experience in carbon capture to invest in new technologies that can potentially reduce emissions at scale without altering its fundamental business model of producing and selling oil, gas, and chemicals. It announced plans to invest more than $15 billion by 2027 on lower emission initiatives, including developing technologies for carbon capture and storage, blue hydrogen production, and biofuels.[46] Exxon Mobil also launched the Low Carbon Solutions business to invest $3 billion in lower-emission energy solutions with a focus on scaling up carbon capture and storage.[47] The International Energy Agency projects carbon capture and storage could mitigate up to 15% of global emissions by 2040 and Exxon Mobil is betting big it will contribute to such mitigations.

Exxon Mobil and 10 other companies are discussing the formation of a carbon capture and storage innovation zone along the Houston Ship Canal, which has a high concentration of petrochemical, manufacturing, and power generation facilities that generate significant GHG emissions. The CO_2 would be captured from these facilities, liquified, cooled, and piped into geologic formations thousands of feet under the sea floor in the Gulf of Mexico where it would be permanently stored. The project has an estimated cost of approximately $100 billion and could capture and store up to 100 million metric tons of CO_2 per year by 2040.[48]

In the meantime, Exxon Mobil continues to make capital expenditures to expand its existing oil and gas business in projects that are not aligned with limiting global warming to 1.5°C. The company's near-term capital expenditure plans include acquiring additional reserves in Guyana, Brazil, and the Permian Basin in the United States.[49] Without including these additional acquisitions, at the end of 2020, Exxon Mobil's total proven reserves of crude oil, natural gas liquids, natural gas, bitumen, and synthetic oil were the equivalent of 15,211 billion barrels of crude oil.[50] Using the EPA's conversion factor of 431.87 kg of CO_2e per barrel of crude oil, this translates to approximately 6.57 billion metric tons of CO_2e.

Exxon Mobil's Pathway One strategy is to focus on eliminating the Scope 1 and 2 emissions from its operations by 2050 through eco-efficiency processes and systems and carbon capture, double down on its existing business model, and address its Scope 3 emissions when carbon capture technologies are available at scale.

CHARACTERISTICS OF PATHWAY ONE

The core assumption for companies on Pathway One is that conforming their business models to a net zero emissions economy will not require them to fundamentally transform their business models. They can just make incremental changes to their existing businesses using eco-efficiency processes and systems to achieve net zero and adapt to the new climate policies and regulations being imposed on them.

Low carbon intensity Pathway One companies such as Weyerhaeuser, Microsoft, and Canada Goose that set science-based emissions-reduction targets include carbon credits and offsets, nature-based carbon sequestration, and carbon capture and storage in their long-term targets to offset any remaining Scope 1, 2, and 3 emissions, which are expected to be reduced by 95% from base year levels under the SBTi.

High carbon intensity Pathway One companies such as Exxon Mobile that wish to retain their core business models likely will not be able to achieve net zero emission using eco-efficiency practices alone. Such companies likely will not achieve net zero emissions across their Scope 1, 2, and 3 emissions unless they fundamentally change their business models or unless carbon capture and storage and other technologies mature in time to scale cost-effectively to mitigate their emissions. In other words, carbon capture and storage and other mitigation strategies are core to their strategy to achieve net zero.

Generally, management of low carbon intensity Pathway One companies will be able to adapt to, and mitigate, the increasing costs of regulatory compliance by finding lower carbon substitutes in their supply chains, continually improving the efficiencies of their processes, reducing costs through technology, and deploying new technologies such as data analytics, artificial intelligence, and machine learning. Pathway One companies with low carbon intensity business models generally will have the pricing power to pass on to their customers any increase in costs due to regulatory compliance, purchasing renewable energy, and buying carbon credits and offsets. As a result, for low carbon intensity companies on Pathway One, conforming their business models to a net zero emissions economy should not have a material impact on earnings and returns to investors.

High carbon intensity Pathway One companies will be less resilient in absorbing the increasing costs of climate-related regulatory compliance and less able to conform their business models to a net zero emissions economy primarily by employing eco-efficiency processes and systems. As discussed in Chapter 5, carbon capture and storage technologies are evolving, largely unproven at scale, and expensive. Pathway One companies with high carbon intensity business models may not have the pricing power to pass on to their customers any increase in costs due to regulatory compliance, buying carbon credits and offsets, and capturing and storing CO_2 at the scale required to achieve net zero emissions across their Scope 1, 2, and 3 emissions or meet their potential carbon short positions. As a result, for high carbon intensity companies on Pathway One, such as Exxon Mobil, the ultimate cost of conforming their business models to a net zero emissions economy could have a material impact on earnings and returns to investors.

Since Pathway One companies' business models remain intact, investors will continue to focus on traditional financial performance metrics and investment returns. Pathway One companies should continue to enjoy access to sources of capital available for companies that meet traditional metrics. For traditional investors, low carbon intensity Pathway One companies' net zero performance will be considered interesting but not critical in making investment decisions. For impact investors, those focused on achieving positive social and/or environmental impact along with financial return, low carbon intensity Pathway One companies could be attractive investments because their route to net zero is relatively straightforward and risk free.

For traditional investors, high carbon intensity Pathway One companies' net zero performance will be considered critical in making investment decisions because of the greater risk exposure to potential carbon taxes and other climate-related regulations and the inherent risk in timely scaling cost-effective carbon capture and storage and other technologies to mitigate emissions. For impact investors, high carbon intensity Pathway One companies may not be attractive investments because their route to net zero is subject to a higher degree of risk and dependent on unproven technologies and, therefore, may not be viable.

The expectation is that government policies will continue to allow Pathway One companies to generate some emissions and they will be able to further reduce their carbon intensity before carbon taxes are implemented or become material. As under the SBTi, the expectation is that low carbon intensity Pathway One companies will eliminate most of their Scope 1, 2, and 3 emissions and offset the remainder by purchasing carbon credits or offsets or through carbon capture or carbon sequestration. On the other hand, high carbon intensity Pathway One companies likely will need to rely on carbon mitigation strategies like carbon capture and storage.

PATHWAY ONE RISK FACTORS

Pathway One is not risk free. For example, costs of achieving net zero may accelerate faster than expected because carbon taxes get implemented sooner than predicted or the price of carbon credits and offsets increases unexpectedly. A company's pricing power may erode so it can no longer pass its net zero emissions compliance costs on to its customers, causing operating costs to increase and profitability to decline.

Existing competitors may develop product alternatives that have a smaller overall carbon footprint, with a lower cost structure, and with features customers prefer. New competitors and potential industry disruptors may emerge with new business models featuring net zero emission products that are less expensive and have more attractive features.

Investors and debt providers may lose confidence in a Pathway One company's climate change strategy, its GHG emissions-reduction targets, its reliance on eco-efficiency processes and systems to achieve net zero, and, therefore, its future earnings potential. Such a company's strategy may be perceived as "old school" with the company not doing enough to contribute to the systemic changes needed to achieve a net zero emissions economy.

CRITICAL SUCCESS FACTORS FOR PATHWAY ONE COMPANIES

All Pathway One companies need to conduct a comprehensive analysis of their carbon footprints, including an analysis of their Scope 1, 2, and 3 emissions. This analysis provides a solid foundation for a board-approved transition plan to conform the company's business model to a net zero emissions economy that will achieve both a net zero business model and commercial success. Pathway One companies that have not conducted such a comprehensive analysis are flying blind and lack the data to create credible transition plans.

A comprehensive net zero transition plan should set forth multiyear objectives and near-term and long-term science-based emissions-reduction targets that will enable the CEO and board to plan investment decisions, monitor progress, learn, and course correct. Companies that fail to inventory their Scope 1, 2, and 3 emissions and set science-based emissions targets may be viewed increasingly as incompetent, especially as investors become more sophisticated about net zero emission business models.

Pathway One companies must have an experienced CEO and management team capable of, and committed to, driving continual improvement in the eco-efficiency of their business processes, aggressively reducing costs, and increasing profitability. This often is reflected in a faster, better, cheaper mindset and culture. Ideally, the board of directors will put in place an executive compensation program with incentives that are aligned with achieving the objectives of the transition plan, including rewards for achieving the company's eco-efficiency and near-term and long-term emissions-reduction targets.

The CEO and management team must be able to efficiently manage compliance with an ever-growing set of complex and often conflicting climate-related laws, regulations, and policies. This requires fluency in the nomenclature and the concepts discussed in Chapters 2 through 4. More importantly, the CEO and executive team must fully support the need to conform the company's business model to a net zero emissions economy to have the internal and external credibility to achieve net zero. The CEO and management team must be able to convince investors and other stakeholders that the company's net zero transition plan is credible and worthy of their continued support. Again, as the investor community becomes more sophisticated, high carbon intensity Pathway One companies that lack a comprehensive analysis of their Scope 1, 2, and 3 emissions and science-based emissions-reduction targets may lose their credibility with investors.

Finally, a Pathway One Company should have, and should be able to continue to generate, sufficient resources and capabilities not only to grow its business but also conform its business model to a net zero economy and comply with changing emissions regulations in the most cost-efficient manner.

SUMMARY

Pathway One may appear attractive in the short-term but requires a continual assessment of a company's evolving carbon footprint and an understanding of how and where its Scope 1, 2, and 3 emissions are produced. Management needs a detailed multiyear and multidecade carbon mitigation plan with appropriate stress testing of key planning assumptions, such as the price of carbon. Unless this is done, the risks identified are more likely to materialize and may prove fatal.

A successful mitigation plan requires multidecade planning, enterprise-wide engagement, and the ability to learn what does and does not work and to course correct. In Pathway One, senior management and the board of directors need to monitor and assess continually whether the critical assumptions that underly Pathway One are still valid or becoming untenable.

If senior management and the board of directors realize the company's choice of Pathway One will not ensure both commercial success and achieving its net zero targets, then a socially responsible, commercially successful company has only two choices: choose another Pathway or develop an exit strategy to wind up operations and return capital to shareholders. On Pathway One, there are no other choices.

(See Appendix 6.1 for some questions Pathway One company directors and investors might ask and for management to consider.)

NOTES

1. Weyerhaeuser. (2021). Weyerhaeuser receives highest designation for its greenhouse gas reduction targets. Press release (20 December). https://investor.weyerhaeuser.com/2021-12-20-Weyerhaeuser-Receives-Highest-Designation-for-Its-Greenhouse-Gas-Reduction-Targets.

2. Weyerhaeuser Company. (2022). Weyerhaeuser Carbon Record B-Side. https://carbonrecord.weyerhaeuser.com/wp-content/uploads/2022/06/CarbonRecord_Bside-methodology_05-16-2022.pdf.

3. Weyerhaeuser. (2022). Estimates based on revenues reported in Weyerhaeuser Company's Form 10-K for the fiscal year ended 31 December 2021. U.S. Securities and Exchange Commission. https://www.sec.gov/ix?doc=/Archives/edgar/data/0000106535/000156459022005707/wy-10k_20211231.htm

4. Weyerhaeuser Company. (2022). Weyerhaeuser Carbon Record B-Side.

5. Ibid.

6. Weyerhaeuser. (2022). Weyerhaeuser Company Form 10-K for the fiscal year ended 31 December 2021. U.S. Securities and Exchange Commission.

7. Weyerhaeuser Company. (2022). Weyerhaeuser Carbon Record B-Side.

8. Weyerhaeuser Company. (2022). Weyerhaeuser Carbon Record (May). https://carbonrecord.weyerhaeuser.com/wp-content/uploads/2022/06/Weyerhaeuser-Carbon-Record-Single1-05-24-2022-1.pdf (accessed 19 August 2022).

9. Weyerhaeuser. (n.d.). Making better energy choices. www.weyerhaeuser com/sustainability/environmental-stewardship/#energy (accessed 19 August 2022).

10. Weyerhaeuser. (2021). Weyerhaeuser's carbon record: methodology (version 1, September). https://www.weyerhaeuser.com/application/files/9916/3232/9591/WY_Carbon_Record_Methodology_V1.pdf (accessed 19 August 2022).

11. Weyerhaeuser Company. (2022). Weyerhaeuser Carbon Record B Side.

12. Weyerhaeuser. (n.d.). Making better energy choices.

13. Carbon Leadership Forum. (n.d.). Wood carbon seminars. https://carbonleadershipforum.org/wood-carbon-seminars/ (accessed 19 August 2022).

14. Building Transparency. www.buildingtransparency.org/ (accessed 19 August 2022).

15. Bipartisan Policy Center. (2021). BPC forms net zero business alliance around key 2050 climate goal. Press release (17 February). https://bipartisanpolicy.org/press-release/bpc-forms-net-zero-business-alliance-around-key-2050-climate-goal/.

16. Microsoft Corporation. (2022). Microsoft Corporation form 10-K for the fiscal year ended 30 June 2022. U.S. Securities and Exchange Commission. https://www.sec.gov/ix?doc=/Archives/edgar/data/789019/000156459022026876/msft-10k_20220630.htm.

17. Smith, B. (2020). Microsoft will be carbon negative by 2030. Microsoft blog (20 June). https://blogs.microsoft.com/blog/2020/01/16/microsoft-will-be-carbon-negative-by-2030/.

18. Microsoft. (2021). 2021 environmental sustainability report. https://query.prod.cms.rt.microsoft.com/cms/api/am/binary/RE4RwfV.

19. Willmott, E. (2022). How Microsoft is using an internal carbon fee to reach its carbon negative goal. Microsoft Industry Blogs (24 March). https://cloudblogs.microsoft.com/industry-blog/sustainability/2022/03/24/how-microsoft-is-using-an-internal-carbon-fee-to-reach-its-carbon-negative-goal/.

20. Microsoft Corporation. (2021). Microsoft Corporation form 10-K for the fiscal year ended June 30, 2021. U.S. Securities and Exchange Commission. https://www.sec.gov/ix?doc=/Archives/edgar/data/0000789019/000156459021039151/msft-10k_20210630.htm.

21. Smith, B. (2020). Microsoft will be carbon negative by 2030.

22. Canada Goose Holdings Inc. (2022). Canada Goose Form 20-F for the fiscal year ended 3 April 2022. U.S. Securities and Exchange Commission. https://www.sec.gov/ix?doc=/Archives/edgar/data/0001690511/000169051122000011/goos-20220403.htm.

23. Canada Goose. (2022). Canada Goose launches sustainable impact strategy and commits to carbon neutrality by 2025. Press release (22 April). https://www.canadagoose.com/on/demandware.static/-/Library-Sites-CG-Flagship/default/dw70754976/press/Canada-Goose-Launches-Sustainable-Impact-Strategy-and-Commits-to-Carbon-Neutrality-by-2025.pdf.

24. Canada Goose Holdings Inc. (2022). Canada Goose form 20-F for the fiscal year ended 3 April 2022.

25. Canada Goose. (2021). Sustainability Report 2020: Humanature: keeping the planet cold and the people on it warm. https://www.canadagoose.com/on/demandware.static/-/Library-Sites-CG-Global/default/dw06bcf87f/pages/sustainability/landingpage/cg-sr-report.pdf.

26. Outdoor Industry Association Climate Action Corps. (2021). The Outdoor Industry aspires to be climate positive by 2030 (June). https://

ip0o6y1ji424m0641msgjlfy-wpengine.netdna-ssl.com/wp-content/uploads/2015/03/OIA-2030-Climate-Positive-Strategy-Announcement-June-2021.pdf.

27. Canada Goose. (2021). Sustainability Report 2020: Humanature: Keeping the Planet Cold and the People on it Warm.

28. Business Roundtable. (2022). Statement on the purpose of a corporation (May). https://s3.amazonaws.com/brt.org/2022.06.01-BRTStatementonthe PurposeofaCorporationwithSignatures.pdf.

29. JAB Holding Company. (2022). JAB Holding Company prices offering of sustainability-linked senior notes. Press release (5 April). https://www.jabholco.com/documents/6/JAB-PricingPressRelease(2022Notes).pdf.

30. Science Based Targets Initiative. (n.d.). Case study – JAB [transcript of interview with Jacek Szarzynski, JAB Holdings ESG Partner]. https://sciencebasedtargets.org/companies-taking-action/case-studies/case-study-jab (accessed 19 August 2022).

31. JAB Holding Company. (2022). JAB Holding Company prices offering of sustainability-linked senior notes. Press release (5 April).

32. Science Based Targets Initiative. (n.d.). Case study – JAB.

33. Ibid.

34. Keurig Dr. Pepper. (2021). Keurig Dr. Pepper corporate responsibility report 2020. https://www.keurigdrpepper.com/content/keurig-brand-sites/kdp/en/our-company/corporate-responsbility/reporting.html.

35. Panera Bread. (n.d.). Climate positive. https://www.panerabread.com/en-us/articles/climate-positive.html (accessed 19 August 2022).

36. Panera Bread. (2021). Panera Bread announces its goal to become climate positive by 2050. Press release (20 October). www.panerabread.com/content/dam/panerabread/integrated-web-content/documents/press/2021/Panera-Climate-Commitment-Release.pdf.

37. JAB Holding Company. (2022). JAB Holding Company prices offering of sustainability-linked senior notes.

38. Exxon Mobil Corporation. (2022). Advancing climate solutions 2022 progress report (July). https://corporate.exxonmobil.com/Sustainability/Sustainability-Report.

39. Exxon Mobil Corporation. (2021). Exxon Mobil Corporation's form 10-K for the fiscal year ended 31 December 2020. U.S. Securities and Exchange

Commission. https://www.sec.gov/ix?doc=/Archives/edgar/data/0000034088/000003408821000012/xom-20201231.htm.

40. U.S. Securities Exchange Commissions. (2021). Majority Action: notice of exempt solicitation (6 May). https://sec.report/Document/0001387131-21-005386/.

41. Exxon Mobil Corporation. (2022). ExxonMobil announces ambition for net zero greenhouse gas emissions by 2050. Press release (18 January). https://corporate.exxonmobil.com/News/Newsroom/News-releases/2022/0118_ExxonMobil-announces-ambition-for-net-zero-greenhouse-gas-emissions-by-2050.

42. Exxon Mobil Corporation. (2021). Sustainability Report (5 January). https://corporate.exxonmobil.com/Sustainability/Sustainability-Report

43. Exxon Mobil Corporation. July (2022). Advancing climate solutions 2022 progress report.

44. Ibid.

45. Ibid.

46. Exxon Mobil Corporation. (2022). ExxonMobil announces ambition for net zero greenhouse gas emissions by 2050.

47. Energy Factor. 12 August (2021). Helping decarbonize industry with carbon capture and storage. Energy Factor by ExxonMobil (12 August). https://energyfactor.exxonmobil.com/insights/voices/low-carbon-solutions-joe-blommaert/.

48. Exxon Mobil Corporation. (2022). ExxonMobil announces ambition for net zero greenhouse gas emissions by 2050.

49. Exxon Mobil Corporation. (2021). ExxonMobil outlines plans to grow long-term shareholder value in lower carbon future. Press release (3 March). https://corporate.exxonmobil.com/News/Newsroom/News-releases/2021/0303_ExxonMobil-outlines-plans-to-grow-long-term-shareholder-value-in-lower-carbon-future.

50. Exxon Mobile Corporation. (2021). Exxon Mobil Corporation's form 10-K for the fiscal year ended 31 December 2020. U.S. Securities Exchange Commission. https://www.sec.gov/ix?doc=/Archives/edgar/data/0000034088/000003408821000012/xom-20201231.htm.

7

PATHWAY TWO, OPTION ONE: INCREMENTAL TRANSFORMATION OF THE BUSINESS MODEL—ZERO-CARBON PRODUCTS AND SERVICES

"The technological innovations our people are pioneering will shape our planet's destiny."[1]

—Warren East, CEO Rolls-Royce

Companies that choose Pathway Two have committed to achieve net zero emission targets. They have concluded that an eco-efficiency, risk mitigation, and compliance-oriented approach to emissions reduction will not be enough to meet their net zero targets. They have embraced the notion that they must transform their business models to thrive in the emerging net zero emissions economy. Pathway Two is transformational.

According to the World Economic Forum, only 9% of the world's publicly listed companies had achieved an actual emissions reduction of more than 4% in 2019, the minimum annual reduction necessary to limit global warming to 1.5°C.[2] Many of these companies are Pathway Two companies.

As part of their plans, companies in Pathway Two deploy eco-efficiency processes and systems, comply with changing climate regulations, and employ effective carbon-risk management practices. They also may use carbon credits and offsets, and carbon capture and storage within a broader plan to achieve a net zero business model outcome. Pathway Two companies not only employ all the eco-efficiency processes of Pathway One companies but, unlike Pathway One companies that remain committed to maintaining their existing business models, they also change their fundamental business models. Pathway Two companies have a higher degree of net zero strategic planning complexity than Pathway One companies and require leaders with leadership capacity in the operational and business systems-thinking domains, as will be discussed in Chapter 13.

Pathway Two companies set clear, measurable, multiyear science-based emissions-reduction targets in their net zero transition plans. Pathway Two companies do not engage in greenwashing and support their pledges to achieve net zero targets with credible board-approved research and development, capital expenditures, and net zero transition plans for achieving them.

Pathway Two companies focus on anticipating and meeting the changing needs of their customers, who increasingly demand sustainable and zero-emission products and services. Their transition priorities include expanding their markets and growing their zero-carbon revenues, as well as reducing or eliminating their carbon dependencies and expenses.

By transforming their products and services, these companies also are transforming their business models for value creation and return on capital.

Ben van Beurden, the Chief Executive Officer of Shell, another one of the world's largest global energy companies, summarizes the focus of Pathway Two companies:

> We must give our customers the products and services they want and need—products that have the lowest environmental impact. At the same time, we will use our established strengths to build on our competitive portfolio as we make the transition to be a net-zero emissions business in step with society.[3]

Pathway Two companies also accept responsibility for their environmental impact on the planet beyond their own core operations. As a result, they are focused on reducing and, in most cases, completely eliminating Scope 3 emissions in their supply chains. Pathway Two companies measure, manage, and reduce their Scope 3 emissions, which requires them to collaborate proactively with their supply chain partners. Pathway Two companies recognize that achieving their science-based targets and re-engineering their business models requires them to work with key customers, supply chain partners, investors, regulators, and other stakeholders. Pathway Two is all about collaboration within and between companies.

Pathway Two companies are more likely to have medium or high carbon intensity but may include some with low carbon intensity. Some industry sectors with high carbon intensity, such as energy, mining, steel, utilities, and automotive, are more likely to choose Pathway Two.

Pathway Two has two transformation strategies. This chapter covers re-engineering for zero-carbon products and services (see Exhibit 7.1), and Chapter 8 covers re-engineering the complete end-to-end business model.

EXHIBIT 7.1 Pathway Two, Option One

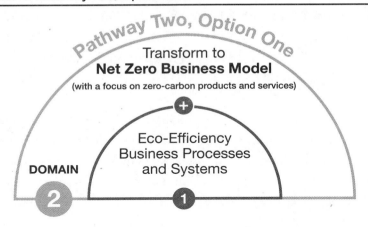

Pathway Two, Option One

Transform to
Net Zero Business Model
(with a focus on zero-carbon products and services)

+

Eco-Efficiency
Business Processes
and Systems

DOMAIN

2

1

Pathway: Strategic Option for Net Zero Business Model Design
DOMAIN: Degree of Strategic Planning Complexity

RE-ENGINEERING WITH A FOCUS ON ZERO-CARBON PRODUCTS AND SERVICES

The first transformation strategy takes an incremental approach to transforming a business model. This strategy creates new zero-carbon products and services and develops markets for them. The objective is to increase revenues and profits from a new portfolio of products and services with lower carbon intensity.

Developing new zero-carbon products requires an investment in innovation and developing the capacity necessary to produce new zero-carbon products and services. The objective is to grow the portfolio of zero-carbon products and services and shrink the portfolio of high carbon products and services. Over time, this rebalancing of the portfolio of products and services in favor of zero-carbon solutions will lead to a restructuring of the overall product and service portfolio. This may entail divesting the higher carbon intensive products or services to free up and allocate capital to expand zero-carbon products and services. This restructuring of product and service portfolios and business units will cause companies sooner or later to rethink their capital allocation strategies and to revise their business models.

NET ZERO TRANSFORMATION STRATEGIES AND TRANSITION PLANS

All companies in Pathway Two pursue a similar long-term strategic objective—to become a commercially successful, net zero emissions enterprise. Each Pathway Two company, however, will have different strategies, tactics, and time frames for achieving this long-term objective.

There are many ways to create a net zero transition plan. The World Economic Forum has suggested four steps for companies and investors to consider in transitioning to a net zero enterprise:

> First, measure current emissions, identify the priority areas where emissions can be reduced, and then map out a strategy to curb climate risks.
> Second, having set a strategy, make net zero emissions pledges, set interim goals, and specify how the pledges will be achieved.
> Third, take immediate action to implement the strategies in the plans to achieve the interim targets and the long-term net zero objective.
> Fourth, measure and monitor progress, disclose results, and adjust strategy or plans as necessary.[4]

The World Economic Forum's suggestions, like most net zero guidance, focus on carbon mitigation and do not address how transitioning to a net zero enterprise will affect a company's business model. Most companies, especially if they do not have low carbon intensity, must transform both their carbon utilization and mitigation practices as well as their business models and competitive strategies to be successful in the net zero economy. The World Economic Forum's catchy phrase "map out a strategy to curb climate risk" oversimplifies what is a complex, multidimensional, high-risk, time-consuming, and demanding strategic initiative.[5]

Achieving net zero emissions is not the only transformation that Pathway Two companies are engaged in. For example, many companies also are engaged in a digital transformation, which is far from complete. As discussed in Chapter 2, tracking a company's GHG emissions data requires a robust data analytics strategy and database architecture to gather, store, monitor, and interpret massive amounts of emissions data. Digital technologies, data analytics, artificial intelligence, machine learning, and cyber security will play an important part in most net zero transformation strategies, including creating a smart power grid as the foundation for the energy transition.

The transition to net zero needs to be integrated with the digital transformation of the business model and products and services provided to customers. On the surface, for example, the automotive industry's transition to electric vehicles looks like a transition from internal combustion engines to electric motors, but it is a much deeper and more profound transformation. Car manufacturers are evolving rapidly into information technology platform companies. The transition to electric and autonomous vehicles will transform General Motors into a software company that just happens to make hardware—cars. GM's transformation to an information technology and computing platform based on smart electric vehicles inspires a new business model: cars become the platform to deliver GM developed software to offer consumers services that go beyond their vehicles. GM's zero-emission electric cars will use machine learning and artificial intelligence to assist drivers, making cars safer and more efficient.

Other industries are responding to the simultaneous digital and net zero transformations. Companies embed artificial intelligence into buildings to reduce power to lights, ventilation, or elevators that are not in use. Home-energy storage solutions allow power from solar panels to be stored, enabling the foundation of a smart, distributed power grid where all buildings contribute and consume power.

COMPLETE TRANSFORMATION OF THE EXISTING PRODUCT AND SERVICES PORTFOLIO TO ZERO CARBON

Walmart, Inc.

Walmart, the world's largest retailer with operations in more than two dozen countries and a supply chain that spans the globe, is committed to addressing climate change. It is committed to achieving net zero emissions across its global operations by 2040 without relying on carbon offsets.

Walmart is a Pathway Two company with low carbon intensity that is transforming its product portfolio without changing its fundamental business model as a retailer. At the same time, however, Walmart is transforming the company "to provide its customers with a seamless omni-channel experience in stores and on-line in a way that is regenerative." This means creating value for people and the planet, including reducing the carbon intensity of the products it sells by enhancing the sustainability of retail supply chains. Walmart believes its regenerative approach creates a virtuous cycle it calls its "flywheel."[6]

In 2016, Walmart became the first retailer to set science-based emissions-reduction targets to reduce emissions in its own operations and supply chain. In 2020, Walmart aligned its science-based emissions-reduction targets to a 1.5°C temperature rise trajectory. Its near-term targets include reducing its absolute Scope 1 and 2 emissions by 35% by 2025 and 65% by 2030 from a 2015 base year. Walmart's long-term target is to achieve net zero emissions across its global operations by 2040 without relying on carbon offsets.

In fiscal 2021, Walmart reported Scope 1 emissions of 7.24 million metric tons and Scope 2 emissions of 9.19 million metric tons. In fiscal 2021, the company's carbon intensity across its Scope 1 and 2 emissions was approximately 29 metric tons per $1 million of revenue.[7]

Walmart reports all applicable categories of its Scope 3 emissions using Carbon Disclosure Project methodologies and reports them through the CDP but focuses primarily on reducing the Scope 3 emissions in its two largest categories: category 1 (purchased goods and services) and category 11 (use of sold products). In fiscal 2021, Walmart estimated its Scope 3 emissions from purchased goods and services and from use of products sold were 130.2 million metric tons and 32.1 million metric tons, respectively. Also in fiscal 2021, Walmart reported total Scope 3 emissions of 171.269 million metric tons. The company's carbon intensity across its Scope 3 emissions was approximately 298 metric tons per $1 million of revenue and its carbon intensity across its Scope 1, 2, and 3 emissions was approximately 327 metric tons per $1 million of revenue.[8]

Project Gigaton, which aims to cumulatively avoid 1 billion metric tons of its Scope 3 emissions by 2030, is Walmart's science-based Scope 3 target. In fiscal 2022, Walmart reported that its suppliers cumulatively had avoided more than 576 million metric tons of GHGs since 2017. To date, more than 4,500 of Walmart's suppliers have formally joined Project Gigaton, making it one of the largest private sector consortiums for climate action. At the current rate of cumulative emissions avoidance, Walmart will achieve Project Gigaton's 1 billion metric ton target by the end of fiscal 2025.

Walmart also is working to reduce the Scope 3 emissions of its private brands and create a circular economy with no waste. It has set a goal to have its private brands use only recyclable, reusable, or industrially compostable packaging by 2025. In 2020, it donated over 745 million pounds of food globally and diverted 81% of its waste from landfills and incineration.[9]

Eco-efficiency processes and systems will play a role in helping Walmart reach its net zero target by 2040. It has identified five primary eco-efficiency targets: renewable energy, energy efficiency, refrigeration, transportation, and stationary fuels. Walmart has committed to power 50% of global operations with renewable sources of energy by 2025 and 100% by 2035. The company will achieve energy efficiencies throughout its facilities through design, replacement of equipment with the latest high-efficiency technology, and the use of technology to monitor and optimize energy use in its buildings. It plans to electrify its fleet to achieve net zero emissions and phase out the use of stationary fuels, including fossil fuels used for heating, cooling, and backup power. Walmart is working to reduce its emissions from refrigerants by eliminating leaks, implementing low global warming potential (GWP) refrigerants, and advocating for scaled adoption of low GWP technology.[10]

Nestlé

Nestlé, the world's largest food and beverage company, is committed to addressing climate change. It is committed to achieving net zero emissions across its global operations by 2050. Nestlé is a Pathway Two company with low carbon intensity that is transforming its entire product portfolio to advance regenerative food systems at scale without changing its fundamental business model as a food and beverage company.

Nestlé believes business should act "as a force for good" and has a business philosophy to create shared value, which means not only creating value for its shareholders but also for society.[11] To advance regenerative food systems at scale, Nestlé is helping to restore the environment, improve the lives of farmers, and enhance the resilience and well-being of the communities in which it does business and where its customers live.[12]

Nestlé has set SBTi-aligned emissions-reduction targets aligned with limiting the global temperature rise to 1.5°C as contemplated by the Paris Agreement. Its near-term targets include reducing its absolute Scope 1 and 2 emissions by 20% by 2025 and 50% by 2030 from a 2018 base year. Nestlé's long-term target is to achieve net zero emissions across its global operations by 2050.[13]

In fiscal 2021, Nestlé reported Scope 1 emissions of 3.37 million metric tons and Scope 2 emissions of 1.61 million metric tons. The company's carbon intensity across its Scope 1 and 2 emissions was approximately 55 metric tons per $1 million of revenue.[14]

Also in fiscal 2021, Nestlé reported total Scope 3 emissions of 113.72 million metric tons.[15] The company's carbon intensity across its Scope 3 emissions was approximately 1,267 metric tons per $1 million of revenue and its carbon intensity across its Scope 1, 2, and 3 emissions was approximately 1,322 metric tons per $1 million of revenue.[16]

More than 95% of Nestlé's GHG emissions come from its Scope 3 emissions. Dairy and livestock ingredients account for about half of the emissions associated with sourcing Nestlé's ingredients. To tackle emissions from its upstream supply chain, Nestlé has developed two strategic approaches: Forest Positive and Regenerative Agriculture.[17]

Nestlé's Forest Positive strategy has three key objectives: establishing deforestation-free supply chains, conserving and restoring forests in its supply chain, and creating sustainable landscapes. The overall strategy is to optimize global forests' ability to continue to sequester approximately 2.6 billion metric tons of CO_2 per year. Nestlé aims to have deforestation-free supply chains for meat, palm oil, pulp and paper, soya, and sugar by 2022 and for coffee and cocoa by 2025. To conserve and restore forests in its supply chain, Nestlé aims to plant 200 million trees by 2030. The company plans to support at least 15 sustainable landscape initiatives by 2023 to introduce sustainable agroforestry crop systems and restore natural ecosystems.[18]

Nestlé's Regenerative Agriculture strategy is an approach to farming that improves soil health and fertility and protects water resources and biodiversity. These practices are foundational for sustainable food production. Nestlé plans to invest over $1.2 billion by 2025 in supporting regenerative agriculture across its supply chain. The company has worked to develop net zero dairy farms employing a variety of practices, including enriching animal diets, using biogas digesters, improving soil health, and installing solar power.[19]

The company has joined the Ellen MacArthur Foundation's New Plastics Economy initiative to create a circular economy for plastic. The company intends to follow the New Plastics Economy's Nine Golden rules to drive packaging toward a circular model.[20] Nestlé also is working to reduce the emissions of its packaging, which accounts for about 10% of its overall emissions. It aims to use only recyclable or reusable packaging by 2025 and reduce its use of virgin plastic by one-third by 2025.

Eco-efficiency processes and systems will play a key role in helping Nestlé reach its net zero goal by 2050. It has identified several primary eco-efficiency targets: renewable energy, energy efficiency, refrigeration, transportation, and logistics. Nestlé has committed to power 100% of global operations with renewable sources of energy by 2025. The company will achieve energy efficiencies throughout its facilities by installing LED lighting systems, optimizing energy consumption during nonpeak hours, and recovering heat. Nestlé is working to reduce its emissions from refrigerants by phasing out refrigerants with high global warming potential and replacing them with low global warming potential refrigerants.[21] It is reducing the emissions of its vehicle fleet by switching some vehicles to liquified natural gas, the fossil fuel with the lowest carbon intensity, and experimenting with electric and hydrogen-powered trucks. Finally, Nestlé plans to use nature-based solutions, including agroforestry, silvopasture, and restoration of forests, to remove 13 million metric tons of CO_2e from the atmosphere by 2030.[22]

Nestlé has taken a systemic approach to achieving its net zero objectives. It has integrated its net zero strategy with a comprehensive strategy to fulfill the UN SDGs and its philosophy to create shared value takes a multiple stakeholder approach to managing its business. Its Net Zero Roadmap is a good example of a plan to conform a business model to a net zero emissions economy.

Roll-Royce Holdings

Rolls-Royce Holdings, a multinational aerospace and defense company based in the UK, has pledged to reduce emissions from its own operations to reach net zero by 2030 and to play a leading role in enabling the sectors in which it operates to reach net zero by 2050. The company believes the transition to net zero is both a societal imperative and the greatest commercial opportunity of our time.

Rolls-Royce is a Pathway Two company with low carbon intensity across its Scope 1 and 2 emissions and high carbon intensity across its Scope 3 emissions that is transforming its product portfolio without changing its fundamental business model as a manufacturer of engines and energy systems. Most of Rolls-Royce's Scope 3 emissions come from its customers' use of its products in the aviation, shipping, and power-generation industries, where reducing GHG emissions is quite challenging.

In fiscal 2021, Rolls-Royce reported Scope 1 and 2 emissions of 585,000 metric tons, including 300,000 metric tons from testing its products.[23] The company's carbon intensity across its Scope 1 and 2 emissions was approximately 42 metric tons per $1 million of revenue.[24]

More than 97% of Rolls-Royce's GHG emissions come from its Scope 3 emissions. In fiscal 2021, Rolls-Royce reported total Scope 3 emissions of 275.28 million metric tons.[25] The company's carbon intensity across its Scope 3 emissions was approximately 20,333 metric tons per $1 million of revenue and its carbon intensity across its Scope 1, 2, and 3 emissions was approximately 20,375 metric tons per $1 million of revenue.[26]

Rolls-Royce has set science-based targets across its Scope 1 and 2 emissions, excluding emissions caused by testing its aircraft engines and other products. In addition to its near-term goal to achieve net zero operations by 2030, it has pledged to become a net zero company across its value chain by 2050. Rolls-Royce also intends to play a leading role in enabling the sectors in which it operates to get to net zero by 2050 and has joined the UN Race to Zero.

Rolls-Royce has adopted a three-stage decarbonization plan.[27] The first stage involves achieving net zero GHG emissions from its operations and facilities, excluding product testing, by 2030. The company currently is precluded from using 100% sustainable biofuels to test its aircraft engines and is awaiting new regulations that would allow the use of 100% sustainable biofuels in such tests.

The second stage involves decarbonizing critical systems at the heart of global society. To this end, Rolls-Royce is designing all its civil aviation engines to be 100% sustainable aviation-fuel compatible by 2023 and demonstrating that all its military aviation engines are compatible with 100% sustainable aviation fuel. Sustainable aviation fuel produces up to 70% less CO_2e than conventional aviation fuel. Rolls-Royce aims to reduce the lifetime emissions of its power system products by 35% by 2030 and integrate 2 million watts of hydrogen fuel cells into microgrids by 2030.

To ensure it reaches its targets, Rolls-Royce plans to increase its research and development spending on low-carbon and net zero technologies to 75% of its total research and development budget by 2025 from about 50% now. The company believes in the "power of technology as a force for good."[28] The company is investing in breakthrough technologies and developing products to de-carbonize the complex, carbon-intensive sectors in which it operates. It is innovating in new product areas with significant growth opportunities such as all-electric urban air mobility and regional aviation, hybrid-electric systems, fuel cells, microgrids, and small modular nuclear reactors.

Rolls-Royce is also restructuring its product and service portfolio to focus on activities aligned with its net zero strategy. It has sold businesses to free up capital to invest in new low- or no-carbon businesses with high-growth potential. It sold its interest in ITP Aero, its Civil Nuclear North America Services business, its Civil Nuclear Instrumentation & Control business, and its Bergen Engines medium-speed gas and diesel engines business.

Rolls-Royce made several acquisitions during 2020 to accelerate its net zero strategy in power systems. It acquired a majority stake in electricity storage specialist Qinous to enhance its microgrid offering; acquired Kinolt, a leader in dynamic uninterruptible power supply, to strengthen its market position in safety-critical applications; and acquired Servowatch Systems, an international supplier of integrated marine automation solutions for navies, commercial vessels, and large yachts, to expand its ship automation activities.

The third stage involves working with customers, regulators, and policy makers to change policies to create the conditions to facilitate a successful transition to a net zero emissions economy, including advocating for an increase in the amount of permissible sustainable aviation fuel from 50% to 100%.

Eco-efficiency processes and systems will play a relatively minor role in helping Rolls-Royce reach its net zero goal by 2050. It has already cut the emissions from its operations in half by improving energy efficiency to reduce demand, installing on-site renewable energy generation, and purchasing renewable energy. The company is working to reduce waste generated from its operations and cut the use of virgin materials. To keep its focus on developing technologies to help achieve a net zero emissions economy, Rolls-Royce does not plan to use carbon offsets to achieve its targets.

SUMMARY

To summarize, Pathway Two, Option One includes a focus on eco-efficiency, regulatory compliance, and risk management. The focus moves beyond compliance by starting to transform the business model by anticipating and meeting the future expectations and needs of customers by engineering and designing new zero-carbon products and services.

(See Appendix 7.1 for some questions Pathway Two company directors and investors might ask and for management to consider.)

NOTES

1. East, W. (n.d.). as quoted on the Rolls-Royce website. https://www.rolls-royce.com/innovation/net-zero.aspx#/ (accessed 19 August 2022).
2. World Economic Forum in Collaboration with Boston Consulting Group. (2022). Winning the race to net zero: the CEO guide to climate advantage (January). https://www3.weforum.org/docs/WEF_Winning_the_Race_to_Net_Zero_2022.pdf.
3. Shell plc. (2021). Shell accelerates drive for net zero emissions with customer first strategy. Press release (11 February). https://www.shell.com/media/news-and-media-releases/2021/shell-accelerates-drive-for-net-zero-emissions-with-customer-first-strategy.html.

4. Ross, J. (2021). Define, target, implement, track: a 4-step program to net-zero. World Economic Forum (22 October). https://www.weforum.org/agenda/2021/10/net-zero-companies-business-cop-26-business/.

5. Ibid.

6. Carbon Disclosure Project. (2021). Walmart, Inc. Climate Change 2021. https://www.cdp.net/en/formatted_responses/responses?campaign_id=74241094&discloser_id=892817&locale=en&organization_name=Walmart%2C+Inc.&organization_number=20402&program=Investor&project_year=2021&redirect=https%3A%2F%2Fcdp.credit360.com%2Fsurveys%2F2021%2Fdbbr64mv%2F141779&survey_id=73557641 [Note: Anyone can obtain a user name and password to access data on the CDP website].

7. Walmart Inc. (2021). Environmental, social & governance reporting: FY 2022 summary. https://corporate.walmart.com/esgreport/.

8. Carbon Disclosure Project. (2021). Walmart, Inc. Climate Change 2021.

9. Walmart Inc. (2021). Environmental, social & governance reporting: FY 2022 summary.

10. Carbon Disclosure Project. (2021). Walmart, Inc. Climate Change 2021.

11. Nestlé. (2021). Annual review 2021. https://www.nestle.com/sites/default/files/2022-03/2021-annual-review-en.pdf.

12. Nestlé. (2022). Creating shared value and sustainability report 2021 (March). https://www.nestle.com/sites/default/files/2022-03/creating-shared-value-sustainability-report-2021-en.pdf.

13. Nestlé. (2021). Annual review 2021. Carbon intensity based on a conversion rate of reported revenue at 1.03 Swiss Francs to the dollar.

14. Ibid.

15. Nestlé. (2022). Creating shared value and sustainability report 2021.

16. Nestlé. (2021). Annual Review 2021.

17. Nestlé. (2022). Creating shared value and sustainability report 2021.

18. Ibid.

19. Ibid.

20. Nestlé. (2021). Accelerate, transform, regenerate: Nestlé's net zero roadmap (February). https://www.nestle.com/sites/default/files/2020-12/nestle-net-zero-roadmap-en.pdf.

21. Carbon Disclosure Project. (2021). Nestlé climate change 2021. https://www.cdp.net/en/formatted_responses/responses?campaign_id=74241094&discloser_id=897156&locale=en&organization_name=Nestl%C3%A9&organization_number=12942&program=Investor&project_year=2021&redirect=https%3A%2F%2Fcdp.credit360.com%2Fsurveys%2F2021%2Fdbbr64mv%2F146106&survey_id=73557641 [Note: Anyone can obtain a user name and password to access data on the CDP website].

22. Nestlé. (2021). Accelerate, transform, regenerate: Nestlé's net zero roadmap.

23. Rolls-Royce. (2022). Leading the transition to net zero carbon. https://www.rolls-royce.com/~/media/Files/R/Rolls-Royce/documents/others/rr-net-zero-full-report.pdf.

24. Rolls-Royce. (2022). Rolls-Royce Holdings PLC 2021 full year results. Press release (24 February). https://www.rolls-royce.com/~/media/Files/R/Rolls-Royce/documents/investors/2021-fy-press-release.pdf [Carbon intensity based on a conversion rate of 1.22 pounds to the dollar].

25. Rolls-Royce. (2022). Leading the transition to net zero carbon.

26. Rolls-Royce. (2022). Rolls-Royce Holdings PLC 2021 full year results [based on a conversion rate of 1.22 pounds to the dollar].

27. Rolls-Royce. (2022). Leading the transition to net zero carbon.

28. Ibid.

8

PATHWAY TWO, OPTION TWO: COMPLETE TRANSFORMATION OF THE BUSINESS MODEL

"We want to create a world that runs entirely on green energy—in a way that works for people and planet."[1]

—Mads Nipper, Group President and CEO, Ørsted

The second transformation strategy of Pathway Two takes a bold, enterprise-wide transformational approach. This strategy develops a long-term strategic plan to transform a company into a net zero enterprise. The objective is to reinvent or redesign completely the company's business model, and quite possibly its purpose and vision. Developing new no- and low-carbon products and services naturally flows from reinventing or redesigning the business model.

Pathway Two, Option Two companies need to combine comprehensive climate risk management over a long-term planning horizon with

EXHIBIT 8.1 Pathway Two, Option Two

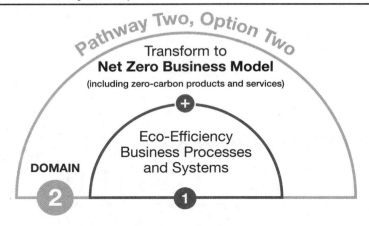

Pathway Two, Option Two

Transform to
Net Zero Business Model
(including zero-carbon products and services)

+

Eco-Efficiency
Business Processes
and Systems

DOMAIN

2

1

Pathway: Strategic Option for Net Zero Business Model Design
DOMAIN: Degree of Strategic Planning Complexity

scenario analysis and cash flow forecasting. Pathway Two, Option Two companies also need to rethink their capital allocation strategies (see Exhibit 8.1).

COMPLETE TRANSFORMATION OF THE BUSINESS MODEL

Ørsted

Fifteen years ago, Ørsted was a fossil fuel–based oil and gas company based in Denmark with high carbon intensity. Since 2006, Ørsted has transformed its business model from being one of the most carbon intensive oil and gas energy providers in Europe to being a global leader in renewable energy. The company has made a complete end-to-end business model transformation from fossil fuel energy to clean and zero-emission electrical power. It has done so by investing heavily in renewable energy—onshore and offshore wind, solar, and biomass—acquiring Danish electrical power producers and phasing out generating power from fossil fuels. The company is on track to achieve net zero emissions by 2040 across its Scope 1, 2, and 3 emissions.

In fiscal 2021, Ørsted reported Scope 1 emissions of 2.142 million metric tons and Scope 2 emissions of 54,000 metric tons. It reported Scope 3 emissions of an estimated 18.174 million metric tons.[2] In fiscal 2021, the company's carbon intensity across its Scope 1 and 2 emissions was approximately 202 metric tons per $1 million of revenue. Its carbon intensity across its estimated Scope 3 emissions was approximately 1,670 metric tons per $1 million of revenue. Ørsted's carbon intensity across all estimated Scope 1, 2, and 3 emissions was approximately 1,872 metric tons per $1 million of revenue.[3]

Ørsted has set scienced-based emissions-reduction targets across its Scope 1, 2, and 3 emissions. As noted in Chapter 4, it was the first energy company to have its targets validated by the SBTi and is one of seven energy companies in the world to have had its targets validated. It has committed to reduce its Scope 1 and 2 emissions by 98% from its 2006 levels by 2025. It has also committed to a near-term target to reduce its Scope 3 emissions by 50% by 2030 from a 2018 base year and a long-term target to achieve net zero emissions by 2040.[4]

Ørsted announced its ambition to become the world's leading green energy major by 2030. It has articulated a comprehensive five-pronged strategy to achieve its ambition that provides a detailed plan of how it will execute upon its strategy and conform its business model to a net zero emissions economy.

First, the company aims to almost quadruple its installed base of gross renewable power capacity from 13.0 gigawatts to 50 gigawatts by 2030. To accomplish this goal, Ørsted aims to maintain its position as the world's largest offshore wind producer with a target of 30 gigawatts of production and to become a top-10 producer of onshore renewables—onshore wind, solar, and storage—with a target of 17.5 gigawatts. It aspires to be one of the world's largest green electricity producers by 2030 and become a global leader in renewable hydrogen and green fuels.

Second, to deliver on its ambitions, Ørsted needs to deploy vast amounts of capital. The company aspires "to be one of the world's largest and most value creating deployers of capital in the green transformation."

Third, to succeed, Ørsted needs to have the best talent. The company aspires to be "the world's leading talent platform in the renewable energy industry."

Fourth, Ørsted wishes to provide global sustainability leadership. The company aspires to be a role model for sustainability and demonstrate that "sustainability and value creation are not opposing, but mutually reinforcing objectives."

Fifth, Ørsted wishes to be a core contributor and catalyst for the change required to create a world that runs entirely on green energy. The company plans to continue to take a leadership role in the transition to a net zero economy by leading by example, setting ambitious targets, and engaging with its stakeholders.

Ørsted has outlined the key components of its strategy. With respect to offshore wind, it aspires to increase the annual rate of expansion of capacity from 2 gigawatts per year until 2025 to 3 gigawatts per year until 2030. With respect to onshore renewables, it aspires to increase the annual rate of expansion of capacity from 0.8 gigawatts per year to 1.5 gigawatts per year. Ørsted will also shift its onshore portfolio to include more solar capacity and pursue additional growth through asset and platform acquisitions. Finally, the company will focus on becoming a leader in renewable hydrogen and green fuels.

Eco-efficiency processes and systems will play a relatively minor role in helping Ørsted reach its net zero goal by 2040 primarily because the company has been engaged in transforming its business model since 2006 and has already achieved many of the benefits of eco-efficiency processes and systems. For example, all power purchased and consumed by Ørsted is certified green power. The company has reduced its GHG emissions by divesting itself of high carbon intensity businesses, including the sale of its natural gas business in 2020. It plans to decommission its remaining coal-fired power plant in 2023.[5]

Shell plc

In 2022, Shell, another one of the world's largest oil, gas, and power producers, is approximately where Ørsted was in 2006 on its journey as a Pathway Two company. Shell is in the early stages of its transformation from a high carbon intensity oil and gas exploration, production, and refining and marketing business into a provider of net zero emissions energy products and services. Shell aspires to become a net zero emissions energy business by 2050, in step with society's progress toward achieving the goals of the Paris Agreement of limiting global temperature rise to 1.5°C. Shell also aspires to be a leading player in developing a global hydrogen economy.

In fiscal 2020, Shell's reported Scope 1 emissions were 98 million metric tons on an equity basis but were calculated on a net basis using carbon capture and storage and nature-based solutions to offset some of its Scope 1 emissions.[6] In fiscal 2020, the company reported 17 million metric tons of Scope 2 emissions, with 8 million metric tons from the energy it consumed and 9 million metric tons from imported energy.[7] Shell reported Scope 3 emissions of an estimated 1,299 million metric tons.[8] As well in fiscal 2020, the company's carbon intensity across its Scope 1 and 2 emissions was approximately 852 metric tons per $1 million of revenue. Its carbon intensity across its estimated Scope 3 emissions was approximately 9,972 metric tons per $1 million of revenue. Shell's carbon intensity across all estimated Scope 1, 2, and 3 emissions was approximately 10,939 metric tons per $1 million of revenue.[9]

Shell has not set scienced-based emissions-reduction targets across its Scope 1, 2, and 3 emissions but it has established emissions-reduction targets from 2016 levels across its Scope 1 and 2 emissions for 2030. It also has committed to work with the SBTi Transition Pathway Initiative and others to develop emissions-reduction standards for the oil and gas industry and align with those standards. Such targets include a 50% reduction, or approximately 41 million metric tons, from 2016 levels in absolute emissions from assets and activities under its control by 2030. Shell has set targets to reduce the overall carbon intensity of products that it sells by 20% by 2030, 45% by 2035, and 100% by 2050, net of carbon capture and storage and nature-based solutions.[10] As discussed in Chapter 1, a Dutch court recently ordered Shell to achieve a net overall emissions reduction of 45%, by 2030 including Scope 3, category 11 emissions from the use of its products.

Although Shell has announced its ambition to become a net zero emissions energy business by 2050, it is still in the process of developing a detailed transition plan that aligns with its overall net zero aspirations. The strategy is based on the belief that by helping its customers, who account for most of its Scope 3 emissions, achieve net zero, Shell will help itself achieve net zero. At the same time, the company believes "ending our activities in oil and gas too early when they are vital to meeting today's energy demand would not help our customers, or our shareholders."

Shell offered its shareholders an advisory vote on its energy transition strategy in 2021 and plans to put it to shareholder vote every three years. The company also has aligned compensation incentives to its strategy by assigning a 20% weight to the energy transition metric in its Long-Term Incentive Plan by adding a GHG abatement target to the annual bonus scorecard, and by increasing the weighting of incentive measures related to GHG emissions to 15%.

Shell's strategy includes plans to invest about $1 billion per year into a portfolio of strategic low-carbon energy initiatives such as charging for electric vehicles, hydrogen, biofuels, sustainable aviation fuels, and electricity generated by wind and solar power. It plans to offer its customers low-carbon alternatives to fossil fuels as demand increases. Shell plans to increase its investments in low-carbon energy to $2 billion per year, provided it can find suitable investments. Shell also plans to increase its current capacity to capture and store CO_2e by an addition 25 million metric tons per year by 2035. Shell plans to use nature-based solutions to offset up to 120 million tons of CO_2e per year by 2030.

Eco-efficiency processes and systems will play a key role in helping Shell reach its net zero goal in 2050. The company expects its emissions will be reduced by declining oil production, which it expects to decline by 1 to 2% per year until 2030. Although it plans to end the routine flaring of gas by 2025 and keep the methane emissions intensity of its operated assets to less than 0.2%, it has identified few other eco-efficiency opportunities it is pursuing.

Shell's Pathway Two strategy is to focus on eliminating its Scope 1, 2, and 3 emissions by 2050 by gradually reducing sales of its oil and gas products while gradually increasing the sales of lower carbon energy products. Although it is short on details, Shell has a clear strategy to transform its business model for success in a net zero emissions economy. Shell has the financial strength and free cash flows to internally finance its business model transformation, especially if oil prices remain high.

Shell, with its global footprint, strong integrated natural gas business, retail operations, and existing power and trading businesses also has the operational strength to grow its no and low-carbon businesses. Shell's strategy, however, is largely dependent on its ability to assist its customers to switch to lower-carbon sources of energy.

What remains to be determined is what kind of returns on capital Shell's no and low-carbon businesses can generate and whether Shell can be more adept at capturing the economic value creation in these businesses than new no and low-carbon energy businesses that do not have legacy oil and gas operations. Shell has the advantages of scale but whether it can capitalize on these advantages to win in the transition to a net zero emissions economy remains to be seen.

Vattenfall

Vattenfall, one of Western Europe's largest producers and retailers of electricity and heat, is on track to achieve net zero emissions across its Scope 1, 2, and 3 emissions by 2040. Before choosing Pathway Two, Vattenfall was an energy utility based in Sweden with high carbon intensity.

For more than a decade, Vattenfall has been transforming its business model from being a fossil fuel–based, carbon-intensive utility to becoming a net zero integrated energy company. It operates a diversified portfolio of green and renewable energy sources, including wind, nuclear, biomass, hydro, and district heating, and conventional coal and gas power plants.

The company's goal is to enable fossil fuel–free living within one generation. Vattenfall is doing so by investing heavily in renewable energy, particularly wind power—and phasing out generating power from fossil fuels and peat.[11]

In fiscal 2021, Vattenfall reported Scope 1 emissions of 10.3 million metric tons and Scope 2 emissions of 100,000 metric tons. It reported Scope 3 emissions of an estimated 17.6 million metric tons.[12] In fiscal 2021, the company's carbon intensity across its Scope 1 and 2 emissions was approximately 577 metric tons per $1 million of revenue. Its carbon intensity across its estimated Scope 3 emissions was approximately 977 metric tons per $1 million of revenue. Vattenfall's carbon intensity across all estimated Scope 1, 2, and 3 emissions was approximately 1,554 metric tons per $1 million of revenue.[13]

Vattenfall has set scienced-based emissions-reduction targets across its Scope 1, 2, and 3 emissions. It has already reduced its Scope 1 and 2 emissions by more than 50% from the 2017 base year. It has also committed to a near-term target to reduce its emissions intensity by 77% by 2030 from the 2017 base year and a long-term target to achieve net zero emissions by 2040.[14]

Vattenfall is committed to its journey to fossil freedom and has articulated a comprehensive strategy to achieve its ambition to reach fossil freedom within one generation and be one of the leaders in developing sustainable energy production. Vattenfall has five strategic focus areas.

First, Vattenfall aims to secure a fossil-free energy supply by quadrupling its installed base of wind and solar capacity from 4.2 gigawatts to over 16 gigawatts by 2030. In addition, the company seeks to double the amount of electricity distributed in its grid and to increase its installed base of 28,700 electric vehicle charging stations by 2,500% to become the leading operator of e-mobility charging points in northwestern Europe.

Second, Vattenfall is committed to connecting and optimizing the energy system. This means promoting stable and cost-effective grid infrastructure, including digitizing the grid and employing artificial intelligence and data analytics to better balance and distribute energy delivered through the grid.[15]

Third, to succeed, Vattenfall needs to collaborate with its customers, partners, and stakeholders to "think beyond the conventional role of energy companies and act together with others." This includes working proactively with customers to reduce their energy consumption and to promote electrification and climate-smart energy solutions in areas where the company has a competitive advantage.[16] Its HYBRIT partnership is working to produce fossil-free steel and its partnership with Shell, Lanza-Tech, and SAS is developing sustainable aviation fuel. Vattenfall also has partnered with Fermi Energia of Estonia to explore the development of small, modular nuclear reactor technology.

Fourth, Vattenfall wishes to empower its people by focusing on securing necessary competence. The company believes acquiring skills in data analytics and digitization, business development, and cross-functional collaboration will be particularly important.

Fifth, Vattenfall aspires to have high-performing, cost-effective, and competitive operations. This entails leveraging opportunities in digitization and taking social and environmental responsibility throughout its value chain.[17]

Vattenfall has outlined the key components of its strategy. Phasing out of fossil fuels will continue to be its top priority. The company plans to phase coal completely out of its operations by 2030. It will phase out its last two coal-fired plants that generate district heat (urban centralized heating systems) in Berlin and replace their heat generation with a likely combination of biomass, waste heat from the City of Berlin's waste incineration operations, hydrogen ready natural gas, heat pumps, and heat storage.[18] It will invest in expanding its wind generation operations, in developing and modernizing its grid, and in district heating networks.

Eco-efficiency processes and systems play a relatively minor role in helping Vattenfall reach its net zero goal by 2040 primarily because the company is engaged in transforming its business model and already has achieved many of the benefits of eco-efficiency processes and systems. The company will achieve additional efficiencies through maintenance, modernization, and replacement of its facilities. For example, the company is working to decarbonize its Berlin district heat facilities by installing new gas turbines with heat recovery boilers and switching to sustainable heat at its two coal-fired facilities.[19]

Vattenfall has taken a systemic approach to achieving its net zero objectives. It has integrated its net zero strategy with a comprehensive strategy to fulfill the UN SDGs. It takes a multiple-stakeholder approach to managing its business and applies the International Integrated Reporting Framework to enhance accountability and stewardship for the broad base of its capitals, including natural, financial, human, manufactured, social and relationship, and intellectual capital. Its 2021 Annual and Sustainability Report provides a good example of a plan to conform a business model to a net zero emissions economy.

General Motors Company

General Motors, the second largest automaker in the United States, is on track to achieve carbon neutrality across its Scope 1, 2, and 3 emissions by 2040. Before choosing Pathway Two, General Motors (GM) was a global manufacturer of internal combustion engine vehicles with high carbon intensity. GM introduced its first modern all-electric vehicle, the short-lived and limited production EV-1, in 1996 and its first electric hybrid vehicle, the Chevrolet Volt, in 2010. After GM introduced its first mass production electric vehicle, the Chevrolet Bolt, in 2016, it decided to go all in on electric vehicles. GM has fully embraced Pathway Two on the journey to transforming its business model from being a manufacturer of internal combustion engine cars and trucks to a manufacturer of smart and autonomous electric vehicles.

The company's vision is a world with "zero crashes, zero emissions, and zero congestion."[20] To fulfill its vision, GM is simultaneously engaged in two transformations. The first is a transformation from a manufacturer of internal combustion engine vehicles to a producer of zero-emissions electric vehicles. The second is a transformation from being a vehicle manufacturer to becoming a fully digitized technology and software business that is fully integrated with its autonomous and electric vehicle business. To achieve its double transformation, GM is acting with a "sense of urgency to get everyone into an electric vehicle."[21]

In fiscal 2021, GM reported Scope 1 emissions of 1.252 million metric tons and Scope 2 emissions of 5.031 million metric tons. GM reported Scope 3 emissions of an estimated 296.411 million metric tons.[22] The company's carbon intensity across its Scope 1 and 2 emissions was approximately 49 metric tons per $1 million of revenue. Its carbon intensity across its estimated Scope 3 emissions was approximately 2,333 metric tons per $1 million of revenue. Finally, GM's carbon intensity across all estimated Scope 1, 2, and 3 emissions was approximately 2,382 metric tons per $1 million of revenue. [23]

GM has set scienced-based emissions-reduction targets across its Scope 1, 2, and 3 emissions. It has also committed to near-term SBTi targets to reduce its Scope 1 and 2 emissions by 72% by 2035 from the 2018 base year and to reduce its Scope 3 emissions from use of sold products (category 11) by 51% per vehicle kilometer by 2035 from the 2018 base year. GM's long-term target is to achieve carbon neutrality by 2040. GM's long-term target of becoming carbon neutral likely will change to a science-based net zero target when the SBTi completes the process of developing guidance for science-based targets for the automotive sector.

GM is committed to its journey to carbon neutrality and has articulated a comprehensive strategy to achieve its ambition to achieve zero crashes, zero emissions, and zero congestion and, ultimately, become the market leader in electric vehicles. General Motors identified three key priorities on its journey to conforming its business model to a net zero emissions economy. In the process, it upgraded its corporate purpose: "We pioneer the innovations that move and connect people to what matters." At the core of its strategy is reimagining the customer experience by delivering world class customer interactions.

First, GM aims to pursue its path to electric vehicle leadership by advancing development of transformative technologies to become a software and technology platform. GM aims to lead in the commercialization of autonomous vehicle technology with Cruise and its successor, Ultra Cruise, the next-generation advanced driver assistance system. It also wants to increase software-enabled subscriptions and services, including Ultifi and OnStar, to enhance the user experience for its customers.

Second, GM aims to reduce its environmental and carbon footprint by pursuing circular design in its products and zero waste in its operations. This means reducing the carbon footprint of all source materials used in its vehicles. The company has launched several initiatives to collaborate with its suppliers and encourage them to set science-based emissions-reduction targets.

Third, to advance its all-electric future, GM is expanding its manufacturing capacity to produce 1,000,000 electric vehicles in each of the United States and China by 2025. It plans to eliminate all tailpipe emissions from new light-duty vehicles by 2035 and have an all-electric vehicle product offering. In addition, it will build four new battery cell manufacturing facilities by mid-decade through Ultium Cells, an equally owned joint venture with LG Energy Solutions. GM intends to invest $35 billion between 2020 and 2025 in electric and autonomous vehicles.

GM also is beginning to take a whole-systems approach to its dual transformations. The company not only recognizes it has the scale to accelerate the widespread adoption of electric vehicles but also to accelerate the transition to a green and renewable power grid in North America. GM is the world's twelfth largest consumer of PPAs and the largest among the automobile industry. "Setting up the grid for a future in which EVs can charge using renewable power for electricity is an essential part of our zero-emission vision."

GM has not specified how it will help accelerate the development of a smart, green, and renewable power grid in North America but is committed to investing in the infrastructure to support electric vehicles. It plans to invest $750 million through 2025 to deploy up to 3,250 EVgo fast charging stalls and 40,000 electric vehicle chargers and provide access to over 100,000 charging plugs through its Ultium Charge 360 mobile app.

Eco-efficiency processes and systems play a key role in helping GM reach its net zero goal by 2040. The company plans to source 100%

renewable energy at all sites in the United States by 2025 and globally by 2035. It conducts annual Energy Star treasure hunts in its facilities to uncover quick ways to save energy. In 2021, for example, it identified 175 opportunities to save over $5 million. GM used concrete made with CarbonCure, a process discussed in Chapter 5 that captures CO_2 and injects it into concrete, in two of its new manufacturing facilities.[24]

General Motors has taken a systemic approach to achieving its net zero objectives. It takes a multiple-stakeholder approach to managing its business and applies the International Integrated Reporting Framework to enhance accountability and stewardship for the broad base of its capitals, including natural, financial, human, manufactured, social and relationship, and intellectual capital. It implicitly incorporates achieving the UN SDGs, tracking its progress toward upholding human rights and building more inclusive communities. Its 2021 Sustainability Report is a good example of a plan to conform a business model to a net zero emissions economy.

CHARACTERISTICS OF PATHWAY TWO

The core assumption for companies on Pathway Two is that achieving net zero will require them to fundamentally and completely transform their business models. They either will need to develop a carbon-free business model or develop new carbon-free products, which naturally will lead to a net zero emission business model. Pathway Two companies will not be able to conform their business models to a net zero economy using only eco-efficiency processes and systems.

Pathway Two companies may have low, medium, or high carbon intensity across their Scope 1 and 2 emissions but tend to have high carbon intensity across their Scope 3 emissions. Pathway Two companies, especially those with relatively low carbon intensity across their Scope 1 and 2 emissions, such as Walmart and General Motors, may be able to achieve net zero emissions in their operations by using eco-efficiency processes and systems and finding lower carbon substitutes in their supply chains.

The challenge for most Pathway Two companies, however, will be reducing their Scope 3 emissions, especially companies such as Rolls-Royce, Shell, and General Motors with high Scope 3 emissions from customers' use of their products. Even if carbon-capture and storage mature to be scalable and cost-effective, the use of such technologies may help Pathway Two companies with high Scope 3 companies achieve net zero but likely will not be enough for them to rely on to achieve net zero. For companies with high carbon intensity across their Scope 3 emissions, it will be difficult, but not impossible, to achieve net zero. Pathway Two companies that are farther along on their net zero journeys, such as Ørsted and Vattenfall, demonstrate, however, that companies with high Scope 3 emissions can achieve net zero.

For traditional investors, Pathway Two companies' net zero performance will be considered critical in making investment decisions. For impact investors, Pathway Two companies could be unattractive investments because their route to net zero faces significant transformation risk and expense and is likely to take years, if not decades.

Profitable Pathway Two companies should continue to enjoy access to sources of capital available for companies that meet traditional metrics but could face higher borrowing costs due to the transformation risk and the expense inherent in transforming their business models to conform to a net zero emissions economy.

As with Pathway One companies, the expectation is that government policies will continue to allow Pathway Two companies to generate some emissions and that Pathway Two companies will be able to further reduce their carbon intensity before carbon taxes are implemented or become material. As under the SBTi, the expectation is that Pathway Two companies will eliminate most of their Scope 1, 2, and 3 emissions by their long-term target dates and offset the remainder by purchasing carbon credits or offsets or through carbon capture or carbon sequestration. For some Pathway Two companies in industries where GHG emissions are hard to abate, such as oil and gas, energy, and aviation, those that have high carbon intensity likely will need to rely on carbon mitigation strategies like carbon capture and storage to achieve net zero.

PATHWAY TWO RISK FACTORS

In addition to the risks discussed in Chapter 6 for Pathway One companies, Pathway Two has its own unique risks because it requires companies to fundamentally change their business models. Corporate transformations are inherently risky. McKinsey & Company and other management consultancies have statistics that indicate most corporate transformations fail. In addition, Pathway Two companies are attempting to transform their business models in the context of industry-wide and economy-wide transformations on a global scale that has never been attempted before.

It is particularly challenging to transform a company's product portfolio or business model while relying on the cash flow from the existing business model to finance the transformation. Disrupting a business model that has served a company well can be destabilizing in particular and create internal resistance if not properly managed. The ultimate cost of conforming business models to a net zero emissions economy could have a material impact on earnings and returns to investors.

Investors and debt providers may lose confidence in a Pathway Two company's climate change strategy, its ability to achieve its emissions-reduction targets, and, therefore, its future earnings potential. If the company's emissions-reduction targets are not science-based or if the company is not holding itself accountable to its targets, its strategy may be perceived as greenwashing with the company not doing enough to contribute to systemic changes needed to achieve a net zero emissions economy or to lead the transformation to a net zero emissions economy.

CRITICAL SUCCESS FACTORS FOR PATHWAY TWO COMPANIES

Our sample of Pathway Two companies employ different strategies to transform their business models to achieve net zero emissions. In addition to the critical success factors for Pathway One Companies described in Chapter 6, Pathway Two companies have some additional success factors that are critical to a successful transformation.

Get started. Most of our sample companies have been engaged in sustainability and eco-efficiency for some time. As a result, they have developed expertise and built relationships they can draw on to transition to a net zero business model. Many may obtain, therefore, a first mover advantage as the net zero transformation of the global economy gains momentum.

Set clear goals and be accountable to them. Our sample companies have set clear goals and emissions-reduction targets and are holding themselves accountable to them. Successful Pathway Two companies back up their goals and targets with strategies and plans to achieve them. Pathway Two companies recognize that developing a plan to become a net zero enterprise is a major undertaking and may involve years of work. They put in the work before announcing their targets and plans.

Have the right leadership. It is critical to have a CEO who can conceptualize and manage the complexities of a complete business model transformation. The CEOs of our sample companies believe in the need to transition to a net zero business model and have the mindset and systems-thinking capacities to guide their companies to let go of their fossil fuel pasts and embrace a net zero future. Leaders of Pathway Two companies need more complex systems-thinking capacities than those required for Pathway One companies, as will be discussed in Chapter 13.

Elevate the Chief Sustainability Officer to the C-Suite. Many Pathway Two companies have transformed the role of the CSO from being a sideline corporate function mostly responsible for ESG to a senior role in the C-Suite, often reporting to the CEO. The transition to net zero will take a decade or two and needs long-term leadership to achieve it, as will be discussed in Chapter 12.

Invest in the transition and transformation. Many Pathway Two companies require major capital investments over a number of years and require management and boards to rethink and revise their capital allocation strategies and practices. Many Pathway Two companies must deliver on big capital bets. As discussed earlier, GM is planning to invest $27 billion in electric vehicles over the next five years.

Collaborate, collaborate, collaborate. Our sample companies recognize they cannot reduce their Scope 3 emissions without engaging their entire value chain. These companies actively collaborate with governments, NGOs, and other companies.

Innovate, innovate, innovate. Pathway Two companies innovate. This includes both big "I" innovation, which is corporate-directed and -funded research and development, and small "i" innovation, which is business unit and individual contributor–generated ideas and projects. Management cannot lead a net zero transformation without thinking out of the box, supporting game changing innovation, and taking calculated risks.

Align the transformation with corporate purpose. Several of our sample companies have refined or reframed their corporate purposes and redefined what businesses they are in, or should be in, and set out new visions for their companies' future. Some also have redefined the fundamental characteristics of their companies. For example, GM is transitioning from a vehicle manufacturer into an information technology platform based on smart electric vehicles.

Align incentive compensation with net zero objectives. Some of our sample companies have aligned their short-, mid-, and long-term incentive compensation with their net zero emissions-reduction targets, eco-efficiency targets, and objectives in their net zero transition plans.

Have a comprehensive communication strategy. Our sample companies place a high priority on effectively communicating their net zero strategies internally and externally. Many have professionally designed annual sustainability reports that track their progress toward achieving their emissions-reduction targets. Many have internal communications strategies to engage their entire organizations in their net zero transition plans and optimize organizational commitment and buy-in.

Have a data analytics strategy. Most of our sample companies put in place key performance metrics and measurement systems along with a data analytics strategy to track progress, learn, and enable course correction. Many also are undergoing digital transformations and adopting digital and artificial intelligence technologies.

Cultivate knowledge building proficiency. Knowledge building proficiency is a critical skill to develop the resilience necessary to navigate a VUCA world. Our sample companies not only focus on developments in eco-efficiency processes and systems and changing regulations but also on scientific developments, how the industry and markets are evolving, competitor strategies and actions, and customer and investor expectations.

SUMMARY

Pathway Two companies have committed themselves to transforming their businesses and business models to achieve both net zero emissions and commercial success. These companies recognize that transitioning to a net zero economy presents significant opportunities and major risks. Governing and managing this transition is a huge challenge, but these companies step up to the challenge. They show other companies the way and often gain a first mover competitive advantage. Time is of the essence, however, and the economy needs many more Pathway Two companies to achieve net zero by 2050.

Pathway Two companies, as established companies, have significant assets, deep industry and business knowledge, relationships, connections, and talent. They also have baggage. Their success in the fossil fuel–based economy may blind some established companies and their leadership from seeing the business risks and opportunities inherent in the transition to a net zero economy. These companies may remain stuck in Pathway One, defending a legacy business model that worked well in the past but will be under increasing stress and harder to defend as the transformation to a net zero economy progresses.

Pathway Two companies have net zero targets and sound strategies to achieve these targets. Companies that announce net zero targets without strategies or plans to attain them may be greenwashing and not true Pathway Two companies.

Pathway Two companies face many internal and external risks. Choosing Pathway Two to transition to net zero is a major undertaking for any company because it entails embarking on a journey of innovation and investment to restructure products, services, business units, and business models that must, in the longer term, be commercially successful. CEOs, senior management, and boards of directors of Pathway Two companies must address complex fundamental issues and address unfamiliar risks and uncertainties as they plan their net zero transitions.

The governance and leadership challenges in the transition to a net zero business model cannot be overstated. This transition is as much about letting go as it is about building something new. Boards of directors and CEOs need courage and determination. They need to focus on what leadership qualities are needed, not only in the near term but also in the long term to ensure the company will develop the next generations of leaders with the right capabilities to complete the task.

Investor engagement and support for Pathway Two companies also will be critical. Investors must understand the net zero transition opportunities and risks and, where appropriate, support net zero transition plans if they are likely to achieve the twin goals of net zero emissions and commercial success. In this regard, investors also will need new skills and better information and reporting from companies about their strategies and plans to achieve net zero emissions, as will be discussed in Chapter 14.

(See Appendix 7.1 for some questions Pathway Two company directors and investors might ask and for management to consider.)

NOTES

1. Nipper, M. (2022). As quoted in Ørsted 2021 sustainability report. https://orsted.com/en/sustainability/esg-ratings-and-reporting/sustainability-report.
2. Ørsted. (2022). ESG performance report 2021. https://orstedcdn.azureedge.net/-/media/annual2021/orsted-esg-performance-report-2021.ashx.
3. Ørsted. (2022). Annual reporting 2021. https://orsted.com/en/investors/ir-material/annual-reporting-2021 [Carbon intensity based on converting revenue of 77.7 billion Danish kroner at a conversion rate of 7.14 kroner to the dollar].
4. Ibid.
5. Ibid.

6. Shell plc. (n.d.). Our climate target: frequently asked questions. http://shell.com/energy-and-innovation/the-energy-future/what-is-shells-net-carbon-footprint-ambition/faq.html (accessed 20 August 2022).

7. Shell plc. (2022). Achieving net-zero emissions. Sustainability Report 2021. https://reports.shell.com/sustainability-report/2021/achieving-net-zero-emissions.html.

8. Shell plc. (2022). Shell plc Form 20-F for the fiscal year ended 31 December 2021. U.S. Securities and Exchange Commission. https://www.sec.gov/ix?doc=/Archives/edgar/data/0001306965/000130696522000012/shel-20211231.htm.

9. Shell plc. (n.d.). Greenhouse gas emissions. https://www.shell.com/sustainability/transparency-and-sustainability-reporting/performance-data/greenhouse-gas-emissions.html (accessed 20 August 2022).

10. Shell plc. (n.d.). Our climate target: frequently asked questions.

11. Vattenfall. (2022). Annual and sustainability report 2021 (19 March). https://group.vattenfall.com/investors/financial-calendar/annual-and-sustainability-report-2021.

12. Ibid.

13. Ibid. (Carbon intensity based on converting revenue of 180.1 billion Swedish crowns at a conversion rate of 10 crowns to the dollar.)

14. Ibid.

15. Ibid.

16. Ibid.

17. Ibid.

18. Ibid.

19. Ibid.

20. General Motors. (n.d.). ESG data center. http://www.gmsustainability.com.data-center.html (accessed 20 August 2022).

21. General Motors. (2022). 2021 sustainability report. https://www.gmsustainability.com/_pdf/resources-and-downloads/GM_2021_SR.pdf.

22. General Motors. (2022). ESG data center.

23. General Motors. (2022). General Motors Company Form 10-K for fiscal year ended 31 December 2021. U.S. Securities and Exchange Commission. 2022 https://www.sec.gov/ix?doc=/Archives/edgar/data/1467858/000146785822000034/gm-20211231.htm.

24. General Motors. (n.d.). ESG data center.

9

PATHWAY THREE: ECO-STARTUPS, NEW VENTURES, SPINOUTS, AND INDUSTRY DISRUPTORS

"If we don't solve the climate issue, aviation will be severely restricted."[1]
—Val Miftakhov, CEO and Founder, ZeroAvia

Pathway Three companies are innovative new ventures with no legacy fossil fuel–based products, organizations, or business models that need to be transformed. They are either eco-startups or have been spun off by established companies as separate eco-startup entities. Pathway Three companies are eco-experiments with exponential growth potential.

Although Pathway Three companies develop and offer "green" zero-emission and eco-friendly products and services to their customers, their business models may not yet be fully developed or immediately capable of achieving net zero emissions. For example, a startup company may be established to penetrate carbon-free markets but is dependent on electricity produced from fossil fuels or supply chain partners that are working to achieve net zero. Pathway Three companies are, however, committed to achieving zero emissions and often have set near-term and long-term science-based emissions-reduction targets. Pathway Three companies have a relatively low degree of net zero transition planning complexity because they tend to have net zero business models from the start and require leaders with leadership capacity in the operational and business systems-thinking domains, as will be discussed in Chapter 13 (see Exhibit 9.1).

Many Pathway Three companies are development-stage startups working on product development that is years and maybe even decades away from generating any material revenue and operating profits. Typically, development-stage startups fund their capital expenditures and working capital requirements through equity offerings until they can generate positive cash flows from operations.

EXHIBIT 9.1 Pathway Three

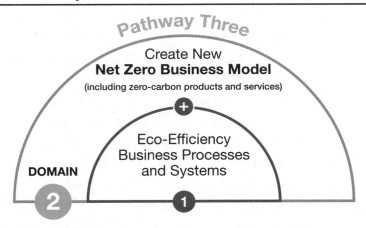

Pathway: Strategic Option for Net Zero Business Model Design
DOMAIN: Degree of Strategic Planning Complexity

CLIMATE TECHNOLOGY AND ECO-STARTUPS

Many eco-startups promote what is known as "climate tech." For example, QuantumScape Corporation, a developer of solid-state lithum-metal batteries for electric vehicles based in California, believes its batteries will charge faster, last longer, go further, and operate more safely than current electric vehicle batteries. The company estimates it will need $2 billion of capital investment to prove its technology and more capital to build production facilities to deliver its batteries to the automotive industry at scale, assuming the technology works as well as expected. QuantumScape has more than 600 scientists and personnel working on its batteries and has more than 300 patents and patent applications.[2] Volkswagen is a major investor and strategic partner and has several representatives on the board of directors. QuantumScape expects to produce prototype batteries for use in test vehicles in 2024 and achieve commercial production after 2025, which is 15 years after it was founded in 2010.

Other climate tech startups aggressively embrace the use of digital and information technologies to create carbon-free, environmentally sound products and business models. For example, Biome Makers, a company dedicated to improving the world's soil health based in San Francisco, provides farmers with detailed reporting and analytics on soil fertility, biodiversity, and health to help them make better-informed decisions. Biome Makers also has developed technologies using artificial intelligence, supported by its expertise in agronomy, to create a virtual assistant that helps farmers increase crop yields and quality. The company is currently piloting a project using its BeCrop technology to restore up to 1 million acres of agricultural fields to health and sequester 500,000 metric tons of carbon in the soil.[3]

Eco-startups no longer face challenges in attracting investors and competing with growth-only IPO-focused startups because interest in impact and ESG investing continues to rise. According to PwC, more than 3,000 climate tech startups were launched between 2013 and the first half of 2021 and received more than $222 billion in funding during that time.[4]

More funding is becoming available every day. For example, the Breakthrough Energy Catalyst, a network organized in 2015 by Bill Gates and a coalition of private investors, is raising up to $3 billion over the next several years and is focused on funding climate tech projects in direct air carbon capture, green hydrogen, long-duration energy storage, and sustainable aviation fuel.[5] Its affiliate, Breakthrough Energy Ventures, has raised over $2 billion in committed capital to support climate tech startups that can reduce emissions from agriculture, buildings, electricity, manufacturing, and transportation.[6]

The goal of many startups, including eco-startups, is to develop a unique product, build and scale a business, and launch an initial public offering (IPO) or get acquired. This game plan continues to look attractive for all startups, including eco- and climate tech startups. In 2021, U.S. stock markets welcomed a record 1,058 IPOs, following a record 480 IPOs in 2020.[7] According to BloombergNEF, $920 billion was invested in energy transition deployment and climate tech companies in 2021.[8]

Although eco-startups can be agile, innovative, and unencumbered by legacy systems and embedded bureaucratic practices, they often lack the resources, data, markets, systems, and management expertise of established companies. As a result, Pathway Three companies have both advantages and disadvantages in competing with established Pathway One and Pathway Two companies.

INNOVATION AND INDUSTRY DISRUPTORS

Reaching net zero by 2050 requires not only the rapid and broad deployment of currently available technologies, but also significant investments in research and development and innovation to develop new breakthrough technologies, new zero-carbon products, and net zero business models.

Pathway Three companies will be a major source of innovation for the transition to a net zero economy. The founders and entrepreneurs in Pathway Three companies often can see the zero-carbon future and will play a critical leadership role in the transition to net zero.

Established companies, particularly those in Pathway One, often focus their research and development and innovation on sustaining innovation, which is innovation directed at continually improving existing processes products, and extending their current business models. It is challenging for many established companies, especially those in Pathway One, to initiate or support creative destruction innovation in which established products and business models are torn apart and replaced by new ones. Sometimes it takes a recession to reveal the weaknesses in old products and business models before established companies re-engineer or replace these old products and business models in a restructuring process. As discussed in Chapter 8, General Motors is engaged in creative destruction by replacing its business model based on producing vehicles with internal combustion engines with one based on information technology and electric vehicles.

Established companies with high carbon intensity and low returns on invested capital will be particularly in need of creative destruction in the transition to net zero. As a result, the transition to a net zero economy will witness many net zero restructurings in established companies. As discussed in Chapter 7, Rolls-Royce is engaged in creative destruction by selling off business units not aligned with its strategy to achieve net zero and acquiring and developing new businesses that are aligned with its strategy.

Innovating to preserve or sustain value in an established company is very different from innovating to create new value in an eco-startup. Innovating to create new value requires different capabilities—people, mindsets, cognitive skills, leadership, organization, risk taking, and funding. There is little, if any, sustaining innovation or creative destruction needed in startup companies because they have no established products or business models to re-engineer or replace. Founders and entrepreneurs focus on capturing the opportunities in unoccupied "white spaces" or, in the case of eco-startups, "green spaces."

Many startups stimulate and enhance innovation by participating in innovation ecosystems or clusters with other startups that bring together entrepreneurs, venture capital firms, post-secondary and research institutions, consultancies, and other players in the startup ecosystem. These ecosystems can provide many benefits, such as encouraging knowledge sharing and collaboration, developing supply chain contacts and relationships, providing sounding boards for solving common business problems, and helping attract and develop talent.

ABOUT DISRUPTION

As startup companies develop new net zero products and services, they may disturb, and in some cases fundamentally disrupt, the markets and business models of established companies.

It is important to differentiate between the concept of ongoing or incremental product improvement and substitution and a full-scale, transformational industry disruption. In a competitive market, established companies continually work to increase their market share by developing and promoting alternative products. Product substitutions may impact how companies compete, but they won't fundamentally change or disrupt the industry.

Clayton M. Christensen, Michael E. Raynor, and Rory McDonald concisely describe the concept of disruption:

> "'Disruption' describes a process whereby a smaller company with fewer resources is able to successfully challenge established incumbent businesses. Specifically, as incumbents focus on improving their products and services for their most demanding (and usually most profitable) customers, they exceed the needs of some segments and ignore the needs of others. Entrants that prove disruptive begin by successfully targeting those overlooked segments, gaining a foothold by delivering more-suitable functionality—frequently at a lower price. Incumbents, chasing higher profitability in more-demanding segments, tend not to respond vigorously. Entrants then move upmarket, delivering the performance that incumbents' mainstream

customers require, while preserving the advantages that drove their early success. When mainstream customers start adopting the entrants' offerings in volume, disruption has occurred."[9]

Christensen, Raynor, and McDonald make another important point—the focus of the disruptor is on the business model, not just the product.

'Disrupters tend to focus on getting the business model, rather than merely the product, just right. When they succeed, their movement from the fringe (the low end of the market or a new market) to the mainstream erodes first the incumbents' market share and then their profitability."[10]

To be discussed in Chapter 10, Tesla is a good example of a Pathway Three Company that evolved into a Pathway Four industry disruptor. Tesla did not invent the electric car, but it disrupted the automobile industry by designing and producing electric cars with leading technologies such as autonomous driving, long-lasting batteries, differentiating features, and a novel business model based on direct sales to customers without middlemen or dealer networks. Tesla even innovated customer service with a direct customer technology support and servicing network where its service people come to customers' homes to service their cars.

THE DISRUPTION OPPORTUNITY MATRIX

Exhibit 9.2 outlines four broad categories of opportunities for eco-disruptors. The axes are the two conditions for a successful transition to net zero namely:

- Transition to net zero emissions by reduction of carbon footprint.
- Generating a return on invested capital greater than the cost of capital.

EXHIBIT 9.2 **The Disruption Opportunity matrix**

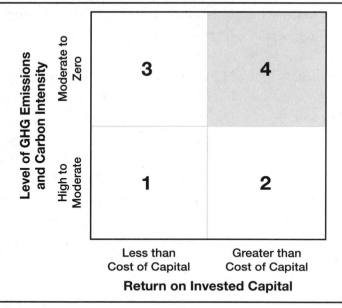

This matrix can be applied to an industry or to specific companies within an industry.

Quadrant 1 contains established companies that have high carbon intensity and returns on invested capital less than their cost of capital, which erodes enterprise value. Companies in Quadrant 1 are ready for an overhaul. These companies are vulnerable to disruptors that produce zero-emissions products with profitable business models. Established companies may be challenged to defend their market position because they may lack the resources to do so.

Quadrant 2 presents great opportunities for disruption, because it contains companies making lots of money with high carbon intensity products and business models. Established companies in Quadrant 2 are vulnerable to disruptors that offer less expensive, no or low-carbon products and then move up market to capture highly profitable customers. Customers of Quadrant 1 and Quadrant 2 companies may tolerate high-carbon products because of a lack of no or low-carbon alternatives, which creates an opening for a disruptor. Disruptors can, however, expect these established companies to vigorously defend their market positions with their most profitable customers.

Quadrant 3 contains established companies that have developed no or low-carbon products but have deficient or broken business models with returns on invested capital below their cost of capital, which erodes enterprise value. Established companies in Quadrant 3 are vulnerable to disruptors that can match their no and low-carbon products and have a superior business model. Companies in Quadrant 3 may be good acquisition targets for other companies or private equity that can provide the managerial expertise to profitably grow market share, build good business models, and scale these companies.

Quadrant 4 comprises successful established companies as well as startups that have developed no or low-carbon products and combined them with business models that create value for investors and other stakeholders with returns on invested capital greater than their cost of capital. It is more difficult for startups to disrupt companies in Quadrant 4, but a startup with no- or low-carbon products and business model may be an attractive acquisition target for larger companies before it takes its products to market.

In summary, eco-disruptors need more than a new no- or low-carbon product or service to be commercially successful. They must understand their market, have a winning strategy for attacking established companies, and have a hard-to-replicate business model that will deliver commercial success and create enterprise value.

Ecolibri Srl

Ecolibri Srl, an Italian company that designs hybrid energy systems, began as an internal project of A.C.E. Srl, a producer of wire harnesses and switchboards for industrial applications. The company began in 2011 as a dream of its co-founder, Donatella Scarpa, to develop clean and renewable energy sources. The first project was a small wind turbine for the international market. Ms. Scarpa's vision was to provide stand-alone renewable energy for developing countries that lack established electrical grids.

After the first prototype was installed at company headquarters in Agrate Brianza, enthusiasm for the project "hit the roof." In 2014, A.C.E. collaborated with the Moldovan Energy Agency to design and construct a factory to build wind turbines in the Republic of Moldova. The factory opened in 2015 and in 2016 A.C.E. spun out the project into a new company, Ecolibri, with the same ownership as A.C.E.[11]

Ecolibri's main products are vertical axis wind turbines. The company's vertical axis design can exploit the power of wind from any direction. This design provides an advantage over horizontal axis turbines, which generally exploit the power of wind from a narrow angle. Unlike noisy horizontal axis turbines, vertical turbines are quiet because the blades cannot rotate faster than the wind. The turbines can be connected to a power grid or used to produce off-grid electricity.[12]

Ecolibri's first wind turbine product is a 3.5 kW generator designed for domestic use. It can provide electricity for a medium-sized home and can be combined with 2 kW of solar panels and battery storage to create a flexible, hybrid system with energy available 24 hours a day. The company is developing 10kW and 20kW versions of its vertical axis turbine for use in areas where it is not feasible to install large horizontal axis generators. Such generators also can be combined with solar panels and battery storage to provide stable and constant power.[13]

The company has focused on selling its products in developing countries that lack fully developed electrical grids, especially in Southern Africa. For example, it installed two hybrid systems to provide electricity to a high school and a university campus under a project with the government of Swaziland.[14]

In addition, Ecolibri offers a variety of products that produce, or run on, renewable energy. It offers solar-powered water pumps, solar-powered gate openers, solar-powered street and garden lights, and portable solar chargers for cell phones and other mobile devices. It also produces solar inverters, photovoltaic systems, solar water heaters, hybrid air conditioning systems, and electric vehicle charging stations.[15]

Like many climate tech companies, Ecolibri has a product portfolio designed exclusively to create solutions for the net zero emissions economy. Like many eco-startups, its business model is already conformed to a net zero emissions economy. Ecolibri has not, however, conducted an inventory of its Scope 1, 2, and 3 emissions, determined its carbon intensity, or set science-based targets. It would be relatively easy for Ecolibri to inventory its GHG emissions and set science-based targets because it has already done the hard work of conforming its core business model to a net zero emissions economy. What remains to be done is to get the carbon out of its business model.

NuScale Power Corporation

NuScale Power Corporation has developed small modular nuclear reactor (SMR) technology. A SMR is a modular light-water reactor nuclear power plant that can supply energy for electrical generation, district heating, desalination, hydrogen production, and other process heat applications. NuScale started with a big goal: to change the power that changes the world. The company aims to redefine nuclear power by delivering safe, scalable, cost effective, and reliable carbon-free power. It is on a mission to improve the quality of life for humankind by continuously improving nuclear power.

NuScale is a 20-year-old eco-startup that began in 2002 as a U.S. Department of Energy (DOE) research project led by the Idaho National Laboratory in collaboration with Oregon State University at Corvallis (OSU). When the DOE-funded project ended in 2003, the research team at OSU continued the project and built a one-third-scale electrical version of an SMR. In 2007, OSU spun out the technology to NuScale and gave it exclusive rights to the technology.[16] Fluor Corporation, a Texas-based global engineering, procurement, and construction company with a 70-year history in commercial nuclear power, became the majority shareholder in 2011 and remains the largest shareholder after NuScale's IPO in 2022.[17]

Since its incorporation in 2007, NuScale has worked toward commercializing the first SMR in the United States. The DOE and NuScale have invested over $1.3 billion toward the development of the NuScale Power Module (NPM) and related VOYGR plant technology. VOYGR is the company's scalable plant design that can accommodate up to 12 NPMs and generate up to 924 megawatts. NuScale also offers the four-module VOYGR-4 (308 MWe) and six-module VOYGR-6 (462 MWe) and other configurations, which allow customers to scale their operations as power demand increases. The company has been issued 443 patents with an additional 196 patents pending.

NuScale's VOYGR's 12-module design is the first and only SMR to have received a U.S. Nuclear Regulatory Commission Standard Design Approval (SDA). NuScale plans to seek an additional SDA for a design with increased NPM power in 2022 and expects approval in 2024.

The company's first contract to deploy a VOYGR system is with the Utah Associated Municipal Power System (UAMPS) at the U.S. Department of Energy's National Laboratory reservation near Idaho Falls, Idaho. Construction of the 6-SMR module system is expected to begin in 2025 with the plant expected to be operational fully in 2029, 22 years after incorporation.[18]

NuScale's SMR has four defining characteristics: it is proven, simple, scalable, and safe.[19] The proven design leverages 60 years of experience with existing light-water nuclear reactor technology and fuel supply. The design greatly simplifies the reactor design by using natural circulation to integrate the reactor core, steam generators, and pressurizers into a single vessel. The simple design eliminates the need for reactor coolant circulating pumps, large bore piping, and other components characteristic of traditional, large-scale nuclear reactors. The design is scalable, allowing customers to add modules as demand increases. The design incorporates many new safety features that allow the SMR to be easily and safely shut down.

Like many eco-startups, NuScale's business model is already conformed to a net zero emissions economy. Although it has signed 20 memoranda of understanding and has over 110 active customer opportunities, it has yet to sell a single NPM.[20] NuScale does not have its own manufacturing facilities and plans to rely on third-party manufacturers to build its NPMs. NuScale has not, therefore, conducted an inventory of its Scope 1, 2, and 3 emissions, determined its carbon intensity, or set science-based emissions-reduction targets. Given that it is still in the research and development stage, it probably has low carbon intensity across its Scope 1, 2, and 3 emissions.

It would be relatively easy for NuScale to inventory its GHG emissions and set science-based targets. It has five years to work with its manufacturing partners and suppliers to reduce the carbon in their processes and products before its first expected commercial sale. During this time, it also could implement the measuring, monitoring, and tracking systems necessary to inventory its Scope 1, 2, and 3 emissions.

Having a clearly articulated net zero strategy and science-based targets in place before the first commercial sale might help NuScale overcome some of the latent resistance to nuclear power caused by accidents at the Three Mile Island, Chernobyl, and Fukushima Daiichi nuclear power plants. Doing so might also inspire its largest investor Fluor, which has committed to achieve net zero across its Scope 1 and 2 emissions from its offices by 2023, to complete a comprehensive analysis of all its GHG emissions and set science-based targets.[21]

Celsius Energy

French startup Celsius Energy was founded by three engineers united by their commitment to the environment and a desire to use their expertise to fight climate change. The inspiration was the realization that heating and cooling buildings generate 25% of global CO_2e emissions. The founders' epiphany was that 70% of the energy needed for heating and cooling buildings is available underground underneath buildings in a constant and abundant supply. The company's concept is simple: utilize geothermal energy for heating and air conditioning buildings. Celsius Energy's solution can reduce the carbon emissions from buildings by up to 90% by using energy readily accessible from inside the earth.[22]

Celsius Energy is a startup spun out of, and wholly owned by, Schlumberger, the world-wide leader in subsurface drilling and development. Schlumberger's expertise in drilling for the oil and gas industry makes it an ideal partner for Celsius Energy. To heat and cool a building, the company places a heat exchanger about 200 meters below the building. A heat transfer fluid circulates in the heat exchanger and a heat pump in the basement allows heat to be exchanged to heat the building in winter and cool it in summer. Generating heating and cooling from the same system reduces the number of components and overall cost. This design complements existing heating and cooling systems and reduces dependence on fossil fuels. The system reduces the carbon footprint of buildings by utilizing a local renewable source of energy. Placing the heat in the basement, which tends to be underutilized space, makes it easy to incorporate the system in new construction and retrofit it into existing buildings.[23]

Like NuScale and Ecolibri, Celsius Energy's business model is already conformed to a net zero emissions economy. It does not appear to have conducted an inventory of its Scope 1, 2, and 3 emissions, determined its carbon intensity, or set science-based targets. Given that it is still in the research and development stage, it probably has low carbon intensity across its Scope 1, 2, and 3 emissions.

It would be relatively easy for Celsius Energy to inventory its GHG emissions and set science-based targets because its parent company, Schlumberger Limited, has set near-term and long-term science-based targets across its Scope 1, 2, and 3 emissions. Schlumberger has committed to reduce its Scope 1 and 2 emissions by 30% by 2025 and by 50% by 2030, including a 30% reduction in Scope 3 emissions. It has committed to achieve net zero by 2050. Since Schlumberger has conducted a comprehensive inventory of its GHG emissions, it would be relatively easy to analyze and sort the data to provide an inventory for Celsius Energy so it could set its own science-based targets. Schlumberger, for example, reported that a Celsius Energy geothermal installation at one of its manufacturing facilities resulted in a 90% reduction in CO_2 emissions, a 60% reduction in energy consumption, and 40% lower annual heating and cooling costs.[24]

Having an inventory of its GHG emissions and setting its own science-based emissions-reduction targets would help Celsius Energy define itself as a leader in the net zero economy.

CarbonCure

CarbonCure, first introduced in Chapter 5, started in 2012 on a mission to decarbonize the concrete industry. Concrete is the world's most resilient building material but has an enormous carbon footprint. The construction and building sector generates about 40% of the world's GHG emissions. More than a quarter of those emissions are in the form of embodied carbon resulting from the manufacturing, transportation, and installation of building materials. Cement accounts for most of this embodied carbon. The concrete industry is responsible for about 7% of global CO_2 emissions, about three times the annual CO_2 emissions of the global civil aviation industry.[25]

To limit global warming to 1.5°C, emissions from embodied carbon need to decline by 65% by 2030 and be eliminated by 2040.[26] CarbonCure's goal is to reduce 500,000 tons of CO_2 per year from the built environment by 2030. The company's core technology injects recycled CO_2 into fresh concrete to reduce its carbon footprint without compromising performance. Once injected, the CO_2 undergoes a mineralization process and becomes permanently embedded, offering permanent carbon storage. CarbonCure's easy-to-adopt technology enables concrete producers to use captured carbon dioxide to produce reliable, lower-carbon concrete mixes.

CarbonCure's technology is based on a four-step process. Waste CO_2 is collected from industrial emitters and purified. The purified CO_2 is stored on-site at a concrete plant and connected to the company's technology. The purified CO_2 is injected into concrete during mixing. The resulting lower carbon, higher performing concrete is then used in building projects.

Injecting purified CO_2 into concrete not only sequesters it but also improves the compressive strength of the mix. The increased efficiency of the cement allows concrete to be produced with less cement—the binder that solidifies the aggregate ingredients such as sand and gravel. The typical mix using CarbonCure's technology will use about 5% less cement. Thus, the technology has a double emissions-reduction benefit by mineralizing waste CO_2 and by avoiding CO_2 emissions from cement. Most of the technology's emissions-reduction benefit comes from avoiding emissions by reducing the use of cement.[27]

The technology has three primary applications in concrete products: ready-mix concrete, precast concrete, and concrete masonry. The technology can also be applied to concrete wash water generated by the washing out of concrete mixers and trucks after concrete has been produced and delivered. Injecting CO_2 into water waste mineralizes the waste cement, making it more stable and less prone to set. The reclaimed water can then be used in making concrete. The reclaimed water also increases the compressive strength of the mix, resulting in reduced emissions and less use of cement.

CarbonCure also sells carbon credits for $235 per ton. Its methodology for calculating CO_2 removal has been verified by Verra, a standard-setting organization whose Verified Carbon Standard Program is the world's most widely used GHG program.[28,29] CarbonCure's technology has been installed in more than 550 sites around the world. To date, its technology has prevented more than 175,000 metric tons of CO_2 from being emitted. As discussed in Chapter 7, General Motors has used its technology to reduce the embodied carbon in two of its facilities.

CarbonCure is a climate tech business whose business model is already conformed to a net zero emissions economy. CarbonCure has not published an inventory of its Scope 1, 2, and 3 emissions, determined its carbon intensity, or set science-based targets other than to achieve net zero emissions. The company claims to have achieved carbon-neutral operations through a combination of eco-efficiency processes and systems, reducing emissions in its supply chain, purchasing renewable energy, and using offsets for its hard-to-avoid emissions. It applies *The Oxford Principles for Net Zero Aligned Carbon Offsetting* in selecting its carbon offset purchases through the Patch platform from Patch Technologies, Inc., a venture capital–financed climate tech startup aiming to scale the carbon removal industry.[30,31] The company aims to achieve net zero by cutting even more of its emissions and removing from the atmosphere as much CO_2 as it emits.

It would be relatively easy for CarbonCure to inventory its GHG emissions, determine its carbon intensity, and set science-based targets. Doing so would give the company more credibility with customers of its technology and carbon credits by leading by example.

Universal Hydrogen Co. and ZeroAvia, Inc.

While Rolls-Royce is working to reduce its carbon intensity by accelerating the transition to sustainable aviation fuels, several climate tech startups around the world are working to revolutionize the aviation industry with zero-emission aviation solutions using electric, hydrogen, and hybrid electric-hydrogen engines. Aviation is the fastest-growing source of greenhouse gas emissions. Although civil aviation currently contributes a little more than 2% of global GHG emissions, its effect is amplified because most aviation emissions are emitted at altitudes where they may have two to four times the warming impact of comparable ground-source emissions.[32] In addition, fossil fuel–powered aircraft emit significant amounts of nitrous oxide (N_2X), contrails, and particulate matter that have their own warming effects.[33]

Two California-based aviation startups, Universal Hydrogen Co. and ZeroAvia, Inc., believe hydrogen-electric propulsion is the only viable, scalable solution for zero-emissions aviation. Both companies are working with alacrity to commercialize their designs for aircraft powered by hydrogen-electric powertrains. Universal Hydrogen's mission is "to decarbonize aviation and put the industry on a trajectory to meet Paris Agreement obligations."[34] ZeroAvia's mission is to "put a hydrogen-electric engine in every aircraft . . . to power a revolution in green flight."[35]

Both companies believe hydrogen-electric powertrains are not only the best way to decarbonize the aviation industry but also offer a better propulsion system with considerable advantages over hybrid electric, battery electric, sustainable aviation fuel, and hydrogen combustion alternatives.

As a fuel, hydrogen has 30 times higher specific energy and lower cycling costs than lithium-ion batteries, whose heavy weight and need for replacement preclude usage on large aircraft. By using a fuel cell in flight to convert hydrogen into electricity to power propulsion, a hydrogen-electric powertrain avoids the NOX emissions and contrails of direct hydrogen combustion propulsion systems. Hydro-electric powertrains generate a fraction of the emissions of hybrid-electric and sustainable aviation fuels, which have the same inflight emissions as conventional aviation fuels. The big challenge is the weight of the powertrain, but that may be a short-term issue that gets resolved as the technology continues to evolve.

Hydrogen fuel is also safer than conventional jet fuels. Hydrogen is nontoxic and dissipates quickly unlike conventional liquid fuel vapors. It is considerably less flammable than jet fuel, which requires far less oxygen to ignite. Hydrogen has been produced, stored, transported, and used safely for more than 50 years.

ZeroAvia estimates hydrogen-electric powertrains have 90% lower life cycle emissions, 60% lower operating costs, and 75% lower hourly maintenance costs than traditional turbine engines.[36] ZeroAvia estimates its hydrogen-electric powertrains will have half the range of standard turboprop planes with equivalent payloads when they enter into service in 2024 but will have the same range by 2026.[37]

Each company's first product is a conversion kit for existing aircraft. Universal Hydrogen's initial focus is converting ATR72s, the most popular in-production regional turboprops, and DeHaviland Canada Dash-8s to fly on hydrogen. It replaces the aircrafts' turboprop engines with a hydrogen fuel cell powertrain. ZeroAvia takes a similar approach. The company retrofits certified fixed-wing aircraft with its hydrogen-electric powertrain.

Universal Hydrogen and ZeroAvia are betting on different approaches to using and storing hydrogen in aircraft. ZeroAvia plans to use green hydrogen produced through electrolysis using locally generated renewable energy. The green hydrogen will be stored at or near airports and used to fill tanks on the aircraft. The company has partnered with Shell, also a strategic investor, to supply compressed, low-carbon hydrogen to its facility and to begin to develop hydrogen airport refueling infrastructure for its hydrogen-electric powertrain retrofits.[38]

Universal Hydrogen, on the other hand, would use green hydrogen also, but takes a modular fuel-distribution approach. The company has designed a lightweight, aviation-grade, hydrogen storage capsule that can be swapped out of an aircraft easily and quickly to refuel it. Universal Hydrogen's approach creates a standard tank form factor, similar in concept to small propane tanks that are widely available for exchange. Using a standard-size storage capsule to store hydrogen not only allows for rapid refueling of aircraft but eliminates the need for fixed hydrogen fuel infrastructure at airports. The storage capsule also can be used in a variety of transportation applications. Universal Hydrogen intends to create a global hydrogen distribution network that can deliver green hydrogen to any commercial airport in the world.

Universal Hydrogen imagines using its powertrains and modular fuel capsules on long-range, single-aisle aircraft, which produce most aviation emissions. Elongating the fuselage of a standard single aisle jet aircraft by 9 meters to accommodate numerous fuel capsules would empower emission-free, transatlantic passenger flight. Universal Hydrogen is blunt in its assessment of the aviation industry's best pathway to net zero emissions: "The only way aviation can meet Paris Agreement emission targets is if the new single aisle airplanes are hydrogen powered."[39]

Both startups are capital intensive and have received funding from a variety of financial and strategic partners. Both have received their first purchase orders. Waltzing Matilda Aviation, a jet charter operator, has placed an order with Universal Hydrogen to convert 75 ATR 72-600s for its new Connect Airlines brand, which has committed to become "the world's first true zero emission airline."[40] Universal Hydrogen will deliver its first retrofitted planes in 2025 and Connect Airlines has rights to purchase an additional 25 planes. MONTE Aircraft Leasing, a zero-emission regional turboprop lessor, has signed an agreement to purchase up to 100 of ZeroAvia's hydrogen-electric powertrains to be installed on four types of new and existing turboprop aircraft. ZeroAvia and MONTE aim to begin retrofitting aircraft for clients in 2024.[41]

Universal Hydrogen and ZeroAvia have business models that are already conformed to a net zero emissions economy. Both companies are in the research and development stage and have not begun to ramp up manufacturing operations. Neither company, therefore, has conducted an inventory of its Scope 1, 2, and 3 emissions, determined its carbon intensity, or set science-based emissions-reduction targets.

It would be relatively easy for each company to inventory its GHG emissions and set science-based targets. Each has two or three years to work with its manufacturing partners and suppliers to reduce the carbon in their processes and products before delivering their first retrofitted planes. During this time, each company could also implement the measuring, monitoring, and tracking systems necessary to inventory its Scope 1, 2, and 3 emissions.

Having GHG emissions inventories and science-based targets in place before delivering their first retrofitted planes to customers would position Universal Hydrogen and ZeroAvia more in alignment with the revolutionary nature of their net zero emissions business models.

INCREMENTAL INNOVATION VERSUS EXPONENTIAL INNOVATION

Our sample companies suggest new technology has great potential to accelerate the transition to a net zero economy. Exponential technologies, which are technologies widely and rapidly adopted, often creating entirely new markets and business models, have the greatest potential. The smartphone, for example, went from invention in 1996 to adoption by 1 billion users in 16 years. It took only four more years to reach 2 billion users. The smartphone enabled the developing world to leapfrog the paired copper wire infrastructure of landline telephony to join the internet world.

An exponential technology causes huge improvement in capability or performance over the incumbent technology. This improvement in capability or performance is not incremental but is at least double, triple, or even orders of magnitude greater. They can become ubiquitous quickly because they are built upon previous technology, which was often exponential in its day. Seasoned venture capital investors look for startups that offer a 10X improvement in capability or performance. Exponential technologies are the innovations upon which their fortunes are made, often providing exponential returns of 10X or more.

Rolls-Royce may be able to provide an incremental improvement in the overall CO_2e emissions from its jet engines by enabling them to run on sustainable aviation fuel. Made from feedstocks such as forestry and agricultural waste and used cooking oil, sustainable aviation fuel may have reduced overall life cycle GHG emissions but, when combusted, still produces emissions comparable to traditional jet fuel. Using sustainable aviation fuel alone will not enable the aviation industry to get to net zero.

Our two hydrogen-electric aviation powertrain companies, Universal Hydrogen and ZeroAvia, are built upon exponential technologies that have numerous advantages over incumbent turboprop and jet turbine aircraft propulsion technologies. While still in the research and development stage, both companies not only have viable paths to market and but also offer the possibly of a new zero-emissions paradigm in aviation. Both companies leverage a foundation of prior aviation technologies to offer the potential of zero emissions, greater safety, and reduced complexity. If their technologies are proven in the marketplace, the global aviation industry might adopt hydrogen-electric propulsion to become net zero by 2050 or sooner.

The technology could revolutionize the aviation industry and have a multiplier effect elsewhere by stimulating the development of the green hydrogen industry that produces hydrogen using renewable or clean energy. Most hydrogen produced today is "gray" and is derived from natural gas using an energy intensive process that emits GHGs. "Blue" hydrogen, which also is derived from natural gas in the same energy-intensive process, is touted as a cleaner alternative to gray hydrogen because emitted CO_2 is captured during production. One easily could imagine a company using NuScale's SMR technology to electrolyze water to produce green hydrogen fuel for the aviation industry and the transportation sector.

EXHIBIT 9.3 Exponential technology matrix

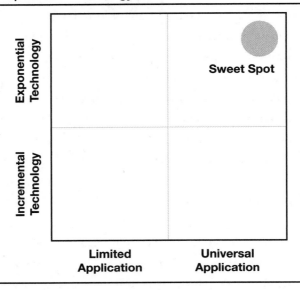

Exhibit 9.3 provides a framework to analyze the potential of an innovation to reduce or eliminate CO_2e emissions.

CarbonCure's technology provides an incremental reduction in CO_2 emissions in the process of making concrete. If universally adopted by the global concrete industry, its technology would reduce its overall emissions by about 10%. This would be a positive result but would still leave the concrete industry a long way from achieving net zero. An exponential innovation in the concrete industry might be a CO_2-sequestering binder to replace the Portland cement that emits CO_2 in the manufacturing process. The point is that incremental and exponential technologies will help the global economy achieve net zero, but exponential technologies will help it achieve net zero faster.

CHARACTERISTICS OF PATHWAY THREE

The core assumption for companies on Pathway Three is that they are out to change the world with a new low- or no-carbon product or service. Pathway Three companies not only assume their business models inherently conform to a net zero economy but also already do business in the net zero economy. Unlike traditional startup companies, which focus on creating a successful business, Pathway Three companies must create a successful business and contribute to achieving a net zero economy.

Pathway Three companies are often so focused on fulfilling their missions that they have not yet conducted a GHG inventory, calculated their carbon intensity, or set science-based emissions-reduction targets. Since their business models already conform to a net zero emissions economy, it should be relatively easy for Pathway Three companies to achieve net zero emissions in their own operations. They should rely on using eco-efficiency processes and systems to eliminate their own Scope 1 and 2 emissions and work with their value chains to reduce or eliminate their Scope 3 emissions.

PATHWAY THREE RISK FACTORS

In addition to the risks discussed in Chapter 6 for Pathway One companies and in Chapter 8 for Pathway Two companies, Pathway Three has its own unique risks. Pathway Three is not for the faint of heart. Startup companies are risky. According to the Bureau of Labor Statistics, 45% of new businesses fail by their fifth anniversary.[42] About 75% of venture capital firms are not able to return their investors' capital, implying a high rate of failure.[43] Although startup companies involve significant risk-taking by their founders and the investors that support them, the payoffs and returns in both financial and nonfinancial terms can be very rewarding.

Eco-startups and potential disruptors should not underestimate how hard established companies will fight to defend their market shares and positions in their industries. Successful startups often start by focusing on an underserved segment of the market that is not of interest to larger established companies. They establish a foothold and then move into higher-end and more profitable market segments. Saving the planet is an admirable goal, but in a competitive market, an eco-startup needs to have a solid plan to launch its product, gain market share, and compete against larger established companies.

Many startups fail because they must work through a significant development phase that drains cash before their products or services are ready to take to market. NuScale, for example, has burned through $1.2 billion over 15 years and still has another 5 years before its first SMR will be operational. A successful startup must successfully manage a long period of negative cash outflows and raise capital before it can generate positive cash flows from operations.

CRITICAL SUCCESS FACTORS FOR PATHWAY THREE COMPANIES

In addition to the critical success factors for Pathway One companies described in Chapter 6 and Pathway Two companies described in Chapter 8, Pathway Three companies have some additional critical success factors to consider.

Have a leadership team with requisite startup skills. Eco-startups, like other startups, typically have high-energy, passionate founders who are on a mission and have the entrepreneurial drive and passion to grow their businesses and help maintain a habitable planet. Unfortunately, many founders lack the managerial experience and expertise in other areas like marketing, finance, and accounting to successfully build and scale a rapidly growing business. Successful eco-startups have a core leadership team that complements and supports the passion and expertise of the founder(s) and has the entrepreneurial skills necessary for success in early-stage companies.

Have a compelling purpose and vision. An eco-startup business needs a compelling purpose and vision to be attractive to investors and employees. Contributing to the transition to a net zero economy can turbocharge an eco-startup's core purpose and vision. The startup must still convince investors that it can deliver on that vision and generate returns that exceed the cost of invested capital.

Have a clear strategy to create economic value. Eco-startups continually develop, revise, and update their business and financial plans to create value for all their stakeholders. Eco-startups need a short-term and long-term funding strategy and financial plan to address their unique funding needs, such as lengthy development phases before they launch commercial operations.

Obtain solid and stable financial backing. An eco-startup needs solid financial backing from investors and sponsors who have a long-term investment horizon. Eco-startups need a transparent and healthy working relationship with their investors.

Have authentic zero-carbon products or services. To be authentic, an eco-startup's products or services need to be clearly aligned with the climate change targets set forth in the Paris Agreement. Being perceived as an opportunistic, greenwashing startup will pose serious reputational and credibility problems.

Understand and meet the net zero needs and sustainable product expectations of customers. Eco-startups need to understand their markets and market opportunities. They need to understand their customers and their needs and ensure their marketing and sales strategies target these customers. An entrepreneur's belief in his or her product is often positively infectious, but a product will not produce commercial success or a commercially successful business if it does not satisfy a real business need at a price that customers will pay. At the end of the day, the successful eco-startup needs to have a product or service that will help its customers achieve their net zero ambitions and succeed in the net zero economy.

Have a scalable business model. Eco-startups have an operating business model that will determine how they will make money as they reach the operational phase and that is scalable to allow them to enter a high-growth phase.

Good discipline. Successful eco-startups put in place reliable management and reporting systems that enable the founders and core leadership team to continually track performance, learn what works, quickly course correct, and provide meaningful and timely reporting to their investors. This includes inventorying GHG emissions, determining carbon intensity, and setting science-based targets.

SUMMARY

As Bill Gates remarked at a recent World Economic Forum:

"The number of companies working on these things is very exciting. Some of them will fail. A lot of them will fail. But we only need a reasonable number, a few dozen of them, to make it through and that's what we have to accelerate."[44]

In short, the world needs a few dozen companies with exponential breakthroughs to lead the charge.

The demand for net zero products and services will continue to accelerate as the world transitions to a net zero economy, creating massive opportunities for eco-startups and disrupters. Policy makers, companies, and investors are all betting on climate tech breakthroughs to transform companies, industries, and society itself to enable humanity to thrive in a net zero economy.

Pathway Three companies will drive much of the innovation for these breakthrough technologies. Pathway Three creates exciting opportunities for eco- and climate tech startups and disruptors. The challenge, however, is to ensure that these companies can access the capital they need to create the innovations and technology breakthroughs essential to facilitate the transition to a net zero world.

(See Appendix 9.1 for some questions Pathway Three company directors and investors might ask and for management to consider.)

NOTES

1. Miftakhov, V. (2022). As quoted in Singer, D. (2022). ZeroAvia aims for 'true zero' instead of net zero. Simpliflying.com blog (22 July). https://simpliflying.com/2022/zeroavia-aims-for-true-zero-instead-of-net-zero/.
2. QuantumScape Corporation. (n.d.). www.quantumscape.com/ (accessed 20 August 2022).
3. Biome Makers. (n.d.). biomemakers.com/ (accessed 20 August 2022).

4. PwC. (2021). State of climate tech 2021. https://www.pwc.com/gx/en/services/sustainability/publications/state-of-climate-tech.html (accessed 20 August 2022).

5. Breakthrough Energy. (n.d.). U.S. requests for proposal. http://breakthroughenergy.org/catalyst-us-rfp (accessed 20 August 2022).

6. Breakthrough Energy. (n.d.). Our story. https://breakthroughenergy.org/our-story/our-story (accessed 20 August 2022).

7. Stock Analysis. (n.d.). All 2021 IPOs. https://stockanalysis.com/ipos/2021/ (accessed 20 August 2022).

8. BloombergNEF. (2022). Energy transition investment trends 2022 (January). https://assets.bbhub.io/professional/sites/24/Energy-Transition-Investment-Trends-Exec-Summary-2022.pdf.

9. Christensen, C., Raynor, M., and McDonald, R. (2015). What is disruptive innovation? Harvard Business Review (December). https://hbr.org/2015/12/what-is-disruptive-innovation.

10. Ibid.

11. A.C.E. (2016). A.C.E.: 50 years of passion. https://www.acecablaggi.com/wp-content/themes/coritheme/pdf/ACE-STORIA.pdf.

12. Ecolibri Srl. (n.d.). Wind generators. https://www.ecolibri.it/hybrid-wind-solar-generators/ (accessed 20 August 2022).

13. Ibid.

14. A.C.E. (2016). A.C.E.: 50 years of passion.

15. Ecolibri Srl. (n.d.). Power of nature. https://www.ecolibri.it/power-of-nature/ (accessed 20 August 2022).

16. NuScale Power Corporation. (n.d.). History of NuScale power. https://www.nuscalepower.com/About-Us/History (accessed 20 August 2022).

17. NuScale Power Corporation. (2022). NuScale Power Corporation Form S-1. U.S. Securities and Exchange Commission: 82. https://www.sec.gov/Archives/edgar/data/1822966/000110465922070702/tm2214378-3_s1a.htm.

18. Ibid.

19. NuScale Power Corporation. (2022). NuScale Power Corporation Form S-1. U.S. Securities and Exchange Commission: 49. https://www.sec.gov/Archives/edgar/data/1822966/000110465922070702/tm2214378-3_s1a.htm.

20. NuScale Power Corporation. (2022). NuScale Power Corporation Form S-1. U.S. Securities and Exchange Commission: 50. https://www.sec.gov/Archives/edgar/data/1822966/000110465922070702/tm2214378-3_s1a.htm.

21. Fluor Corporation. (2022). Q1 2022 progress report. https://www.fluor.com/SiteCollectionDocuments/fluor-net-zero-report-2022-q1.pdf.

22. Celsius Energy. (n.d.). About us. https://celsiusenergy.com/en/about-us/ (accessed 20 August 2020).

23. Celsius Energy. (n.d.). Our geothermal energy solution. https://celsiusenergy.com/en/our-solution/ (accessed 20 August 2020).

24. Schlumberger Limited. (2021). 2020 sustainability report. https://www.slb.com/sustainability/pdf/SLB_2020_Sustainability_Report.pdf.

25. Schlumberger Limited. (n.d.). Carbon mineralization in concrete. https://www.carboncure.com/carbon%20mineralization-in-concrete/.

26. CarbonCure. (n.d.). *CarbonCure's Path to the Decarbonization of Concrete.* https://go.carboncure.com/rs/328-NGP-286/images/CarbonCure%27s%20Path%20to%20the%20Decarbonization%20of%20Concrete%20eBook.pdf.

27. CarbonCure. (n.d.). CarbonCure's 500 megatonne CO_2 reduction technical roadmap. In: *CarbonCure's Path to the Decarbonization of Concrete.* http://go.carboncure.com/rs/328-NGP-286/images/CarbonCure%27s%20500%20Mt%20CO2%20Reduction%20Technical%20Roadmap%20eBook.pdf.

28. CarbonCure. (2021). An introduction to CarbonCure's verified carbon dioxide removal program. https://www.carboncure.com/carbon-removal/an-introduction-to-carboncures-verified-carbon-removal-program/ (accessed 20 August 2022).

29. Verra. (n.d.). The world's leading voluntary GHG program. https://verra.org/project/vcs-program/.

30. University of Oxford. (2020). *The Oxford Principles for Net Zero Aligned Carbon Offsetting* (September). https://www.smithschool.ox.ac.uk/sites/default/files/2022-01/Oxford-Offsetting-Principles-2020.pdf.

31. Patch Technologies, Inc. (n.d.). www.patch.io/ (accessed 20 August 2022).

32. Morgan, S. (2020). Climate-busting plane pollution revealed by new EU study, Euractiv (24 November). https://www.euractiv.com/section/aviation/news/climate-busting-plane-pollution-revealed-by-new-eu-study/.

33. Ibid.

34. Universal Hydrogen. hydrogen.aero/ (accessed 20 August 2022).

35. ZeroAvia, Inc. (n.d.). Our mission: a hydrogen-electric engine in every aircraft. https://www.ZeroAvia.com/about-us (accessed 20 August 2022).

36. ZeroAvia, Inc. www.zeroavia.com/ (accessed 20 August 2022).

37. Ibid.

38. Alcock, C. (2022). Shell will provide hydrogen refueling equipment for test flights. FutureFlight (10 May). https://www.futureflight.aero/news-article/2022-05-09/shell-will-provide-hydrogen-refueling-equipment-test-flights.

39. Universal Hydrogen Co. (n.d.). Product. https://hydrogen.aero/product/ (accessed 20 August 2022).

40. Universal Hydrogen. (2022). Universal Hydrogen and Connect Airlines announce firm order for conversion of 75 ATR 72-600 regional aircraft to be powered by green hydrogen. Press release (9 June). https://www.businesswire.com/news/home/20220608006035/en/Universal-Hydrogen-and-Connect-Airlines-Announce-Firm-Order-for-Conversion-of-75-ATR-72-600-Regional-Aircraft-to-Be-Powered-by-Green-Hydrogen.

41. ZeroAvia, Inc. (2022). ZeroAvia and MONTE strike deal for 100 hydrogen-electric powertrains to enable zero-emission aircraft leasing. Press release (8 June). https://www.zeroavia.com/monte-deal (accessed 20 August 2022).

42. U.S. Bureau of Labor Statistics. (2016). Entrepreneurship and the U.S. economy. https://www.bls.gov/bdm/entrepreneurship/entrepreneurship.htm (accessed 20 August 2022).

43. Gage, D. (2012). The venture capital secret: 3 out of 4 start-ups fail. *The Wall Street Journal* (20 September). https://www.wsj.com/articles/SB10000872396390443720204578004980476429190.

44. Huddleston, T. (2022). Bill Gates on climate tech startups. CNBC Small Business Playbook (20 January). https://www.cnbc.com/2022/01/20/bill-gates-on-exciting-climate-start-ups-a-lot-of-them-will-fail.html.

10

PATHWAY FOUR: INDUSTRY ECOSYSTEM(S) TRANSFORMERS

"The world cannot reduce GHG emissions without addressing both energy generation and consumption."[1]

—Tesla Impact Report 2021

Pathway Four companies lead, shape, and drive the transformation of their industries to achieve net zero emissions. They build on their own Pathways to net zero to take a leadership role in transforming their industries and even the larger economy. A Pathway Four company may start out as a large, incumbent, mature organization transforming its business model on Pathway Two or as an innovative startup or disruptor on Pathway Three but then decides to increase its net zero ambitions by optimizing its impact and seizing the opportunity to gain competitive advantage by leading a larger transformation of its industry. In short, Pathway Two and Pathway

EXHIBIT 10.1 Pathway Four

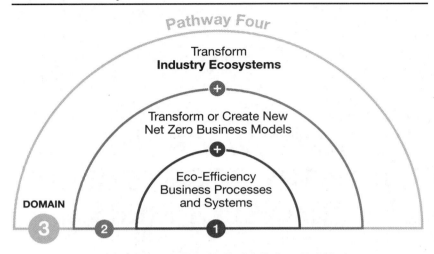

Pathway Four

Transform
Industry Ecosystems

Transform or Create New
Net Zero Business Models

Eco-Efficiency
Business Processes
and Systems

DOMAIN

3   2   1

Pathway: Strategic Option for Net Zero Business Model Design
DOMAIN: Degree of Strategic Planning Complexity

Three companies that also choose to transform their industries are true disruptors that may reap the rewards for their vision and courage.

Pathway Four companies have a high degree of net zero transition planning complexity and require leaders with leadership capacity in the operational, business, and global systems-thinking domains (see Exhibit 10.1), as will be discussed in Chapter 13.

THE FOUR STAGES OF INDUSTRY ECOSYSTEM(S) TRANSFORMATION

The starting point in an industry's transition to net zero is the status quo in which Pathway One companies stick with their existing business models and rely on eco-efficiency processes and systems and compliance with regulations to achieve net zero. The next stage occurs when innovative Pathway Two and Pathway Three companies emerge and begin to move their industries beyond eco-efficiency processes and systems and compliance into new net zero business models.

In the next stage, transformational industry leaders emerge. These leading Pathway Four companies are either established incumbents successfully transforming themselves in Pathway Two or startups or disrupters in Pathway Three. Pathway Four companies have developed net zero products and business models that provide a competitive advantage and give them the experience and wisdom to lead. These companies lead their entire industries to a tipping point where most established companies choose Pathway Two to achieve net zero.

In the final stage, Pathway Four companies realize they must cooperate and work with each other and with governments for their industry to achieve net zero. Pathway Four companies also realize they must work across industry ecosystems (i.e., from mining to steel to automotive to semiconductors to smart cars) and with governments for the entire economy to achieve net zero.

Pathway Four companies recognize there are several transformations occurring at once. Many are transforming their products and business model, which occurs within an industry that is itself transforming, which in turn occurs within an economy that is transforming. The transformation to a net zero economy occurs simultaneously with the digital transformation. Pathway Four companies understand the complex dynamics of these simultaneous transformations and their interdependencies and recognize these dynamics will become more complex and intense as the transition to a net zero economy gathers momentum.

THE TRANSFORMATION OF THE AUTOMOBILE INDUSTRY

The automobile industry has been dominated by vehicles with internal combustion engines. In its early days, however, electric vehicles enjoyed a significant market share until Henry Ford introduced the mass-produced gasoline-powered Model T in 1908. By 1912, his gasoline car cost only $650, while an electric roadster sold for $1,750. The electric car was dead. The internal combustion engine became the propulsion technology of choice for more than a century.[2]

Henry Ford's mass-production techniques enabled the United States to dominate the automobile industry for the first half of the twentieth century. The competitive landscape changed in the second half of the century as western European countries and Japan became major producers and exporters of vehicles with internal combustion engines.

Today, the automobile industry is dominated by Pathway Two and Pathway Three companies. The industry seems to have reached a tipping point in the transition from internal combustion engines to electric motors. The idea that electric vehicles might be a solution to the problem of automobile emissions is not new, but it was never considered practicable.

Switching to electric vehicles has been embraced as a solution to reduce greenhouse gas emissions in the transportation sector. Transportation is at the leading edge of the transformation from fossil fuels to clean energy because it accounts for an estimated 15% of worldwide GHG emissions.[3] In the United States, transportation activities accounted for 27% of net GHG emissions in 2020.[4] Passenger cars and light-, medium-, and heavy-duty freight trucks accounted for about 74% of these emissions.[5]

Suddenly, things have changed. Public perception of electric vehicles has shifted. Government regulations, such as California's ban on the sale of new gasoline-powered vehicles starting in 2035, have stimulated major manufacturers to rethink their strategies for vehicles with internal combustion engines. Manufacturers are making massive investments now to build electric vehicles. The electric car has been reborn and is developing rapidly. Electric vehicles have become generally accepted as "the future" for the automotive industry and all players are rushing to get on board.

The electrification of the transportation sector will achieve an overall reduction in tailpipe emissions over time as electric vehicles replace the installed base of vehicles with internal combustion engines, but such reduction will be limited if the power grids that recharge electric vehicles are powered by power plants that combust fossil fuels. As will be discussed in Chapter 13, to achieve even more progress in achieving the Paris Agreement targets to limit global warming to 1.5°C, automakers need to work with power generators and policy makers to transform power grids to produce clean, zero-carbon electricity.

TESLA THE DISRUPTOR

The story starts with an innovator and market disruptor: Tesla, Inc., a Pathway Three company that evolved into a Pathway Four company. Pathway Four companies can lead their industries to a net zero tipping point. Once attitudes change, and customer expectations shift to embrace the new, there is no going back to the incumbent technology. A Pathway Four company that can sense, anticipate, and help drive an industry to a net zero tipping point can gain a first mover advantage over other companies.

Tesla's success drove the industry to a net zero tipping point. Tesla was the first new company in the United States to successfully enter the automobile industry since Walter Chrysler launched Chrysler Corporation in 1925. Tesla changed the consumer's perception of the electric car from something small and slow to something fast and sexy. Tesla moved public perception in favor of electric vehicles with innovations such as long-range batteries and networks of supercharging stations. Tesla's success inspired other startups, such as Rivian and Lucid, to enter the industry.

Tesla may have been the catalyst to drive the global automotive industry into electric vehicles, but there are other forces that have driven the automobile industry to its net zero tipping point.

One of those is the decision by various state and national regulators to impose bans on the sale of new vehicles with internal combustion engines at some point in the future. These prospective bans, together with various packages of government loans, grants, and tax incentives for both manufacturers and customers, has helped stimulate investment in electric vehicles.

The transformation of the automotive industry is much more than just building electric cars. Success in the transformation requires major capital investments, innovation, vision, and courage. Another driving force has been the disruptive impact of new entrants, such as Tesla, Rivian, Lucid, and BYD, that have developed new electric vehicle designs and better battery technologies, promoted autonomous driving technologies, introduced new ideas for mobility, and coded new software for in-car experiences that are transforming the traditional automotive business model. Currently, investment in research and development for electric vehicles is ahead of both the production of electric vehicle models and customer demand.

Who will dominate the electric car industry of the future? Deloitte expects that by 2030 China will hold 49% of the global electric vehicle market, Europe will account for 27%, and the United States will hold 14%.[6]

TESLA: A PATHWAY FOUR INDUSTRY ECO-SYSTEM(S) TRANSFORMATION LEADER

For now, however, Tesla is the undisputed leader in electric vehicles. The founders, Martin Eberhard and Marc Tarpenning, incorporated Tesla in 2003 to build a successful electric car by leveraging the favorable reaction markets had had to General Motors' experimental electric vehicle, the EV-1, in the 1990s. Tesla produced its first fully electric car, the Roadster, in 2008. It proved the feasibility of electric vehicles as a viable alternative to vehicles with internal combustion engines. It could travel almost 250 miles on a single charge, could out accelerate most sports cars, and had plenty of speed for highway driving. Unfortunately, the Roadster's sticker price was over $100,000, putting it out of reach of most consumers, and charging its batteries took 24 to 48 hours.

Elon Musk, an early Tesla investor, become its CEO and product architect in 2008. That year, Tesla announced the development of the Model S, which would retail for $76,000. The company went public in 2010 and acquired the old New United Motor Manufacturing Inc. (NUMMI) automobile assembly plant in Fremont, California. NUMMI, which had been jointly owned by Toyota and General Motors, is a large manufacturing facility that had produced 428,633 vehicles in its peak year in 2006. The Model S went into full production in 2012 with base prices of $57,400 for the 160-mile version and $77,400 for the 300-mile version. The Model S could be charged faster than the Roadster.

To support its vehicles, Tesla opened its own charging stations, called Superchargers, in 2012. Now, Tesla owns and operates the largest fast-charging network in the world with over 30,000 Superchargers in use. Its Superchargers can charge up to 200 miles of range in 15 minutes. Tesla also has developed an app that shows where the nearest Supercharger is located and whether a Supercharger stall is available. Tesla has placed its Superchargers on major routes near convenient amenities to optimize the charging experience and eliminate range anxiety.

In 2014, Tesla broke ground on Gigafactory 1, a massive manufacturing facility east of Reno, Nevada, to produce lithium-ion batteries for its electric vehicles. Recognizing that ramping production of its vehicles could quickly consume the entire global supply of lithium-ion batteries, Tesla decided to secure its own supply by entering the battery business. The Gigafactory, the world's largest lithium-ion battery factory, has produced more than 1,000,000 batteries. Gigafactory 1 also produces Model 3 motors and Tesla's Powerwall and Powerpack energy-storage products.

Today, Tesla has evolved into a global, vertically integrated manufacturer of electric vehicles and power systems. It delivered more than 911,000 Model 3 and Model Y electric vehicles in 2021 and has sold more than 2 million electric vehicles since 2008. Gigafactory 2, a 1.2 million-square-foot manufacturing plant in Buffalo, New York, produces solar cells and modules, and electrical components for its Supercharger and energy-storage products. Gigafactory 3, a 9.3 million-square-foot manufacturing facility in Shanghai, China, is the second factory to assemble Tesla vehicles. There are two additional Gigafactories under construction: Gigafactory 4 in Berlin, Germany, and Gigafactory 5 in Austin, Texas, where Tesla plans to produce the Model 3 and Model Y, its Cybertruck pickup truck, and the Tesla Semi. The Semi, a heavy-duty truck designed to haul tractor-trailers, is expected to hit the market in 2023 with four independent motors, rapid acceleration, and a range of 300 to 500 miles between charges.

Tesla is on a mission "to accelerate the world's transition to sustainable energy."[7] Its vertically integrated business model that designs, develops, manufactures, sells, and leases electric vehicles and energy generation and storage systems is already conformed to a net zero emissions economy. Tesla's business model takes a holistic, ecosystem approach to addressing climate change by designing and manufacturing a complete energy and transportation ecosystem. Its strategy recognizes that the world cannot reduce its GHG emissions without simultaneously addressing both energy generation and consumption. This means that to make progress in reducing GHG emissions, the world must reduce emissions in both the transportation and energy sectors.[8]

Tesla has published an inventory of its Scope 1 and 2 emissions using the operational control methodology under the *GHG Protocol*. The company has begun measuring its two largest categories of Scope 3 emissions, those from category 11 (use of products sold) and category 1 (purchased goods and services). Tesla has not set near-term and long-term science-based emissions-reduction targets but in 2021 it committed to join the SBTi.

In 2021, its Scope 1 and Scope 2 emissions were 185,000 metric tons and 403,000 metric tons, respectively.[9] In fiscal 2021, the company's carbon intensity across its Scope 1 and 2 emissions was approximately 10.9 metric tons per $1 million of revenue.[10] Tesla reported 1,954,000 metric tons of Scope 3, category 11 emissions in 2021 and is working with its suppliers to incentivize them to report their emissions and energy data.[11]

Eco-efficiency processes and systems will play a role in helping Tesla reach whatever short-term and long-term science-based net zero targets it ultimately sets. It acknowledges that its carbon intensity across its Scope 1 and 2 emissions may rise temporarily as it adds manufacturing capacity, but Tesla already employs eco-efficiency processes and systems across its facilities to optimize their operational efficiency and sustainability.

The company designs its manufacturing facilities with eco-efficiency in mind. For example, it installed highly efficient, insulated, low-emissivity windows at Gigafactory 3 in Texas to reduce the building's cooling and heating demands. It recovers waste heat from compressors to offset natural gas consumption for process heating. Tesla covers the roofs of its facilities with solar panels and installed solar panels with

21,045 kW of capacity by the end of 2021. It plans to shift its energy consumption to renewables as quickly as possible and uses artificial intelligence to control HVAC equipment and reduce energy consumption. It has innovated a new dry electrode process for manufacturing batteries that may reduce overall energy consumption in the manufacturing process by 70%.

Tesla's solar panels have produced an estimated cumulative total of 25.39 terawatt hours of emissions-free energy, which more than offset the cumulative total of 25.27 terawatt hours of energy consumed at its manufacturing facilities and used by its vehicles since 2012.[12] Tesla's global Supercharger network is 100% renewable by using a combination of on-site generation and renewable energy matching. In California, home charging is 100% renewable through annual renewable matching. These renewable matching offsets mean Tesla's Scope 3, category 11 emissions occurred from home charging outside of California and from the use of third-party charging stations. Tesla hopes to reduce these emissions further by selling its vehicle customers solar panels and power storage systems to enable emissions-free home charging.

Tesla thinks strategically to look for opportunities to amplify the emissions-reduction attributes of its technologies. It designs its battery packs to outlast the expected useful life of the vehicle, which is approximately 200,000 miles in the United States and 150,000 miles in Europe. Its batteries are recycled at the end of their useful life and used to build new ones. Tesla observed that a relatively small number of vehicles, including taxis, delivery vans, trucks, and buses, account for a disproportionate amount of vehicle miles driven and, therefore, create a disproportionately high share of emissions in the transportation sector. If such vehicles were electric and had batteries with a 1,000,000-mile life, which Tesla aspires to produce, the emissions per mile of such vehicles would be dramatically reduced.[13]

Similarly, heavy-duty trucks account for only 1.1% of vehicles on the road in the United States but account for approximately 18% of vehicle emissions.[14] Electrifying the world's heavy-duty truck fleet will be critical to achieve a net zero emissions economy. Tesla's Semi could help reduce these emissions and make long-haul trucking sustainable. The company is developing a Semi charger network at trucking rest stops across the United States and Europe where Semis could top off their range.

Tesla is a mature data analytics competitor in the digital transformation. It has primary access to massive amounts of real-world energy consumption data based on over 25 billion miles travelled in its Model 3 and Model Y vehicles.[15] This enables it to provide comprehensive analyses of its vehicles' energy usage compared to vehicles with internal combustion engines. Tesla estimates that one of its vehicles will emit approximately 30 metric tons of CO_2e emissions over its useful life as opposed to approximately 70 metric tons of CO_2e emissions emitted by the average vehicle with an internal combustion engine over its useful life.[16] Most of Tesla's vehicles' emissions come from fossil fuels combusted to power electric grids, which in North America, for example, derive approximately 52% of their energy from combusting fossil fuels. As power grids become cleaner and greener and use less fossil fuels, the carbon impact of Tesla's vehicles will continue to improve and provide an even greater advantage over vehicles with internal combustion engines. At the core, Tesla recognizes that having a clean grid is an essential component in achieving a net zero economy.

Tesla has taken a systemic approach to achieving its net zero objectives. Its 2021 Impact Report provides a good example of what a business model that is already conformed to a net zero emissions economy looks like. With its prowess in big data, data analytics, and artificial intelligence, Tesla should have a relatively easy time conducting a full inventory of its Scope 3 data and setting near-term and long-term science-based emissions-reduction targets.

THE RISE OF ELECTRIC VEHICLES

Tesla may be the company that catalyzed the transformation of the automotive industry, but it is not the only disruptor. New entrants, such as Rivian, Lucid, and BYD in China, also are having a substantial impact as are incumbents, such as General Motors, Ford, and Volkswagen, that bring their size and scale to the race to electrification.

For now, Tesla is the global market leader in electric vehicles. Its differentiation strategy is working, and the company is on a rapid growth trajectory. Tesla has not had an easy path, however. Like most emerging technology companies, Tesla had several near-death experiences. There

EXHIBIT 10.2 Tesla's historical revenue growth

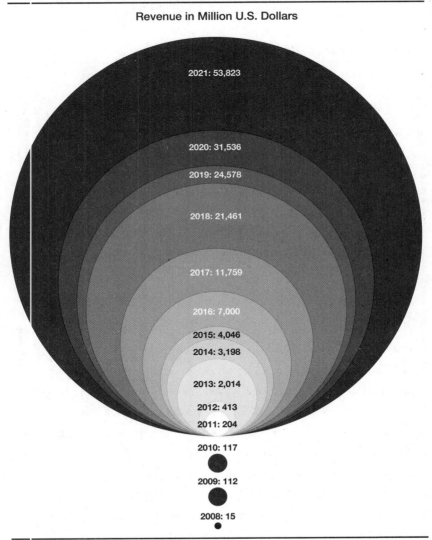

Revenue in Million U.S. Dollars

2021: 53,823

2020: 31,536

2019: 24,578

2018: 21,461

2017: 11,759

2016: 7,000

2015: 4,046

2014: 3,198

2013: 2,014

2012: 413

2011: 204

2010: 117

2009: 112

2008: 15

Source: Statistica.com.

have been missed deadlines, near bankruptcies, emergency capital raises, and product failures. Notwithstanding these challenges, Tesla has posted exponential growth in consolidated revenues since it released its first electric car in 2008 (see Exhibit 10.2).

How does Tesla stack up against other companies in the industry? Exhibit 10.3 is a global breakdown of electric vehicles sales by region. China and Europe lead in the sales and registrations of electric vehicles.

EXHIBIT 10.3 Global electric vehicle registrations

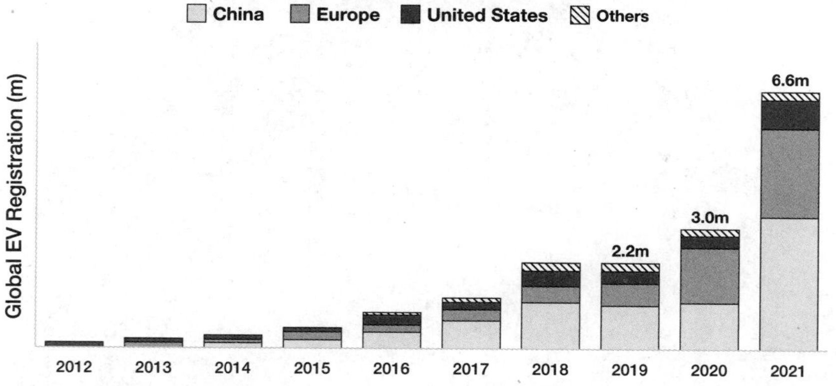

Source: Statistica.com.

At the manufacturer level, Tesla is the global leader and produces only all electric vehicles and no hybrids, which are vehicles with both an electric motor and an internal combustion engine. A significant portion of the total electric vehicle sales of the second- and third-leading manufacturers, Volkswagen and BYD, are hybrid vehicles. General Motors, which places number four, is the second-leading producer of all electric vehicles. While Tesla, the disruptor, sets the pace for the transformation to electric vehicles, incumbents such as General Motors have launched their own transformations, as discussed in Chapter 8. Exhibit 10.4 is a breakdown of electric vehicles sales by the leading manufacturers of electric vehicles.

EXHIBIT 10.4 Global sales of battery and plug-in hybrid global electric vehicles by leading electric vehicle manufacturers

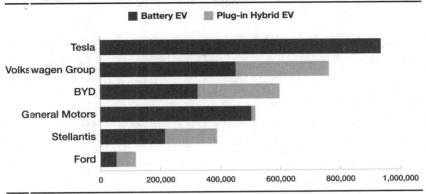

Source: Statistica.com.

How have investors responded to the transformation of the automotive industry? Exhibit 10.5 shows how Tesla's consolidated revenue and market capitalization compares to other established automobile manufacturers in Europe and the United States.

EXHIBIT 10.5 Revenues, multiples of enterprise value to revenues, and percentage shares of industry enterprise value of leading electric vehicle manufacturers

Rank	Company	Revenue in Billions (USD) 2022	Enterprise Value / Revenue Multiple	Enterprise Value 2022 – July	Enterprise Value / % of Peer Group
1	Tesla	$ 67.20	13.6X	$ 916.46	44.08%
2	Toyota	$ 272.40	1.4X	$ 362.35	17.43%
3	BYD	$ 37.70	2.7X	$ 96.40	4.64%
4	VW	$ 291.40	0.78X	$ 215.19	10.35%
5	Mercedes-Benz Group	$ 155.60	0.81X	$ 122.74	5.90%
6	Ford	$ 148.10	1.06X	$ 154.59	7.44%
7	BMW Group	$ 136.90	0.22X	$ 25.00	1.20%
8	General Motors	$ 132.10	1.07X	$ 145.00	6.97%
9	Rivian	$ 0.50	34.8X	$ 16.14	.78%
10	Lucid	$ 0.20	1.41X	$ 25.20	1.21%
	Total	$ 1,242.10		$ 2,079.07	
	Median	$ 134.50	1.24X	$ 133.87	6.44%

Source: FutureZero analysis with source data from YCharts and Capital Cube.

Volkswagen was the industry leader in 2021 in terms of sales, and its consolidated revenues were almost six times greater than Tesla's. Tesla's market capitalization, however, was more than four times larger than Volkswagen's. In fact, Tesla's market capitalization was almost as large as the combined market capitalization of the next six largest automobile manufacturers and two other disruptors, Lucid and Rivian. This is the reward for being a successful disruptor.

Tesla is not the only new entrant to the automotive sector. There are other new electric vehicle companies like Wrightspeed, which makes heavy-duty electric trucks, Rivian, which makes pickup trucks, Zero, which makes electric motorcycles, and Proterra, which makes electric buses. There are also new entrants in complementary automotive technologies such as Mountain View, which makes smart car infrastructure for the connected car, Reviver, which makes digital license plates, and Naruto, which develops artificial intelligence systems for autonomous driving. All these startups are playing a role in the transformation of the automotive industry and hope to join Tesla as industry disruptors.

The automotive industry's net zero transformation, however, is not just about startups. The established industry giants have joined the race to produce electric vehicles and are fighting back. Here's how Ford describes its vision and transformation:

"Just like the Model T revolutionized mobility, we believe electrification can do the same for reducing carbon emissions. So, we have been transforming our business to lead the electric revolution at scale, creating distinct but complementary businesses—Ford Model e, Ford Blue and Ford Pro—that will help us compete and win in the new era of electric and connected vehicles . . .

Around the world, we are dedicating more than $50 billion through 2026 to accelerate our zero-emission plan and create an ultra-efficient manufacturing system for our vehicles and the batteries that power them, helping us achieve our goal of carbon neutrality by 2050."[17]

The incumbent giants in the auto industry have scale, decades of creating knowledge and expertise, loyal customers, and government relationships. They can be a powerful force for change in the transition to a net zero economy if they can innovate, let go of what has generated success in the past, and transform their large organizations, business processes, and institutional knowledge. The emerging battle for industry leadership between the incumbents and the disruptors will be fascinating to watch and could provide a model of industry-wide transformation for other industries to follow.

TESLA'S BUSINESS MODEL

From an investor point of view, Tesla is the clear interim leader in this race. Why have investors allocated so much value to Tesla? It has enormous market capitalization not only because it produces attractive zero-emission, smart electric cars but also because it has a competitively differentiated business model. This combination of zero-emission electric cars and a differentiated business model has created investor excitement and has Tesla shaping the future of the automobile industry.

Here are eight components of Tesla's business model that combine to make it both distinctive and disruptive in the automotive industry:

Smart product design. First and foremost, Tesla changed the image of electric cars from being small, slow, and sluggish to being high-performance and sexy. Tesla has industry-leading product design capabilities that enable it to produce high performance, tailpipe emission-free and noise-free electric vehicles embedded with advanced technologies. Their well-designed cars appeal to multiple market segments such as high-end luxury consumers, commercial transport, environmentalists, and sports car enthusiasts.

State-of-the-art manufacturing. Tesla is transforming how vehicles are built. It currently operates or is building five Gigafactories (Nevada, New York, Texas, Shanghai, and Berlin) of such massive size that all assembly operations can be completed in one location. The Gigafactory in Texas is a $1.1 billion investment on a 2,100-acre site that is the biggest factory in the United States by size and reported to be the second largest building in the world. It is powered entirely by renewable energy sources, primarily solar.

Great software. Tesla is as much a software company as it is a car manufacturing company. Its cars feature a massive touch screen driven by a Tesla-built computer and software developed in-house that serves as the vehicle's command and infotainment center. The company invests heavily in developing software to automate driving and maintenance tasks and constantly improve its electric vehicles. It provides customers with regular software updates that are delivered over the air just like those delivered to smart phones. Tesla's commitment to continually improve the driving experience through software and provision of regular software updates post purchase are appreciated greatly by its customers. Tesla is a leader in autonomous driving software and its data analytics software captures data from both in-vehicle software, customers, and consumer databases to target and enhance the customer experience.

Industry-leading batteries. Tesla currently produces more batteries in terms of kWh than all other car makers combined. It is perceived to produce higher-quality batteries than those of its competitors, thanks to the quality of its partner Panasonic's cells. Tesla continues to drive down the cost of its batteries through economies of scale, reduction of waste, and locating manufacturing processes under one roof. Along the way, Tesla created the Powerwall 2, which is one of the most advanced residential energy-storage systems.

Proprietary charging system. Tesla has developed a proprietary, low-cost charging station network of Superchargers that are designed to charge Tesla vehicles in just 30 minutes. The charging network and the company's industry-leading battery technologies combine to create a powerful competitive advantage.

Powerful brand. Tesla's business model is driven by its powerful brand, which leverages the enduring reputation of Nikola Tesla, whose many inventions included alternating current (AC) generation and transmission technology that is the foundation of the electric power system. Tesla the company has established a reputation for continuous innovation and design that is unmatched in the automotive industry. It built its brand from the top down, starting with high-performance vehicles for high-end customers and then moved down market.

Sales and marketing. Tesla's marketing, sales, and service strategy is unique. It does not operate a traditional dealer network like most other manufacturers but instead has a retail organization that sells cars online and through company-owned stores and galleries. It can provide vehicle maintenance and service directly to a customer's residence, over the internet, and at service centers known as "service plus."

Collaborative partners. Tesla's business model includes several strategic partners, such as Daimler, that gives Tesla access to superior research capabilities, and Panasonic, that provides Tesla with leading-edge battery technology. Tesla is rumored to be exploring a partnership with Toyota to jointly develop an electric vehicle platform for lower-cost electric vehicles.

CHARACTERISTICS OF PATHWAY FOUR

It is too early to identify all the core characteristics of Pathway Four companies because all industry transformations to net zero are currently in an early stage and will take many years to complete. Based on our assessment of the automotive industry, however, the core assumption for companies on Pathway Four is that they are out to change the world with a new low- or no-carbon product or service and business model and transform their industry to net zero in the process. Pathway Four companies have business models that inherently conform to a net zero economy and are already doing business in the net zero economy.

Pathway Four companies lead by example from the net zero future and encourage their competitors to join in transforming their industries to net zero. Tesla, for example, states in its 2021 impact report: "We hope that every car manufacturer will strive to produce hundreds of thousands of

EVs per year, as significant reductions of emissions will only be achieved if all carmakers push for an industry-wide shift to EVs."[18] Pathway Four companies strive to be the catalysts that get their entire industries to follow their lead. Pathway Four companies aim to get their industries to a tipping point where the net zero future becomes the norm.

PATHWAY FOUR RISK FACTORS

It may be particularly difficult for a Pathway Four company to inspire the dominant industry players in some industries, such as oil and gas and energy, to transform the industry to net zero. The dominant players may continue to operate in a state of denial with respect to the impact of GHG emissions on global warming and climate change and the need to adopt net zero transition strategies and plans. This resistance could make it particularly difficult to transform the industry to net zero.

In addition, the worry about a chaotic and disorderly transition to net zero in the oil and gas and energy sectors could prevent or delay companies in a Pathway Four company's industry from initiating net zero planning and target setting. Concerns about cannibalizing their existing high-carbon businesses and restructuring their workforces could cause companies to be reluctant to initiate needed net zero transition strategies and join a Pathway Four company in an industry-wide transition to net zero.

The financial sector may be unwilling to provide sustainable financing to enable potential Pathway Four companies to launch and finance their businesses, especially when positive cash flow may be several years away.

Finally, government policies, regulations, and incentives are a collection of confusing, unclear, and conflicting programs and could cause companies to avoid or delay supporting a transformation of their industries and follow a Pathway Four company in an industry-wide transition to net zero. For example, countries may make net zero pledges or implement carbon taxes while continuing subsidies to the high-carbon intensity oil and gas industry.

CRITICAL SUCCESS FACTORS FOR LEADING AN INDUSTRY TRANSFORMATION

An assessment of the pending net zero transformation of the automotive industry has identified eight factors or capabilities that are important in leading an industry transformation to net zero. The term "industry leader" can refer to a company or to a specific senior transformational executive.

Strategic and systems thinking. Industry leaders must operate at a high level of strategic and systems thinking, as will be discussed in Chapter 13. They must create an inspiring vision not only for their companies but also for their industries and perhaps even for society and civilization itself. It is not enough to see around corners. Industry leaders must have a long-term perspective and be able to see beyond the horizon.

Compelling purpose. Industry leaders must create an authentic, credible, and compelling business purpose for their companies and their net zero transformation strategies that are meaningful to all stakeholders. Tesla's original purpose to accelerate the advent of sustainable transport by bringing compelling mass market electric cars to market as soon as possible may have been authentic, credible, and compelling to its founders but too narrow to appeal to everyone. Today, Tesla's purpose "to accelerate the world's transition to sustainable energy" is authentic, credible, and compelling to all its stakeholders.[19] There is no mention of electric cars.

Courage. Industry leaders must challenge, transform, or abandon business models with high carbon intensity that have been successful in the past. Leaders must have the courage of startup entrepreneurs to go all in when required and make long-term, bet-the-farm decisions for both their companies and their industries.

Knowledge-building proficiency. Industry leaders ensure their organizations build and utilize a superior knowledge of the opportunities and risks inherent in net zero transformations, embrace business model innovation, develop expertise in transformational processes and technologies, and are very clear about what works and what does not.

Walking the talk. Industry leaders develop a compelling net zero vision for their industries and can inspire other companies and their industries to achieve net zero. Industry leaders are obsessed with execution. They lead by example with respect to the execution of net zero transition strategies in their own companies.

Collaboration. Industry leaders understand when companies in the industry need to collaborate and work together to achieve net zero and when they need to compete. They are adept at forming, participating in, leading, and leveraging strategic partnerships, public/private partnerships, joint-ventures, knowledge networks, and other collaborations. Industry leaders can work effectively with governments and regulators and earn their trust in setting net zero transformation policies for their industries and, where appropriate, obtaining grants, loans, and incentives.

Investor support. As with corporate transformations, industry transformations will require a significant level of capital investment and investor support. Industry leaders must have the ability to communicate, and help investors understand why investing in an industry-wide net zero transformation makes sense. They also can work with governments to put in place regulations that will facilitate the transition to net zero and provide appropriate funding support, grants, and incentives when needed.

Top talent. Industry leaders must attract and retain top talent to play a leadership role in an industry-wide net zero transformation. Tesla, for example, is the second choice behind SpaceX for engineering students,[20] and attracted over 3,000,000 job applicants globally in 2021.[21] Industry leaders have effective programs for attracting, retaining, and developing exceptional talent in their companies to avoid losing talent to other companies in their industries.

SUMMARY

An industry's transition to net zero may be orderly or chaotic. The degree of complexity, difficulty, and challenges involved will vary greatly across industries. Whatever the circumstances, there are, and will be, many opportunities for individual companies, executives, and forward-thinking directors to play a leadership role in leading and shaping industry-wide transformations to net zero.

More and more companies aspire to be Pathway Four companies and lead the transformation of their industries to achieve net zero. Canada Goose is a member of the Outdoor Industry Association, which aims to become the world's first climate positive industry by 2030. Ørsted is a member of the Green Hydrogen Catapult, which aims to transform the energy sector by greening the hydrogen industry and making green hydrogen a leading source of carbon-free energy, as will be discussed in Chapter 13. NextEra not only aspires to decarbonize its business but also the power industry and, ultimately, the entire U.S. economy (see Appendix 1.1), and Intel aspires to lead the technology industry ecosystem to "Carbon Neutral Computing" (see Appendix 5.1). These aspiring Pathway Four companies recognize the enormous opportunity for their companies to help transform their industries to achieve net zero and to accelerate the transition to a global net zero economy.

(See Appendix 10.1 for some questions Pathway Four company directors and investors might ask and for management to consider.)

NOTES

1. Tesla, Inc. (2022). Impact report 2021. https://www.tesla.com/ns_videos/2021-tesla-impact-report.pdf.
2. Matulka, R. (2014). History of the electric car. U.S. Department of Energy (15 September). https://www.energy.gov/articles/history-electric-car.
3. Center for Climate and Energy Solutions. (n.d.). Global emissions. https://www.c2es.org/content/international-emissions/ (accessed 20 August 2022).
4. U.S. Environmental Protection Agency. (2022). Greenhouse gas (GHG) emissions and removals (updated April 14). https://www.epa.gov/ghgemissions (accessed 20 August 2022).
5. Ibid.
6. Walton, B., Hamilton, J., Alberts, G. et al. (2020). Electric vehicles: setting a course for 2030. Deloitte Insights (28 July). https://www2.deloitte.com/us/en/insights/focus/future-of-mobility/electric-vehicle-trends-2030.html.

7. Tesla, Inc. (2020). Tesla, Inc. form 10-K for the fiscal year ended 31 December 2021. U.S. Securities and Exchange Commission. https://www.sec.gov/ix?doc=/Archives/edgar/data/1318605/000095017022000796/tsla-20211231.htm.

8. Telsa, Inc. (2022). Impact report 2021.

9. Ibid.

10. Tesla, Inc. (2020). Tesla, Inc. form 10-K for the fiscal year ended 31 December 2021. U.S. Securities and Exchange Commission.

11. Telsa, Inc. (2022). Impact report 2021.

12. Ibid.

13. Ibid.

14. Ibid.

15. Ibid.

16. Ibid.

17. Ford Motor Company. (2022). Integrated sustainability and financial report 2021. https://media.ford.com/content/dam/fordmedia/North%20America/US/2021/03/31/Ford-Integrated-Report-2021.pdf.

18. Telsa, Inc. (2022). Impact report 2021.

19. Ibid.

20. Universum Communications Sweden AB. (2022). World's most attractive employers 2021. https://universumglobal.com/wmae2021/ (accessed 20 August 2022).

21. Telsa, Inc. (2022). Impact report 2021.

Part IV

Implementing a Pathway to Net Zero

11

A FOUNDATIONAL FRAMEWORK TO CHOOSE A PATHWAY

"Value is created by earning economic returns above the cost of capital."[1]

—Bartley Madden

THE INNOVATION AND RETURN ON CAPITAL LIFE CYCLE

Analyzing a company's performance using Bartley Madden's four value quadrant innovation and life cycle framework will guide companies strategically to choose the appropriate Pathway to net zero.[2] The framework has four stages: (i) Value Quadrant 1, early growth, the high-innovation stage; (ii) Value Quadrant 2, high-performance, the competitive fade stage; (iii) Value Quadrant 3, cash cow, the mature stage; and (iv) Value Quadrant 4, the failing business model stage.

Applying this strategic framework for innovation and capital allocation will also inform a company about its transition plan, clarify its transition burden, and suggest how to finance it. Depending on a company's stage of growth, it may finance its net zero transition plan in three ways: reinvesting profits in the business, borrowing money (debt) or selling equity. This framework may be particularly helpful for companies inclined to choose Pathway One as the path of least resistance because it would allow them to continue business as usual and maintain their current business models.

Exhibit 11.1 depicts how companies generally move through these four stages over their lifetime.

EXHIBIT 11.1 **The four stages of innovation and return on capital life cycle**

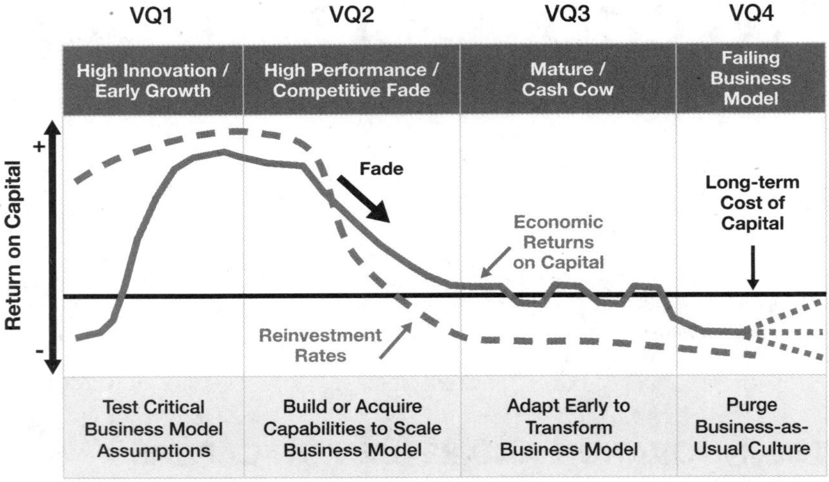

Sources: Adapted from *Value Creation Principles* by Bartley Madden and *Beyond Earnings: Applying the Credit Suisse HOLT CFROI and economic profit framework* with permission from the authors.

Value Quadrant 1: The High-Innovation/Early-Growth Stage

The high-innovation/early-growth stage is characteristic of young growth companies such as technology startups coming from Silicon Valley and the Pathway Three companies described in Chapter 9. High-innovation/early-growth stage companies need to move quickly to prove their investment thesis and business model. These companies have a return on capital less than their cost of capital but have a higher future value because their business models are expected to create value in the future with positive returns on capital and economic profit. If a high-innovation/early-growth stage company can scale its business, then high reinvestment in the business is possible.

The company's value is its story and its expected future value. A high-innovation/early-growth stage company, for example, may enjoy a high market capitalization but still be losing money.

Only 13% of companies at the high-innovation/early-growth stage successfully transition to Value Quadrant 2, the high-performance/competitive-fade stage, within five years.[3] A carbon shock would lower these odds for companies at the high-innovation/early-growth stage to transition to become high-performance/competitive-fade stage companies in the net zero economy.

Value Quadrant 2: The High-Performance/Competitive-Fade Stage

Companies that are successful at the high-innovation/early-growth stage attract competitors and become high-performance/competitive-fade stage companies. This stage is marked by significant growth in revenues that generate and grow returns on capital greater than their cost of capital, also known as positive economic profit. Their high economic returns and reinvestment rates signal an opportunity for competitors to enter the market. Tesla's success in the high-innovation/early-growth stage in the electric vehicle market, for example, has inspired a legion of competitors.

As competitors enter the market, returns on capital for high-performing companies at the high-performance/competitive-fade stage fade over time as their cost of capital and their capital reinvestment rate tends to decline toward industry norms. How quickly the returns on capital fade depend on a host of factors, including a company's ability to continue to innovate and build on its competitive, first-mover advantage. Many companies in the high-performance/competitive-fade stage continue to innovate, which stops the fade in returns on capital. Amazon, for example, acquired a whole new set of capabilities to develop the Kindle and continued to invest heavily in new businesses and technologies to minimize its fade.

High-performing companies at the high-performance/competitive-fade stage have sustained returns on capital greater than their cost of capital, maintained a high future value, and have positive cash flow to reinvest in the business. For these companies, it is all about sustained innovation to continue to grow their competitive advantage for as long as possible. Such companies are valued based on the estimated future cash flows of their existing businesses and the future value of their growth assets. With ample positive cash flow, high-performing companies in Value Quadrant 2 can finance their net zero transition plans from operations or debt or equity financing.

Value Quadrant 3: The Mature/Cash Cow Stage

Over time, most high-performing companies at the high-performance/ competitive-fade stage start to lose their innovation edge, their expected future value is approximately zero, and they enter the mature/cash cow stage when their returns on capital decline toward their cost of capital and may even be negative. Companies at the mature/cash cow stage can only justify selective reinvestment as part of board-approved capital allocations. Given the inconsistency of positive returns on capital (current and future) for companies at the mature/cash cow stage, returning risk capital to shareholders through dividends and share buybacks is often the optimal capital-allocation strategy.

Companies in Value Quadrant 3 need to sustain their core competencies while improving operational efficiency and selectively investing capital to develop new businesses, products, and services.

Companies at the mature/cash cow stage that have solid returns on capital above their cost of capital but no future value have a 35% probability of transitioning to the failing business model stage within five years.[4] Companies at the mature/cash cow stage with high carbon intensity business models likely have a higher probability of transitioning to the failing business model stage if they fail to redesign their business models for the net zero economy.

Value Quadrant 4: The Failing Business Model Stage

Companies at the mature/cash cow stage transition into the failing business model stage when their returns on capital are sustained below their cost of capital and generate negative economic returns for at least five years. These companies also have a negative future value because the capital markets expect that their disclosed business strategies and business models will continue returns on capital well below the cost of capital in the future. Companies in the failing business model stage tend to be bureaucratic and unresponsive to changes in their external environments. Competition has intensified and competitors are better at providing similar goods or services.

Some companies at the failing business model stage will wind down, sell off their pieces, and distribute assets to shareholders. Other companies at this stage restructure and attempt a turnaround. Such companies may transition from the failing business model stage to the high-innovation/early-growth stage.

Companies in Value Quadrant 4 are particularly vulnerable to carbon shocks because they are generating sustained negative economic profit already, and the market interprets their business strategies and business models as having no future value. Companies in the failing business model stage with insufficient cash flow and no future value have trouble attracting new capital. Companies at the failing business model stage have a 59% probability to still be in that stage in five years.[5]

HOW THE INNOVATION AND RETURN ON CAPITAL LIFE CYCLE EFFECTS VALUATION

Bartley Madden's research found that the percentage of a company's market value attributable to the implied value of its growth assets declines and fades as it progresses through the four stages of innovation and growth.[6] Generally, a company's enterprise value and market value is the sum of the value of its invested assets—plant, equipment, inventory—and the estimated future value of its growth assets. The present value of future cash flows from existing assets provides a good estimate of the value of its invested assets. Subtracting the present value of a company's existing assets from its enterprise value or market capitalization yields an approximation of the present value of its future investments and thus its future value (see Exhibit 11.2).

EXHIBIT 11.2 The effect of the four stages of innovation and return on capital life cycle on the future value of a company

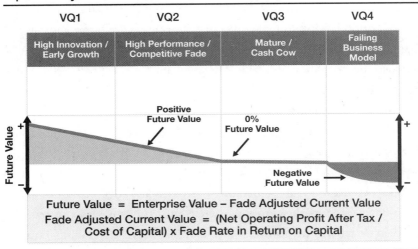

Source: Adapted from *Value Creation Principles* by Bartley Madden.

At one end of the spectrum, high-innovation/early-growth stage companies have a high percentage of their market value attributable to their growth strategy and their stories. At the other end of the spectrum, companies at the failing business model stage, including oil companies such as ExxonMobil and ENI and automotive companies such as Volkswagen, General Motors, and Ford, will have to transform their business models totally to achieve net zero and a positive return on capital. As discussed earlier, some high-performing companies at the high-performance/competitive-fade stage, however, such as Microsoft and Amazon, remain innovative and still have high future value.

THE FOUR DOMAINS OF CARBON INTENSITY, THE INNOVATION AND RETURN ON CAPITAL LIFE CYCLE, AND VALUATION

Applying a carbon tax of $100 per metric ton of CO_2e emissions may accelerate a company's progression through the four stages of the innovation and return on capital life cycle depending on its carbon intensity. A high-performing company at the high-performance/competitive-fade stage or a company at the mature/cash cow stage may suddenly find itself in the failing business model stage because its business model is no longer fit for purpose for a net zero economy and its return on capital is now less than the cost of capital and its future value is negative.

Based on a review of the reported Scope 1 and 2 emissions of over 18,000 global, publicly traded companies, Future Zero identified four levels of carbon intensity with increasing transition burden and carbon shock risk as a company's carbon intensity increases. The four levels of carbon intensity are: low carbon intensity (0 to 10 metric tons of CO_2e per $1 million of revenue), medium carbon intensity (10 to 50 metric tons of CO_2e per $1 million of revenue), high carbon intensity (50 to 100 metric tons of CO_2e per $1 million of revenue), and very high carbon intensity (over 100 metric tons of CO_2e per $1 million of revenue) (see Exhibit 11.3). The general rule is that companies with low carbon intensity at the high-innovation/early-growth stage have a lower transition burden and carbon shock risk than companies with high carbon intensity at the failing business model stage.

Placing a company's GHG emissions on this matrix in one of the four domains of carbon intensity and in one of the stages within the innovation and return on capital life cycle framework provides a preliminary indication of which of the strategic options, the four Pathways discussed at length in Chapters 5 through 10, will be its most appropriate option.

Companies with the highest carbon intensity that are already in the failing business model stage before applying a carbon shock stress test will be

EXHIBIT 11.3 The innovation, return on capital life cycle, and carbon intensity business model performance matrix

Innovation and Return on Capital Life Cycle		25,000-101	100-51	50-11	10-0	
High Innovation / Early Growth	VQ1	7	5	3	1	WINNERS
High Performance / Competitive Fade	VQ2	11	8	4	2	
Mature / Cash Cow	VQ3	14	12	9	6	SURVIVORS
Failing Business Model	VQ4	16	15	13	10	CASUALTIES

Business Model Carbon Intensity
(CO_2e Tons / $1M revenue – Scope 1, 2, and 3)

Source: FutureZero.

especially challenged when the cost of carbon becomes real over the next 5 to 10 years.

Exhibit 11.4 suggests the correlation between carbon intensity and innovation and capital returns life cycle stage before a carbon shock for Ørsted and Vattenfall, discussed in Chapter 8, and NuScale, discussed in Chapter 9.

The scope of this potential problem is huge. For example, FutureZero identified 228 high-performing companies at the high-performance/competitive-fade stage in North America with very high carbon intensity of more than 100 tons of CO_2e per $1 million of revenue. FutureZero estimates approximately 80 companies in this group, when stress tested for a carbon tax of $100 per ton of CO_2e, will have a return on capital less than their cost of capital and less than their cost of carbon. Such companies are especially vulnerable to a carbon shock.

FutureZero estimates that a carbon shock would transition 97 of the 228 high-performing companies at the high-performance/competitive-fade

EXHIBIT 11.4 NuScale, Ørsted, and Vattenfall on the innovation, return on capital life cycle, carbon intensity, and business model performance matrix

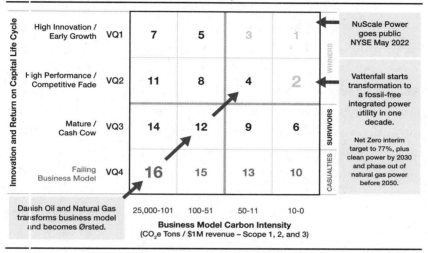

Source: FutureZero.

stage into the failing business model stage, unless they completely redesign their business models to eliminate their Scope 1, 2, and 3 emissions, because they have very high carbon intensity.

FutureZero also identified 178 larger North American companies currently in the failing business model stage with both negative economic profit and negative future value. After applying a carbon stress test of $100 per ton of CO_2e emissions on the current economic model of the company, 161 of these companies would have a negative return on capital after cost of capital and after the cost of carbon. These companies will require a major redesign of their business models to not only achieve net zero emissions but also to achieve a positive return on capital after cost of capital and cost of carbon.

FutureZero also reviewed 1,902 public companies in the global materials sector (mining, metals, steel, cement, glass, and chemicals). Many of these companies will transition into the failing business model stage after applying a carbon stress test of $100 per ton of CO_2e emissions. Of these companies, 915, or 48% of the global materials sector, had a price-to-book value ratio of less than one before the carbon stress test. The capital markets indicate that these companies' disclosed strategies have no value or any expectation of a positive return on capital. When stress tested for a carbon tax of $100 per ton of CO_2e, FutureZero estimates that 1,300 of these companies will have a carbon-adjusted return on capital of less than 5%, which is close to or below their cost of capital. This means that approximately 1,300 materials companies will need to not only develop a strategy that achieves net zero emissions but also restores a positive return on capital.

The technology sector, with over 2,600 public companies globally, is in a unique position to lead the transition to a net zero emissions economy. The sector is profitable and has higher returns on capital compared to other sectors. It also tends to have low-to-medium carbon intensity with the median technology company emitting 19.5 tons of Scope 1 and 2 CO_2e emissions per $1 million of revenue compared to the median for all North American and European public companies of approximately 27.5 tons of Scope 1 and 2 CO_2e emissions per $1 million of revenue.[7] Many technology companies have sufficient internally generated positive cash flow, premium returns on capital, and growing enterprise value to finance the achievement of a carbon-negative business model as Microsoft has committed to do by 2030.

SUMMARY: HAVE GOOD PROCESSES TO PRESERVE AND GROW SHAREHOLDER VALUE

A board of directors should have a measurement and reporting process for return on capital, cost of capital, economic profit, and future value to guide effective capital allocation policies and strategies. Bartley Madden's four value quadrant innovation and life cycle framework will not only help companies to choose the appropriate Pathway to net zero but also provides a tool that boards can use to monitor, preserve, and enhance shareholder value. To be a winner in the net zero emissions economy, a company's net zero transition plans must be fully integrated with its fundamental business and financial strategies.

NOTES

1. Madden, B. (2020). *Value Creation Principles: The Pragmatic Theory of the Firm Begins with Purpose and Ends with Sustainable Capitalism.* Hoboken, NJ: Wiley.
2. Ibid.
3. Holland, D. and Matthews, B. (2018). *Beyond Earnings: Applying the HOLT CFROI and Economic Profit Framework.* Hoboken, NJ: Wiley. See life-cycle probabilities table on p. 278.
4. Ibid.
5. Ibid.
6. Madden, B. (2020). *Value Creation Principles.*
7. Analysis by FutureZero from their Net Zero Transition Database.

12

PREPARING TO LEAD THE TRANSFORMATION: KEY ELEMENTS OF SUCCESSFUL TRANSFORMATIONS

'A transition to net-zero emissions would entail an economic transformation that would affect all countries and all sectors of the economy.'[1]

—McKinsey & Company

Before a company chooses its Pathway, it must understand the process of change to achieve net zero. According to Dean and Linda Anderson, the co-founders of the transformation consultancy Being First, there are three types of change: developmental change, transitional change, and transformational change.[2]

THE THREE TYPES OF CHANGE

Developmental change. Developmental change improves what already exists. It is incremental and usually can be accomplished through existing leadership processes. Developmental change is common. It is what good leaders do on an ongoing basis to improve the performance of their existing operations[3] (see Exhibit 12.1).

EXHIBIT 12.1 Developmental change

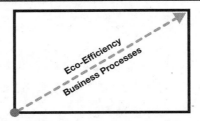

In the context of net zero, eco-efficiency processes and systems represent developmental change. A Pathway One company with low carbon intensity, such as Microsoft, may be able to get to net zero by making incremental changes in its business, such as electrifying its fleet, consuming renewable energy, and revising its employee travel policy. If a company can get to net zero solely by making incremental changes, then its complexity of change is low, and its current leadership likely is to be capable of leading and making such incremental changes.

Transitional change. Transitional change involves building something new rather than simply improving the old. Transitional change requires dismantling the old state while simultaneously creating the new one. A defining factor in transitional change is that the future state can be known and designed before initiating the change. The changes are not radical or paradigm shifting. The future state can be conceived and implemented within the same worldview or way of thinking that currently exists. Classic project and change management are useful to guide transitional change[4] (see Exhibit 12.2).

EXHIBIT 12.2 Transitional change

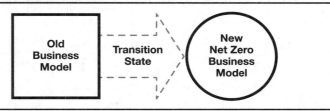

In the context of net zero, a Pathway Two, Option One company will achieve net zero through a combination of eco-efficiency processes and systems and by getting the carbon out of its products either by reinventing them or removing the carbon from the manufacturing process. Such a company will transition from its current state of offering products with high carbon intensity to a new state offering a suite of products with no- or low-carbon intensity. As discussed in Chapter 7, Rolls-Royce plans to reduce the carbon intensity of its jet engines by enabling them to run on sustainable aviation fuel while exploring new emissions-free products such as small, modular nuclear reactors. If a company chooses Pathway Two, Option One, then its complexity of change is medium, and its current leadership may be capable of leading and making such a transitional change process.

Transformational change. Transformational change involves a shift in paradigm. It is far more complex than developmental or transitional change. First, the change often begins before the vision has been fully developed. Transformational change bears a quality of "stepping into the unknown." The destination and the process to get there are emergent because companies learn new information and adjust their strategies along the way. Second, the process is nonlinear. The learning and discovery process means it is full of course corrections. Third, it always requires shifts in leadership mindset, behavior, and the company's culture. Successful transformational change comes from innovation, maximum stakeholder commitment and engagement, and new ways of thinking and doing things. Transformational change demands breakthroughs in conventional wisdom[5] (see Exhibit 12.3).

EXHIBIT 12.3 **Transformational change**

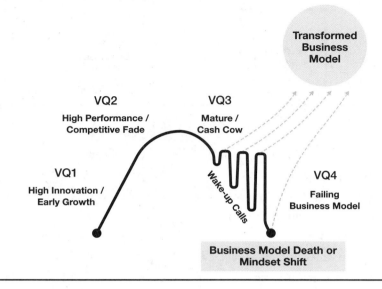

In the context of net zero, a Pathway Two, Option Two company that chooses to transform its business model and a Pathway Four company that chooses to transform its industry are engaged in transformational change. A transformation creates something completely new through an emergent, creative, iterative process in which a company replaces a business model with high carbon intensity with a net zero business model or an entire industry transforms to transition to net zero.

Because transformational change is messy and nonlinear, it requires its participants to figure it out as they go. Collaboration and co-creation are essential. Heroic, top-down leadership rarely succeeds. A Pathway Two, Option Two company such as General Motors, which is transforming its fundamental business model, is engaged in transformational change. If a company chooses Pathway Two, Option Two, then its complexity of change is high. It must finance its transformation to a new business model from the revenues of its old one. This is not an easy task. There is a high probability that its current leadership may not be capable of leading and making such a transformational change. Transformational change requires new leadership mindsets, strategies, and skills.

HEARING THE CALL

The prerequisite for any change process is to have heard the call to change. In the context of net zero, this can take a while. According to Karina Litvak, Non-Executive Director and Chairman of the Sustainability and Scenarios Committee of Eni, the Italian energy company, the CEO wanted to lead the company to net zero eight years ago, but the board of directors was not ready. It took six years for Eni's board to develop and approve a plan to get to net zero by 2050. Ms. Litvak had to improvise because there was no how-to manual. She brought in outside experts to educate the board about the science of climate change and macroeconomics.

The Eni board of directors' biggest hurdle was their fear that a plan to achieve net zero would breach their fiduciary duties to shareholders. While she educated the board, the legal objections lifted. An international study was published that supported directors applying the business judgment rule to weigh the pros and cons of adopting a net zero target. This alleviated the board's concerns and empowered them to set a net zero target.

Today, Eni's board of directors and management team are fully committed to achieving carbon neutrality by 2050. The company has set near-term and mid-term targets to achieve a 35% reduction in its net Scope 1, 2, and 3 emissions by 2030 and an 80% reduction in such emissions by 2040, in each case from 2018 levels. The company is increasing the proportion of its investments in new sustainable energy solutions from 30% by 2025 to 60% by 2030 and to 80% by 2040. Its Plenitude subsidiary will develop over 15GW of renewable energy capacity by 2030.[6]

Eni has embraced working toward fulfillment of the UN SDGs and has incorporated environmental awareness into its business operations. For example, Eni was planning to convert an oil refinery in Sicily to process palm oil into biofuels until it realized it would be supporting deforestation in Indonesia to make room for palm plantations. It switched to processing organic waste into biofuel for jets and is phasing out palm oil. By 2023, Eni will be producing biofuel from food and agricultural waste and plans to increase production to 6 million metric tons per year by 2030.[7]

Before a company can begin its change process, its leadership team and board of directors must have not only heard the call to net zero but be prepared to act on it. Most directors and executives have accepted the scientific consensus that humanity needs to limit the global rise in temperature caused by human generated GHGs, but their companies may not have acted yet on the call to conform their business models to a net zero emissions economy.

Some companies heard the call 20 years ago. Some are just hearing it now. Some companies have heard the call but ignore it. Some have not heard it yet. Companies hear the call when they hear the call. There are many ways for companies to hear the call. They might hear it in a customer's request for its emissions data so the customer can inventory its Scope 3 emissions. They might hear it from prospective employees who ask about why the company has not set science-based emissions-reduction targets. They might hear it when the Chairman of the Board's granddaughter asks her what her company is doing about climate change. They might hear it when a climate activist investor proposes a slate of candidates for the board of directors. They might hear it when a wildfire burns down a company facility.

The truth is that humans have been pouring GHGs into the atmosphere for centuries. Humanity did not know any better. Now, humanity has woken up to the likelihood that such emissions are warming the planet and threatening the economy and civilization itself. Hearing the call to net zero is not about blaming, shaming, or finding fault, it is about deciding whether to believe in the science and do something about it.

The reality is that most companies are early in the change process to conform their business models to a net zero emissions economy. The laggards in the transition to a net zero emissions economy will either run with their current business models and attempt to get to net zero with eco-efficiency processes and systems, carbon credits, and offsets, or be in denial. Those in denial will lobby to maintain the status quo. Only regulations or a severe climate disaster will get them to change.

When a company hears the call, it is important to have a process to analyze it, discern the facts, and neutralize the emotions. The climate science is what it is. The truth is that humanity is engaged in a giant collective science experiment by emitting more than 50 billion metric tons of CO_2e into the atmosphere every year. The evidence seems to indicate that temperatures are rising as a result. Temperatures likely will continue to rise with potentially disastrous consequences if the economy keeps emitting massive quantities of GHGs into the atmosphere. The question is: What will a company's leadership do about it?

PREPARING TO LEAD TO NET ZERO

Once a company's leadership has heard the call to net zero and is fully committed to act, the first step is to prepare to lead the company to net zero, which is largely what Parts II and III of *Net Zero Business Models* are about. Being First estimates that 50 to 60% of decisions are made at this stage of any transformation. For the transition to net zero, these decisions include taking an inventory of a company's GHG emissions, determining its carbon intensity, estimating its carbon short, and setting science-based emissions-reduction targets.

These processes are labor intensive. The SBTi gives companies two years to set science-based emissions-reduction targets after they make a general commitment to net zero. This process provides an opportunity to prepare people within a company for the journey to net zero. For most companies, choosing the appropriate Pathway to conform their business models to a net zero economy will be the biggest decision. This means that by the time a company is ready to lead its transformation to net zero, most of the major decisions will be behind it.

According to McKinsey, 70% of corporate transformations fail, but a company's transformation to net zero should have a higher probability of success because it can build on the experience of hundreds of companies that are far along in their journey.[8] Happily, companies can draw on the best practices these companies have employed in designing their net zero transition plans. These plans are accessible in publicly available documents such as annual reports, sustainability reports, impact reports, and road-maps to net zero. There are companies in every industry at the forefront of the race to net zero that companies can look to for inspiration.

Having good examples to follow, however, will not guarantee a transformation will be successful. A company still needs to execute well. According to Being First, most transformations are unsuccessful because they fail to address all three key aspects of any transformation: content, people, and process. Most transformations fail because they focus on the content—the solution—and under attend to people and process. Most transformations fail because they go right to implementing the solution without ensuring the CEO, board of directors, executive team, and key stakeholders—including employees—have bought in to the change. Most companies march ahead without helping leaders and staff first make the paradigm shift required. Old, outdated worldviews stifle the required innovations and out-of-the-box thinking. The strategies required to succeed never get developed.

This often keeps leaders from putting in place the people-oriented engagement processes needed to build stakeholders' commitment to support the transformation. Conventional ways of leading developmental or transitional change, which rely on low levels of engagement and communication and are geared for speed to design a solution, fail. In a successful transformation, a company must go slow to go fast. Companies need to take the time to get people aligned behind the transformation. A quickly designed net zero transition plan will not be implemented successfully unless the company gets people behind it and championing the cause. Fundamentally, most transformations fail because the leaders fail to walk the talk of the transformation. They do not model its desired behaviors and fail to design and implement the high engagement processes required to support it.

Successful transformations focus on people, process, and content in equal measure. Successful transformations get as many people as possible engaged in the conversation from the beginning and keep them engaged. The good news about transformations to net zero business models is that the process of inventorying GHG emissions and setting science-based emissions-reduction targets often takes several years. This gives companies the opportunity to use these processes as a means of creating alignment behind the transition to net zero over several years.

This may be more challenging for Pathway Two and Pathway Four companies, because these Pathways require people to change how they work. This often creates resistance because people are used to how things are done currently and usually want to maintain the consistency and apparent safety of the status quo. The transformation will require people to stop doing business the old way.

General Motors, Ford, and Volkswagen, for example, have enormous workforces that know how to build vehicles with internal combustion engines. Their transformations into makers of smart electric vehicles requires every worker to rethink how he or she approaches making cars. Since the overall purpose and mission of their companies have shifted, the cultures need to shift, too.

To shift individual mindsets and the collective mindset of a corporate culture, a company needs to have a compelling vision and a clear, well-articulated strategy to carry it out. A plan to conform a business model to a net zero economy can form the basis for that vision and strategy. Achieving net zero provides a unifying, common goal and achieving near-term and long-term science-based targets and eco-efficiency targets provide a basic structure. This will take care of a lot of the content so that companies can focus more on the people and process.

Taking the time to design a thorough net zero transition plan has many benefits and optimizes the probability of success. A good plan accelerates the transformation and reduces costs. A good plan keeps leaders and everyone else engaged, especially if they are involved in its design and evolution. A good plan minimizes fear and anxiety and helps align the culture behind the transformation.

To consciously design a net zero transition plan, it helps to first identify the conditions for its success. What needs to be in place for the company to get to net zero? Who needs to be involved? What leaders need to buy-in? What actions need to be taken and in what sequence? What resources are needed? How long will things take? Do people have the capacity to take on the transformation? How will the company make course corrections? How will the company hold people accountable to the plan?

Startup and Staff

The first step is starting up and staffing the change effort. How to staff up depends in part on which Pathway is appropriate for a company. For example, a Pathway One company may already have the right people in place. A Pathway Four company, however, may need to bring in outside talent with the right level of strategic and systems-thinking capabilities to lead a transformation of its industry. Chapter 13 examines the domains of systems thinking needed to lead a transformation.

Create the Case for Net Zero

The next step is to create the case for net zero and establish the initial desired outcomes. In the context of net zero, many of the desired outcomes are relatively clear: achieve net zero by a target date and get there by achieving near-term and long-term science-based targets and eco-efficiency goals. The foundation of the strategy to achieve these objectives will be largely determined by the Pathway chosen. This leaves companies to focus on creating the case for change.

Creating the case for change starts by identifying a company's key internal and external stakeholders, including the board of directors, the C-Suite, employees, customers, suppliers, and investors. In addition to the timeline for achieving its science-based targets, it needs to optimize and prioritize participation, communicate timelines for meeting other objectives such as transitioning to a clean fleet, articulate clear roles and responsibilities, educate leaders to set the tone, and have a clear articulation of all desired outcomes.

As discussed in Chapter 1, having a net zero business model has many clear advantages. First, eco-efficiency processes and systems can save lots of money. Second, having a net zero transition plan can help companies attract and retain top talent, especially younger talent who often seek sustainable employers. Third, having a net zero business model gives companies more resiliency from prospective regulations such as carbon taxes. Fourth, investors who are looking increasingly to optimize the social and environmental impacts of their investments may reward a company with a net zero business model with a higher market capitalization than its competitors. Fifth, achieving net zero may give a company a competitive advantage in its industry and enable it to take a leadership role in shaping it.

Whatever the case for change may be, a company's employees and other stakeholders need to understand the rationale so that they can buy in and support the change.

Assess and Build the Organization

The next step is to assess the company's readiness and capacity to get to net zero. It is helpful to think of the transformation from two perspectives: down-and-in and up-and-across. Down-and-in accounts for the work streams on the various projects and subprojects relating to the transformation. Up-and-across identifies the relationship between the company's transformation to net zero and its other initiatives and priorities. How ready are the employees to be all-in? How will the company align the culture with the transformation?

Build Leadership Capacity to Change

Do a company's leaders have the capacity to lead it to net zero, or will it need to bring in outsiders that have the capacity? Do its leaders understand the change process? Are they committed to the outcome? Companies need to build the infrastructure and conditions to support the change effort.

Have Clear Roles

Generally, companies aiming to achieve net zero create special roles for those leading and designing the transformation process. Having clear roles eliminates conflict and establishes responsibilities. It increases speed and efficiency and lends credibility to the change process. This helps avoid confusion about who is in charge, reduce political struggles, and minimize conflicts between leaders. It also avoids some of the common outcomes that stem from lack of clear direction, including poor follow-through, numerous restarts and re-dos, redundancy of projects, and poor decisions.

Designate an Executive Sponsor

Every successful transformation needs an executive sponsor. Generally, the highest-ranking officer in the company, the CEO or Chairman of the Board, should sponsor the transformation. Ideally, the board of directors will endorse the transformation, too. This sets the transformation up for success by giving it the requisite authority and power to succeed.

Establish a Parallel Governance Structure

An essential innovation is to create a parallel net zero change leadership team to run the change process. If a company tries to run it through its existing hierarchy, the operational "fire of the day" will keep its net zero work from getting much traction. A parallel governance structure that reports into the CEO or executive team is the solution.

Successful transformations have parallel change leadership teams to run the process. Again, because achieving net zero may take decades, companies need a robust governance structure to support the net zero transition through turnover on the executive team and on the board of directors. The change leadership team runs in parallel to the executive team, whose primary role is to keep operations going. The executive team should also buy in and support the transformation. Some members of the executive team should be on the net zero change leadership team, but they will be wearing two hats. There will often be dynamic tension between operations and the change leadership process that requires political skill to manage well because it can disrupt operations. Operations and net zero governance run in parallel. The company still needs to run operations, but operations needs to adjust to the net zero transition plan. The change leadership team needs to lead the transition to net zero but it needs to adjust to operations.

There are hundreds of companies that have established governance architecture to manage their transitions to net zero. Companies can draw inspiration from their examples to develop the appropriate governance structure for their change process, define the needed roles, determine how decision-making will work, and design the net zero transition plan and its governance interface with operations. Company filings with the Carbon Disclosure project contain detailed descriptions of how they have designed the governance architecture for their net zero transition plans.

As discussed in Chapter 2, the *GHG Protocol* was designed to encourage collaboration among companies to achieve a net zero economy. Inventorying a company's Scope 3 emissions, for example, requires it to get information from its suppliers. These conversations encourage the sharing of best practices to optimize a company's transition to net zero.

Designate a Net Zero Leader

The net zero change leadership team needs a designated leader to orchestrate the process. This role is critically important because the leader sets the tone of the transformation. The journey to net zero is a creative, iterative process that will have its own challenges and vicissitudes. Change is scary to humans. Change of the scale required to conform a company's business model to a net zero economy will be terrifying for many employees. The designated leader needs to understand how to guide employees through these emotions.

A company's designated net zero leader should be a great communicator, relational, and very good with people. He or she needs to have a solid strategic mind and know how to get things done operationally. The designated leader needs to have top notch systems and process thinking skills to handle the complexity of the transition to net zero. It can be tough to find all these skills in one person, but the more of these skills the designated net zero leader has, the smoother a company's journey to net zero will be.

Ideally, the designated leader understands change leadership and knows how to design the process from start to finish, own the process, and model the values needed to drive the change. Often the designated net zero leader is a new C-Suite position, the Chief Sustainability Officer, who reports directly to the CEO.

Appoint Individual Net Zero Process Leaders

A well-run transition to net zero has individual net zero process leaders. In the context of net zero, this means there is a change process leader to lead each aspect of the company's chosen eco-efficiency processes. One change process leader, for example, may lead the process of procuring renewable energy for company facilities, while another may be responsible for electrifying the company's vehicle fleet.

Use Experts as Needed

The overall net zero change leadership team will have content experts, communication experts, and change management experts. Sometimes net zero teams retain change management or change leadership consultants to help educate, advise, coach, and course correct.

Align Incentive Compensation with Achieving Net Zero

To optimize the probability that a company will achieve its short-term and long-term science-based emissions-reduction targets, compensation incentives should be aligned to achieving those objectives. If a significant portion of variable compensation is tied to achieving a company's eco-efficiency targets, emissions-reduction targets, and other climate-related goals, then management takes achieving those goals seriously. According to Willis Towers Watson, a multinational insurance advisor, only 11% of top European companies and only 2% of United States S&P 500 companies tie incentive compensation and bonuses to achieving net zero goals.[9]

Have Adequate Financial Resources to Get to Net Zero

The net zero transition plan should detail how the company will allocate financial and other resources to support the transformation. Many Pathway Two transformations, such as General Motors' and Ford's, require tens of billions of dollars of investment. Such capital expenditures require board approval. The plan should have detailed budgets for each initiative and explain where the money is coming from. The plan helps determine whether reviewing the latest renewable power purchase agreement comes out of the legal department's budget or be part of the overall net zero transition budget.

Some companies, such as Rolls-Royce, will need to sell non-essential assets to finance their transition plans. Others, such as General Motors and Ford, may be able to finance their transition plans from a combination of cash flow from operations and debt and equity financing. Allocating sufficient capital for the transformation is critical for its success. Having approved budgets and capital allocations sends a powerful signal to a company's stakeholders that it is serious about getting to net zero. Having a dedicated budget for the transformation minimizes the usual internal political jockeying for budget dollars and helps create alignment.

Have a Flexible Plan

The net zero transition plan should be flexible to adjust to changes in circumstances. A lot will happen between now and 2040, 2045, or 2050 when a company commits to achieve net zero. Pandemics, wars, recessions, and other challenges will come and go. A company's fortunes will wax and wane. The plan should be subject to continuous improvement and allow a company to course correct as it learns from the transformation process. Many companies, for example, have adjusted their near-term and long-term science-based targets and eco-efficiency targets to be more ambitious as they obtain more primary data about their Scope 3 targets and make good progress toward their initial targets.

Meet People's Psychological Needs

A transformation pushes people out of their comfort zones, but everyone needs to be on board to succeed. A clear transition plan empowers people to feel comfortable with the process and encourages more innovation and risk taking. A good plan helps provide the psychological safety people need to get behind it. A well-designed net zero transition plan, coupled with a designated leader who knows how to guide employees through the uncertainty of change, helps meet employees six core psychological needs: security, power, control and order, competence, inclusion, and justice and fairness.

Having a clear net zero transition plan helps employees feel safe about the journey to net zero. Involving employees in designing the plan and giving them clear roles in the transformation empowers them. Having a clear roadmap with clear timelines and objectives provides employees with order and a reliable process to follow. Educating employees about the case for net zero and the expected benefits of the transformation makes them feel competent and capable about contributing to achieving net zero. Including employees in the process by soliciting their ideas for eco-efficiency improvements, for example, makes them feel included.

LAUNCHING THE TRANSFORMATION

By the time a company has a formal net zero transition plan, its transformation is well underway. A company should treat the decision to inventory its GHG emissions as the informal launch of its transformation. As discussed in Chapter 2, inventorying a company's greenhouse gas emissions is a massive undertaking that involves the entire company. This process gives a company a chance to start a buzz. Eco-efficiency processes and systems are a great way to get everyone involved. Many companies have "treasure hunts" to encourage employees to find ways to reduce energy consumption and save money. Such treasure hunts get people engaged and demonstrate getting to net zero is good for the bottom line. Rewarding employees for finding ways to improve processes to reduce emissions builds the habit of continuous improvement into the process.

Most companies that have committed to net zero produce an annual sustainability report that tracks their progress against their targets. Tracking progress requires company-wide systems to track and analyze GHG emissions data and keeps everyone continually engaged in the transition. Having an annual sustainability report independent of, and complementary to, the annual report helps signal a company is committed to achieving net zero. Chapter 14 discusses how companies can tell their net zero stories.

SUMMARY

A company's net zero transition plan helps it avoid many of the common problems of transformations. Often, the schedule is king, and speed takes priority over what is required, creating unrealistic timetables and budgets that drive a transformation to failure. An unclear leadership structure and vague chain of command create ambiguity and confusion that can doom a transformation. The lack of a holistic company-wide approach can create internal silos that compete for resources and mindshare, creating a lack of alignment. A top-down comprehensive transformation strategy can avoid having a disempowered project team isolated from senior management that lacks the authority and power to drive the transformation. Engaging stakeholders early and often in the design process sets up two-way communications that helps accelerate buy-in.

A net zero transition plan also serves as an implementation plan. It should include all the company's key initiatives, including its eco-efficiency programs and their anticipated start dates and completion dates. Ideally, the net zero transition plan provides a framework to manage the overall transformation and provides a common dashboard to track a company's progress to net zero. The plan also establishes priorities not only among a company's net zero initiatives but also among its other initiatives and projects. The plan establishes how other silos within the company will support the transition to net zero.

(See Appendix 12.1 for some questions for the leader, the change leadership team, and the company to consider about a transformation.)

NOTES

1. McKinsey & Company. (2022). Charting net zero: Insights on what the transition could look like. McKinsey Sustainability (21 April). https://www.mckinsey.com/business-functions/sustainability/our-insights/charting-net-zero-insights-on-what-the-transition-could-look-like.
2. Anderson, D. and Anderson, L. (2010). *Beyond Change Management: How to Achieve Breakthrough Results Through Conscious Change Leadership*. San Francisco: Pfeiffer.
3. Ibid.
4. Ibid.
5. Ibid.
6. Eni.com. (2022). Eni for 2021. Our sustainability report. https://www.eni.com/static/en-IT/infographics/eni-for-2021/.
7. Ibid.
8. McKinsey & Company. (2019). Why do most transformations fail? A conversation with Harry Robinson (July). https://www.mckinsey.com/~/media/McKinsey/Business%20Functions/Transformation/Our%20Insights/Why%20do%20most%20transformations%20fail%20A%20conversation%20with%20Harry%20Robinson/Why-do-most-transformations-fail-a-conversation-with-Harry-Robinson.pdf.
9. Ganu, S. and Geiler, P. (2020). Combating climate change through executive compensation. WTW Executive Pay Memo (30 September). https://www.wtwco.com/en-GB/Insights/2020/09/Combating-climate-change-through-executive-compensation.

13

THE THREE DOMAINS OF SYSTEMS THINKING

"Decarbonization needs to take place across the whole economy and it is something that needs to be done by all of us, not just by oil and gas companies, because everything relates to everything else."[1]

—Lord John Browne, Chairman, BeyondNetZero

Companies need the right leadership to achieve net zero. The right leadership for a Pathway One company may not be the right leadership for companies in Pathway Two, Pathway Three, or Pathway Four because those Pathways have net zero transition plans with tougher challenges that require more complex strategic leadership capacities. The right leadership has the systems-thinking capacities appropriate for the chosen Pathway and the skills to lead a commercially successful enterprise.

The transition to a net zero economy requires leadership with three distinct domains of systems thinking: operational, business systems, and global systems. The domains progress through increased levels of complexity for strategic planning that have increasingly complex problems to

EXHIBIT 13.1 The three domains of systems thinking

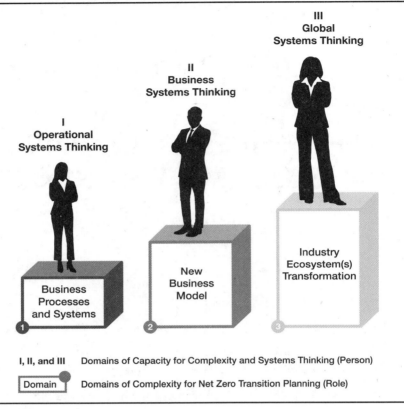

I, II, and III — Domains of Capacity for Complexity and Systems Thinking (Person)

Domain — Domains of Complexity for Net Zero Transition Planning (Role)

Source: FutureZero

be solved, strategic decisions to be taken, and more elements, subsystems, and industry ecosystems to be integrated together. The domains progress to transcend and include the systems-thinking capacities of the prior, less-complex domains (see Exhibit 13.1).

THE OPERATIONS DOMAIN

The operations domain is the least complex and covers fundamental businesses processes and systems. Operational systems thinking is commonly applied in operations to improve existing products and processes. The quality of operational systems thinking required in this domain is relatively linear. A problem requiring operational systems thinking generally has a cause and an obvious effect. The solutions tend to be tangible, simple, and straightforward. The feedback loop for prospective solutions is relatively quick and the time horizon for implementing them is relatively short.

In the context of net zero, the operations domain covers most eco-efficiency processes and systems, which generally will only require operational systems thinking. Companies in every Pathway require leaders with strong operational systems-thinking capacities because companies on every Pathway will employ some combination of eco-efficiency business processes and systems to achieve net zero, and traditional operational skills will be needed to be commercially successful. Operational systems thinking is adequate to manage developmental change, as discussed in Chapter 12.

The basic objective of eco-efficiency processes and systems is to reduce GHG emissions with relatively simple solutions. Again, operational systems thinking is linear. The problem has a cause—a fleet of delivery vehicles with internal combustion engines—and an obvious effect—GHG tailpipe emissions. To reduce or eliminate the emissions, the solution is simple and straightforward—replace the fleet with electric delivery vans. Such a cause-and-effect solution can be managed using operational systems thinking and does not require complex leadership capacities.

THE BUSINESS SYSTEMS DOMAIN

The business systems domain is more complex than the operations domain and covers a company's core business model. Systems thinking is commonly applied to design new business models and create new zero-carbon products and services. The quality of business systems thinking required in the business systems domain is nonlinear, abstract, multidimensional, and multilevel and transcends and includes the qualities of operational systems thinking. A problem requiring business systems thinking is novel, conceptual, and unstructured with multiple causes and effects that may not be immediately obvious. The feedback loop for prospective solutions can take years and the time horizon for implementing them can be 2 to 10 years for impact on innovation and positive return on capital.

In the context of net zero, the business systems domain covers changes to a company's fundamental business model to achieve net zero, which generally require business systems thinking. Companies in Pathway Two and Pathway Four require leaders with strong business systems thinking capacities because these companies will change their fundamental business models to achieve net zero. Companies in Pathway Three also require leaders with strong business systems-thinking capacities, especially those with novel, industry-disrupting business models. Business systems thinking is adequate to manage transitional change, as discussed in Chapter 12.

THE GLOBAL SYSTEMS DOMAIN

The global systems domain is more complex than the business systems domain and covers industry-wide and economy-wide systems and ecosystems. Global systems thinking is applied to transform the global economic system and entire industries and to establish new global business and industry norms. The quality of global systems thinking required in the global systems domain transcends and includes the qualities of business systems thinking and operational systems thinking. Like problems requiring business systems thinking, a problem requiring global systems thinking is novel, conceptual, and unstructured with multiple causes and effects that may not be immediately obvious but is more complex, requiring an understanding of interdependencies between systems and systems of systems. The quality of global systems thinking required in the global systems domain is more multidimensional and multilevel than business systems thinking. It requires the ability to conceptualize systems within systems. The feedback loop for prospective solutions can take years and the time horizon for implementing them can be over several decades.

In the context of net zero, the global systems domain covers transformations of the global economic system and entire industries to achieve net zero and the establishment of new global business and industry norms regarding climate change, sustainability, and circularity. Companies in Pathway Four require leaders with strong global systems-thinking capacities because these companies will lead the transformation of their industries and ecosystems to achieve net zero. Global systems-thinking capacities are helpful to companies in all Pathways, especially those in Pathway Three that aspire to disrupt their industries. The transition to a net zero economy invites leaders with strong global systems-thinking capacities to step up to lead within companies and in business, politics, economics, and other fields because global systems thinking will help the world achieve net zero. Global systems thinking is adequate to manage transformational change, as discussed in Chapter 12.

CULTIVATING SYSTEMS-THINKING CAPACITY FOR THE TRANSITION TO NET ZERO

Systems thinking starts with seeing the whole and then discerns how the parts and other systems interact and affect each other. The basis of systems thinking is that complex problems have multiple, interrelated causes and delayed feedback loops that must be understood before they can be solved.

Complex systems are comprised of many interconnected parts. Changing one interconnected part tends to affect the whole system. This means systems are constantly evolving as their component parts change. Their behavior is characterized as emergent. Applying systems thinking often can identify the smallest possible changes that will have the greatest positive effect on solving a complex problem. Conversely, systems thinking also can expose vulnerabilities in a system and help identify the small events that can disable an entire system.

Systems-thinking capacity for complexity develops in leaders over time. Successive promotions with ever-increasing complexity and scope enlarge a leader's ability to take in perspectives, which then allow the leader to see systems and their interdependencies from increasingly expansive points of view.

An engineer, for example, applies operational systems thinking to improve a product and earns a promotion to manage a team to develop a suite of products. In her role as a manager, the engineer interacts with other business functions, such as sales and marketing, and customers. These interactions lead to the development of business systems thinking as the engineer develops an understanding of how the products interact with other functions and the market. If she develops sufficient business systems thinking to juggle the competing needs and priorities of other internal functions and the customers, she may be promoted to a more complex role managing several teams developing several suites of products that further develop her business systems-thinking skills. A posting in Germany to manage engineering operations in Europe would provide the engineer with another linguistic and cultural perspective and develop her global systems-thinking capacity.

One of the obstacles to achieving a net zero economy is the lack of leadership with the requisite levels of global systems-thinking capacities because these skills are relatively rare. The U.S. Armed Forces and other leadership researchers have identified that less than 5% of the world's adult population has the potential for business systems and global systems-thinking capacities.[2] The U.S. Armed Forces understands this problem acutely because, unlike companies that can recruit executives from other companies, the military cannot recruit one-, two-, three-, and four-star generals and admirals from the outside: it must develop these strategic leaders internally to have the requisite levels of global systems thinking required for senior and complex strategic leadership positions. The military identifies personnel with high leadership and global systems-thinking potential and puts them on an executive developmental track with increasingly complex and demanding assignments designed to expand their leadership and systems-thinking capacities through key career pathways and gateways career paths for strategic leadership talent assessment, selection, and development.[3]

Companies that invest in the assessment and development of leaders with the requisite levels of systems-thinking capacities optimize their probability of success in their journeys to net zero. This means having a long-term plan to develop the next three-to-five generations of executive leadership with the systems-thinking capacities to lead business model and industry transformations. Companies need to create robust talent pipelines because it will take decades for them to achieve net zero (see Exhibit 13.2). Many companies, such as Salesforce, have extensive developmental curricula to develop leaders at all stages of development and create a robust pipeline of leadership talent.[4]

EXHIBIT 13.2 The three domains of systems thinking and the four Pathways

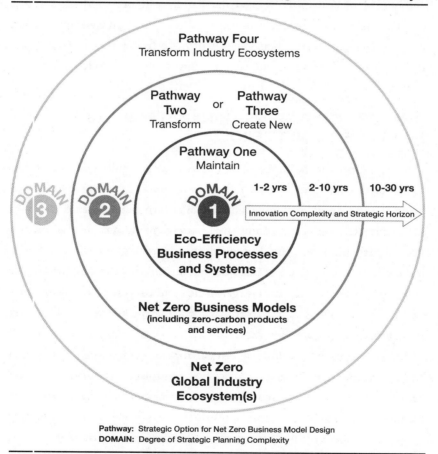

Pathway: Strategic Option for Net Zero Business Model Design
DOMAIN: Degree of Strategic Planning Complexity

The relative rarity of leaders with global systems-thinking capacities makes the overall transformation to a net zero economy more challenging, but it is not necessarily a limiting factor. One transformational leader with global systems-thinking capacity, such as Tesla's Elon Musk, can precipitate the transformation of an entire industry. Happily, there are many companies with transformational leadership with global systems-thinking capacity that have committed to net zero that have created roadmaps and strategies that can be emulated and followed. A few transformational leaders of Pathway Two, Pathway Three, and Pathway Four companies with global systems-thinking capacities can have an oversized effect on the overall transition to a net zero economy. These pioneering companies and their leaders can show others the blueprint to follow and the best practices to deploy since all corporate transitions to net zero follow one of the four Pathways.

DOMAINS OF SYSTEMS THINKING FOR THE PATHWAYS TO NET ZERO

Understanding the domains of systems thinking will help companies transition to net zero by giving them a framework to work with their internal and external systems. The parallel governance structure discussed in Chapter 12 to support a company's strategic planning, innovation, and net zero transition plan, for example, needs to interact well with operations to be effective. This requires business systems thinking to understand the company's various functions—legal, human resources, accounting, sales, and marketing—and how the process of achieving net zero will impact these functions (see Exhibit 13.3).

Business systems thinking is critical for companies such as General Motors, which is experiencing a double transformation not only to net zero but also to a completely new business model. General Motors' net zero leadership team, for example, must employ business systems thinking to interact effectively not only with the business units that make smart, electric vehicles but also with the legacy business units that make vehicles with internal combustion engines. The legacy business units may use operational systems thinking to deploy their own eco-efficiency processes and systems to decarbonize their processes.

EXHIBIT 13.3 Systems thinking in the four Pathways

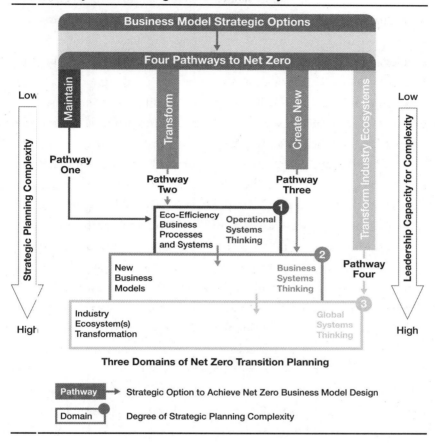

Three Domains of Net Zero Transition Planning

| Pathway → | Strategic Option to Achieve Net Zero Business Model Design |
| Domain ● | Degree of Strategic Planning Complexity |

On a larger scale, systems thinking can help companies identify the principal risk factors that can impact their businesses. These risk factors include business risks, competitive risks, supply chain risks. climate risks, and geopolitical risks. Business systems thinking can help companies identify the business risks, such as the loss of a major customer, disruptions in their supply chains, or the rise of new competitors. Global systems thinking can help companies identify the risks affecting their industries, such as government regulations or the rise of new technologies, and the geopolitical risks that may affect them, such as a civil war that disrupts supplies of raw materials in their supply chains.

Risk factors are dynamic, and the potential danger posed by an individual risk may rise or fall depending on external circumstances. A comprehensive collection of risk factors provides a dashboard that enables a board of directors and management team to constantly monitor and assess the risks across all domains of systems thinking.

Systems thinking can help companies monitor their business risks. Not only do systemic risks shift in priority and magnitude as internal and external circumstances shift, but they also vary in time horizon, which also can shift quickly and unexpectedly. Few companies anticipated the disruption in the global energy market and the West's coordinated response to Russia's invasion of Ukraine. With the resulting rise in the prices of oil, gas, and coal and the interruption of fossil fuel supplies to Europe, the geopolitical risks inherent in the global economy's supply chains became starkly apparent. Companies need to anticipate such unexpected shifts in circumstances in their scenario planning because such shifts may, for example, accelerate the transition to net zero and invite carbon taxes sooner than expected to accelerate the development of renewable energy sources.

Global systems thinking enabled Tesla to gain market share during the Covid-19 pandemic. Tesla increased its sales 87% in 2021, while the three traditional manufacturers of vehicles with internal combustion engines in the United States, General Motors, Ford, and Stellantis (the amalgamation of Chrysler, Fiat, and Peugeot) saw their sales decline.[5] Telsa's competitors failed to anticipate how quickly demand would rebound during the pandemic and cut back orders for semiconductors, which are ubiquitous in smart cars. When demand returned, their suppliers had reallocated semiconductors to other customers. Factories idled and showrooms were empty while these automakers waited for semiconductors.

Global systems thinking enabled Tesla to identify the risks in its global supply chain to disruptions in supplies of semiconductors and other components. Tesla created resilience by developing internal capacities. Unlike General Motors, Ford, and Stellantis, which rely primarily on third-party software, Tesla builds its own software. When certain semiconductor chips were in short supply, Tesla simply ordered different semiconductors and applied operational systems thinking to rewrite its code to run on the substitute chips. Its business never skipped a beat and gained market share. Tesla's competitors now recognize their vulnerability and are starting to design their own semiconductors and software internally.

Cultivating systems-thinking capacity makes a company more resilient and has other benefits. Systems-thinking capacity can increase enterprise value. Investors often pay premiums for companies like Tesla that have strong systems-thinking skills in their leadership ranks.[6]

Systems Thinking Meets Electric Vehicles and Gray Electrons

A North American company on any of the Pathways may employ operational systems thinking by switching to an all-electric delivery fleet to eliminate tailpipe emissions. This may eliminate its fleet's tailpipe emissions but not the indirect emissions that come from combusting the fossil fuels that provide 52% of the electricity supplied by the grid.

A company may employ operational systems thinking to purchase renewable energy to charge its vehicles, but this does not solve the indirect emissions problem. Purchasing renewable energy to recharge those vehicles may create more demand for renewable and carbon-free sources of energy, but the electrons that charge those vehicles will still be mostly gray electrons now and for the foreseeable future.

Installing on-site solar and wind generation may not fix the problem either. Many jurisdictions require private renewable energy installations to contribute their power to the grid and require the owner to purchase gray electrons from their local utility. The result is an offset that does not fix the systemic problem with the grid.

These issues are not unique to companies receiving their power from the North American grid. Companies in other geographies face the same issue. The European grid produces 44% of its electricity from fossil fuels.[7] The Chinese grid produces about 85% of its electricity from fossil fuels.[8] The grid in India produces 75% of its electricity from fossil fuels[9] (see Appendix 13.1). Companies may eliminate the tailpipe emissions of their vehicles by electrifying their vehicle fleets but not emissions from the grids that charge those vehicles.

A truly emissions-free electric fleet requires a clean and carbon-free energy power grid. Achieving a clean grid, however, is not a simple problem with a simple, linear solution that can be solved with operational systems thinking, but a complex problem arising from a complex system with many interdependent components that can only be solved with higher levels of systems thinking.

Systems Thinking and the Electric Power Sector—the Foundation to the Net Zero Economy

The transformation of the electric power industry to net zero requires all three domains of net zero systems thinking. The power systems and grids of the world are engineered as hierarchies of complex systems within systems for power generation, power transmission, and electric power distribution to the customer with the electric meter as the demarcation point between the power grid and the end consumer.

The North America power system and electrical grid has been called the "largest machine on earth" and is comprised of power systems within systems within systems.[10] At the top of the hierarchy of systems is the not-for-profit North American Electric Reliability Corporation (NERC), which governs eight regional power coordinating councils for the continent, which are organized into three regions, the Eastern Connection, the Western Connection, and ERCOT for Texas (see Appendix 13.2).

At the next level of systems in the North America power system are either independent system operators (ISOs) and or regional transmission operators. In short, the nine ISOs operate each region's electricity grid, synchronize with the other ISOs, direct the hourly, daily, weekly, and monthly dispatch of power generation onto the grid, administer the region's wholesale electricity power markets, and provide reliability planning for the region's bulk electricity system.

At the next level of systems in the North American power system is a complex network of 9,200 electricity generating facilities connected to more than 300,000 miles of transmission lines operated by hundreds of companies.[11] NERC ensures the reliability of the power system, which is a collection of eight synchronous grids. The totality of the grid is a complex network of power producers, asset owners, service providers, and state, local, and federal government entities.

Exhibit 13.4 depicts the power generation mix of the overall North American grid, including Canada, in 2020.

EXHIBIT 13.4 The power generation mix of the North American grid

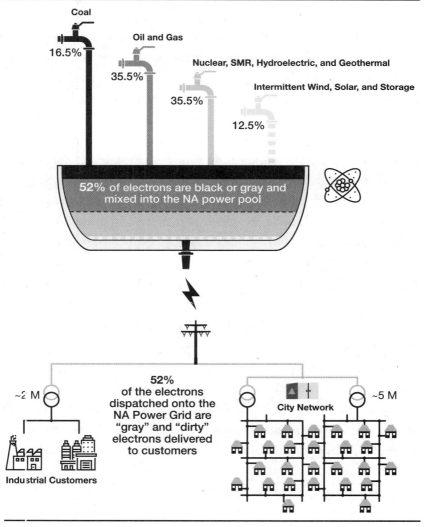

Source: FutureZero, Statistics Canada, U.S. Environmental Protection Agency, Standard & Poor's CAP Q with power.

249

The United States may have set a goal to have a clean grid by 2035 but there is no clear strategy to achieve this goal. Achieving a clean North American grid requires global systems-thinking and business systems-thinking skills.

A simple, linear solution such as adding more wind and solar capacity to the grid to replace fossil fuel plants will not fix the problem. Solar and wind are renewable but intermittent sources of energy. To have a stable, consistent, reliable, 24/7 supply of electricity requires fossil fuel power plants for the near-term. Switching coal-fired power plants to natural gas turbines is only an incremental solution because natural gas produces about 25% less emissions per kilowatt produced than coal. Natural gas may be cleaner than coal but still produces a lot of GHG emissions.

The automobile industry may have reached a tipping point and be in the process of transitioning from vehicles with internal combustion engines to electric ones, but it will not be able to eliminate its Scope 3, category 1 (use of products) emissions without a clean grid. Tesla may be leading this industry-wide transformation, but an opportunity remains for the automobile industry to help lead the transformation of the North American grid from producing gray electrons to clean ones. The intention of Scope 3 is to encourage companies and their supply chains to collaborate to reduce emissions. Walmart's Project Gigaton, discussed in Chapter 5, illustrates the kind of collaboration that can be highly effective in reducing Scope 3 emissions. The invitation inherent in Scope 3 emissions is to scale this kind of collaboration across entire industries, ecosystems, and economies to address systemic emissions.

Scaling this kind of collaboration requires business systems thinking to transform business models within the power industry and global systems thinking to transform the North American and other global power systems.

Transforming a power grid into a clean, carbon-free energy power grid requires a holistic understanding of the entire power system and systems within systems (regional and microgrids). This requires identifying all the gric's components and constituent stakeholders and understanding the relationships among the components. Some stakeholders, such as operators of transmission lines, will be unaffected relatively by the decarbonization of the grid and likely will be supportive of the transition. Other stakeholders, such as operators of coal-, gas-, and oil-powered power plants and the companies that supply them with fossil fuel, may feel threatened by decarbonization and work against the transition. Just as there was an opportunity for Tesla to lead the transformation of the automobile industry, there is an opportunity for leaders to emerge to unite all the grid's stakeholders behind a common vision and strategy to achieve a clean grid.

Systems Thinking and the Development of the Smart Grid

The application of systems thinking does not stop with developing a strategy and plan to achieve a clean grid. The grid also needs to be transformed into a smart grid. Achieving a smart grid requires business systems thinking to transform and digitize business models within the power industry and global systems thinking to transform and digitize the North American and global power systems.

The current North American grid may be an engineering marvel, but its current patchwork architecture dates to the 1890s and is stretched to capacity.[12] The grid needs an upgrade to enable two-way communication between utilities and their customers and to add sensors throughout to enable data collection, new measurements, and data analytics that will improve its efficiency and reliability. The grid also needs to be modernized to protect it from natural disasters, hackers, and foreign actors.

A smart grid will enable demand response and advanced metering. With a smart grid, utilities will be able to work with their customers to limit or delay their consumption of electricity during periods of high demand. With advanced metering, customers will reduce their energy costs by switching their usage to off-peak times when electricity costs less.

A smart grid will also accommodate new technologies such as microgrids and grid-scale energy-storage devices. A microgrid is a self-sufficient constellation of renewable energy sources that supports a local community such as a hospital or college campus. When the grid is down, a microgrid can operate independently, thereby increasing resilience of the entire system. Energy-storage devices can help utilities meet demand during peak loads when the grid may not be able to generate enough electricity to meet demand.

On a macro level, a smart grid will enable load balancing among the eight synchronous regional grids that comprise it. A smart grid, for example, would allow a solar installation in the Nevada desert to send electricity in the afternoon to the East Coast in the early evening to meet air conditioning demand during a heat wave.

The smart grid is an emergent process that will evolve over the next decade. According to the U.S. Department of Energy, the smart grid "will consist of millions of pieces and parts—controls, computers, power lines, and new technologies and equipment."[13]

Systems Thinking and the Double Transformation of the Grid

Just as General Motors' transformation into a software platform for smart electric vehicles is part of the larger double transformation of the economy from analog and fossil fuels to digital and clean energy, the smart grid also requires a simultaneous double transformation. It requires global systems thinking to coordinate the dynamic interaction between the power system and the emergent information system that will make the clean grid smart.

In addition to identifying all the power grid's components and constituent stakeholders and understanding the relationships among them, creating the smart grid will require identifying all the information system's components and constituent stakeholders. Applying global systems thinking will identify the relationships between systems and the components and stakeholders of each system. Not only is there an opportunity to unite all the grid's information system stakeholders behind a common vision and strategy to achieve a smart grid, but there is also an opportunity to unite all the grid's power system and information system stakeholders behind a common vision to create a smart and clean grid.

Just as the resulting clean and smart grid will be more resilient, global systems thinking will make the emergent process of creating the new grid more resilient. On a macro level, this transformation is occurring in an increasingly VUCA context affected by ever-shifting economic, environmental, political, geopolitical, health, and technology risks. In addition, the transformation is occurring during a period of rapid technological innovation. Thus, the emergent process of creating a smart and clean grid needs to be flexible to adjust to changing circumstances and new technologies.

Systems Thinking, Smart Grids, and Green Hydrogen

The emergent process of creating a clean and smart grid may accelerate the development of complementary technologies. Hydrogen, for example, is widely expected to be a significant source of energy in the net zero economy. Most currently available hydrogen, however, is "gray," made in an energy-intensive process from natural gas that results in about 7.05 kilograms of CO_2 per kilogram of hydrogen. As discussed in Chapter 9, so-called "blue" hydrogen is also made from natural gas, but the CO_2 emissions are captured in the manufacturing process.

A clean grid could enable more production of "green" hydrogen, which is hydrogen produced through electrolysis whereby water atoms are split into oxygen and hydrogen. Producing green hydrogen this way is also an energy-intensive process. It takes approximately 52 megawatts of electricity to produce one metric ton of hydrogen. If the entire annual production of hydrogen, which is currently about 70 million metric tons, were green, it would consume more power than currently is consumed in all of Europe.[14]

Recently, a coalition of the world's largest green hydrogen project developers, including Ørsted, Iberdrola, ACWA Power, CWP Renewables, Envision, Snam, and Yara, launched the Green Hydrogen Catapult initiative using global systems thinking.[15] The objectives of the initiative include the short-term goals of increasing the production of green hydrogen 50-fold by 2026 and driving the cost of green hydrogen to below $2 per kilogram, which the group believes is the tipping point that will make hydrogen the fuel of choice across many sectors. Goldman Sachs estimates that developing the green hydrogen market in Europe alone could attract over €2 trillion of investment by 2050.[16]

Such investments include dedicated renewable power sources—onshore and offshore wind and solar, electrolyzers, hydrogen turbine power plants, and gas infrastructure to deliver hydrogen. Existing natural gas pipelines can be repurposed to transport a mix of natural gas and hydrogen and gas-fired power plants could be converted to run on hydrogen. Goldman Sachs estimates that the green hydrogen market could potentially reach €10 trillion per year, or 13% of global GDP by 2050.[17] The Green Hydrogen Catapult estimates that hydrogen could supply 25% of the world's energy by 2050.[18]

The promise of a hydrogen economy has stimulated innovation, such as Universal Hydrogen and ZeroAvia's hydrogen-powered powertrains for aviation discussed in Chapter 9. Toyota already offers a hydrogen-powered automobile, the Mirai,[19] and has partnered with Paccar, the maker of Kenworth and Peterbuilt trucks, to produce a hydrogen fuel cell to power heavy-duty trucks. Prototypes of these hydrogen-powered trucks are already on the road.[20] The hydrogen fuel cells in these vehicles convert compressed hydrogen from their fuel tanks into electricity that powers an electric motor, providing a similar range to vehicles with internal combustion engines while emitting only water vapor.

Universal Hydrogen and ZeroAvia show that the technology to use hydrogen as a power source for transportation applications is already here. Making enough green hydrogen at scale and then distributing it at scale remains a challenge. Solutions to scale the hydrogen economy are emergent. Heliogen, Inc., a renewable energy company in California, produces hydrogen by using smart, adjustable mirror arrays to reflect and concentrate sunlight to a target on a tower. The generated heat, when combined with an electrolyzer, can produce green hydrogen.[21] KU Leuven in Holland has produced hydrogen panels, similar in concept to solar panels, that produce green hydrogen from sunlight and water vapor from the air.[22] Hydrogen panels would allow for the distributed production of hydrogen by enabling individual consumers to produce their own.

Producing green hydrogen remains energy intensive and requires dedicated sources of renewable energy, such as wind or solar, or new clean energy sources at scale. A network of NuScale's small modular nuclear reactors, for example, could power electrolysis at scale to produce green hydrogen at scale. The point is that while the clean smart grid is emergent, the green hydrogen economy is simultaneously emergent. A high level of global systems thinking needs to be applied to create a unifying vision and strategy to create a clean and smart grid that can accommodate parallel developments in the green hydrogen market, which because of the energy intensity of producing green hydrogen, could place extraordinary new demands on power grids.

SUMMARY

Achieving a net zero economy requires all three domains of systems thinking. Global systems-thinking capacities are in short supply, but this does not have to be a limiting factor in the creation of a net zero economy. Many of the companies discussed in this book, including Honeywell, Mitsubishi Heavy Industries, Shell, Ørsted, Vattenfall, NextEra, Microsoft, Salesforce, Paccar, and Nestlé, apply all three domains of systems thinking in their transitions to net zero as evident in their publicly available disclosures. These disclosures provide models of how to apply systems thinking that other companies can follow on their journeys to net zero.

NOTES

1. Brown, J. (2022). Lord John Browne's speech to the City of London corporation's investment committee. Beyond Net Zero (26 January). https://beyond-net-zero.com/lord-john-brownes-speech-to-the-city-of-london-corporations-investment-committee/.

2. Personal correspondence between Mark Van Clieaf and T. Owen Jacobs (retired Chief Strategic Leadership Technical Area, U.S. Army Research Institute) and Theo Dawson (President, Educational Testing Service).

3. McGuire, M. (2011). *Pulling Back the Curtain: Developing Strategic Thinkers at the Industrial College of the Armed Forces*. Washington D.C.: National Defense University Press.

4. Sostrin, J. (2022). Want to prepare your employees to lead from anywhere? Salesforce reveals its playbook. Salesforce.com (13 June). https://www.salesforce.com/blog/leadership-development/ (accessed 22 August 2022).

5. Ewing, J. (2022). Why Tesla soared as other automakers struggled to make cars. *The New York Times* (8 January). https://www.nytimes.com/2022/01/08/business/teslas-computer-chips-supply-chain.html.

6. Intel. (2022). Intel names David Zinser Executive Vice President and Chief Financial Officer. Business Wire (10 January). https://www.businesswire.com/news/home/20220110005917/en/Intel-Names-David-Zinsner-Executive-Vice-President-and-Chief-Financial-Officer.

7. Eurostat. https://ec.europa.eu/eurostat (accessed 22 August 2022).

8. ChinaPower. (n.d.). How is China's energy footprint changing? https://chinapower.csis.org/energy-footprint/ (accessed 20 August 2022).

9. International Energy Agency. (n.d.). India energy outlook 2021: energy in India today. https://www.iea.org/reports/india-energy-outlook-2021/energy-in-india-today (accessed 22 August 2022).

10. Angwin, M. (2020). *Shorting the Grid: The Hidden Fragility of Our Electric Grid*. Wilder, VT: Carnot Communications.

11. SmartGrid.gov. (n.d.). The smart grid. U.S. Department of Energy. https://smartgrid.gov/the_smart_grid/smart_grid.html (accessed 22 August 2022).

12. Ibid.

13. Ibid.

14. Gandolfi, A., Patel, A., Della Vigna, M. et al. (2020). Green hydrogen: The next transformational driver of the utilities industry. Goldman Sachs Research (22 September). https://www.goldmansachs.com/insights/pages/gs-research/green-hydrogen/report.pdf.

15. Alvirá, M. (2021). *The Hydrogen Revolution: A Blueprint for the Future of Clean Energy*. London: Hodder & Stoughton.

16. Gandolfi, A. et al. (2020). Green hydrogen: The next transformational driver of the utilities industry.

17. Ibid.

18. RMI. (2021). The green hydrogen catapult announces expansion of world-leading green hydrogen deployment. Press release (4 November). https://rmi.org/press-release/the-green-hydrogen-catapult-announces-expansion-of-world-leading-green-hydrogen-deployment/.

19. Toyota. (n.d.). Mirai. https://www.toyota.com/mirai/ (accessed 22 August 2022).

20. Quimby, T. (2021). 'Not a competition:' Paccar's electric and fuel cell trucks prove impressive in Rockies. CCJ (18 February). https://www.ccjdigital.com/alternative-power/article/14972957/not-a-competition-paccars-electric-and-fuel-cell-trucks-prove-impressive-in-the-rockies.

21. Heliogen, Inc. heliogen.com/ (accessed 22 August 2022).

22. FuelCellsWorks. (2021). Solar panels that may revolutionize hydrogen production (19 December). https://fuelcellsworks.com/news/solar-panels-that-may-revolutionize-hydrogen-production/.

14

TELLING THE NET ZERO STORY

"We cannot get to net zero without proper climate reporting."[1]
—Mark Carney, Former Governor of the Bank of England

Every company, large and small, public and private, will be affected by the Great Transformation, but each company has a unique story to tell. Regulations requiring publicly listed companies to disclose how they will achieve net zero are emergent in jurisdictions around the world. The consensus is that uniform and globally recognized disclosure standards with respect to companies' net zero transition plans, their Scope 1, 2, and 3 emissions, their science-based emissions-reduction targets, and their progress toward those targets will emerge by 2025.

As more and more publicly listed companies commit to achieve net zero, inventory their Scope 1, 2, and 3 GHG emissions, and set near-term and long-term science-based emissions-reduction targets, one could argue that this information is material to the future value and performance of publicly listed companies and should be disclosed now for shareholders.

Many reporting companies already take this approach and provide full disclosure of all this information in their securities filings, on their websites, and in sustainability and impact reports.

Parts II and III of *Net Zero Business Models* outline the general narrative arc of conforming a business model to a net zero economy and suggest elements of the common pattern language that companies use to describe their journeys to net zero. It starts with an inventory of a company's GHG emissions using the *GHG Protocol*, which has emerged as the leading GHG emissions and value chain accounting reporting standard. Most issuers use the *GHG Protocol* and its three scopes and categories of emissions to inventory their emissions.

In terms of setting emissions-reduction targets, the SBTi approach appears to be the emergent standard in the industries where targets and methodologies to achieve them have been established. The SBTi approach is systemic and encourages the setting of targets in line with the ambition to limit global temperature rise to 1.5°C by 2050. As the SBTi completes target setting standards for all industries, momentum toward universal acceptance of the SBTi framework likely will build.

COMPANIES NEED GOOD DATA TO TELL THEIR NET ZERO STORIES

To tell their net zero stories, either voluntarily or as may be mandated by securities regulation, companies need accurate GHG emissions and other related ESG and business model performance disclosures, much of which needs to be third-party verifiable. CEOs, C-Suites, and boards of directors need good information to ensure their companies' net zero transition plans are comprehensive, credible, and on track with near-term and long-term GHG emissions-reduction targets, eco-efficiency targets, other climate-related goals, business plans, and budgets. Most companies should be on a path to achieve a reduction of at least 45% to 60% of their overall GHG emissions by 2030. Their board-approved net zero transition plans should include year-over-year GHG emissions-reduction targets after 2030 in a range of 6% to 8% until they achieve a business model with zero, net zero, or net negative GHG emissions on or before 2050.

Capital providers, including institutional investors, commercial banks, and insurance companies, also need high-quality and comprehensive ESG and GHG disclosures that are reliable and decision-useful about the short-, medium-, and long-term financial implications of companies' net zero transition plans and progress toward achieving net zero. As companies embark upon their chosen Pathway to achieve net zero, they need to enhance their regular management reporting systems and scorecards to include additional metrics that track and report on financial and nonfinancial performance toward achieving their net zero transition plans, including climate-related objectives. These additional data and performance metrics are critical for boards of directors and executive teams to measure the associated financial impacts and to inform spending decisions and capital allocation strategies.

The CFO and Chief Sustainability Officer are generally accountable for implementing such enhanced financial and nonfinancial reporting systems. These systems help a company stay on track with its net zero transition plan and to meet its business strategy, innovation, growth, return on investment, and other financial and nonfinancial performance targets material to value creation and enterprise value.

The Board of Directors' Role in Telling the Net Zero Story

Boards of directors need to ensure these new performance metrics, targets, and reporting processes are in place and aligned with the transition plan. Boards also need to ensure long-horizon institutional investors, such as pension funds, that are transforming their investment portfolios into net zero portfolios receive decision-useful disclosures and information to enable them to distinguish the future winners in the net zero economy from the future survivors and casualties.

In effect, boards of directors and the C-Suite together are the gatekeepers for these corporate governance and communication processes.

On the one hand, boards of directors need to receive the key financial and nonfinancial performance metrics related to achieving net zero transition plans for effective strategic oversight of management. On the other hand, directors need to ensure the information provided to investors is accurate, timely, and material for investment research and securities selection purposes. Directors also need to ensure disclosures to investors about net zero transition plans and progress toward achieving them, both voluntary and mandatory, are consistent with information provided in any voluntary sustainability reporting by the company to broader audiences of stakeholders.

Investors Expect Comprehensive and Credible Net Zero Stories

Institutional investors, including asset owners and asset managers, are becoming increasingly sophisticated about the terminology and taxonomies related to GHG emissions, the *GHG Protocol*, SBTi-verified science-based emissions targets, and accepted asset classes for investment. A company that fails to tell the story about its transition to net zero using the emergent common pattern language may be sending a signal to investors that it is not serious about addressing climate-related risks or that its commitment to achieve a net zero business model is just greenwashing.

A sophisticated institutional investor who understands the *GHG Protocol* will question a company's commitment to net zero, for example, if it only sets and discloses targets for its Scope 1 and 2 emissions and does not report its Scope 3 emissions, claiming that such information is misleading or not available. Such a company might find itself subject to shareholder proposals or facing a slate of climate activist candidates for its board of directors. Investors who are informed by relevant metrics and other disclosures about companies' net zero transition plans and progress toward achieving them can be highly influential catalysts for strengthening board oversight and management performance.

The global financial services sector is acting increasingly as an enabler and accelerator of the transformation of the global economy to net zero. Going forward, asset owners, such as pension funds, asset managers, commercial banks, and insurance companies, quickly are becoming net zero savvy and acting as fiduciaries of the financial capital they manage to support the transition of the global economy to net zero. These actions include reviewing companies' net zero–related disclosures, proxy voting, say-on-pay voting, and say-on-climate voting. Asset owners are putting forth shareholder resolutions calling for better net zero transition plan disclosures, are engaging proactively with investee companies, and are exploring the potential litigation risk for boards of directors whose companies make net zero commitments without having credible and defensible net zero transition plans. Asset owners with more than $130 trillion dollars of financial capital under management are seeking better disclosures on net zero transition plans from companies listed on stock exchanges and privately held companies.[2]

THE EVOLUTION OF VOLUNTARY ESG AND CLIMATE-RELATED DISCLOSURE—THE ALPHABET SOUP

There is a growing recognition of the need for global standards and requirements for mandatory sustainability and corporate climate-related reporting. The movement toward mandatory climate-related reporting is accelerating. As the former Governor of the Bank of England, Mark Carney stated, "We cannot get to net-zero without proper climate reporting."[3]

Climate-related external reporting has evolved from its initial focus on corporate GHG emission mitigation initiatives and results. More recently, following the Paris Agreement in 2015, the focus has been on how to reduce global GHG emissions by 2050 to limit global warming to well below 2°C, preferably to 1.5°C, compared to pre-industrial levels. Nation-states committed to this goal will not be able to reach it without significantly reducing emissions from companies listed on stock exchanges and privately held companies.

A common pattern language for companies' external reporting about climate-related targets, plans, progress, and results is still in the formative stage, despite gradual advances over the last 25 years and significant progress in the last 5 years. During this time, institutional investors have become interested in the relationships between sustainability, climate change, company performance, and enterprise value. Today, they have a major influence on corporate board and management decision-making about vision, strategy, plans, targets, performance, and governance regarding the transition to a net zero global economy.

This interest formally emerged in 1997 when Ceres, a U.S. nonprofit sustainability advocacy organization, and the Tellus Institute, a nonprofit that strives to advance a planetary civilization rooted in justice, well-being, and sustainability, formed the Global Reporting Institute (GRI). GRI was the first international organization to develop a sustainability-reporting framework. Its first sustainability-reporting guidelines were released in 2000 and have evolved into today's formulation as the *GRI Standards*, which are the world's most widely used sustainability-reporting standards.[4] The *GRI Standards*, although voluntary, provide a useful common language for internal and external communication about corporate sustainability issues and enterprise impacts on the planet and people.

Information in a *GRI Standards*-compliant sustainability report may be of limited value to investors, however. A general, multitopic sustainability report intended for all stakeholders may not be the ideal way to present institutional investors with the decision-useful information most relevant and material to their assessment of business risks and possible impacts on a company and its enterprise value posed by the transition to a net zero business model.

In 2002, a relatively small group of institutional investors collaborated to form the Carbon Disclosure Project (CDP), a nonprofit based in the UK. The CDP asked a cross-section of listed companies around the world to complete a questionnaire about their annual GHG emissions. The compiled results from this survey were then publicly reported, creating the first publication at scale about corporate GHG emissions. Today, over 13,000 companies disclose their carbon emissions data and other information to the CDP, which maintains a publicly accessible online database of their submissions.

The United Nations released its Principles for Responsible Investing (PRI) in 2005, which added momentum to investors' desire for company disclosures about key sustainability issues, of which climate change was emerging as a front-runner.[5] At about this time, the widely used acronym ESG entered investors' lexicon, referring to any environmental, social, and governance issue, information about which might, for a given company, be material to an investor's decision-making.

In 2007, the Climate Disclosure Standards Board (CDSB) was initiated at the World Economic Forum to develop standards for companies to disclose annually in mainstream annual reports not only their GHG emissions, but also the associated financial risks and impacts, their strategies for managing these risks and impacts, and governance oversight for such matters. CDSB standards were released in 2010 and set out an approach for reporting environmental information in standard corporate reports such as annual reports. The CDSB standards later became the basis of the *Recommendations of the Task Force for Climate-Related Financial Disclosures* (the *Recommendations*).

In 2013, the International Integrated Reporting Council promulgated the *International Integrated Reporting Framework* (the *IR Framework*) with the goal of creating a universally accepted framework companies could use to report primarily to investors on value creation over time. The *IR Framework* is based on the concepts that companies depend on multiple forms of capital to create, preserve, or erode value and such value is reflected in a company's stores of financial, manufactured, intellectual, human, social and relationship, and natural capitals. The *IR Framework* begins to take a multicapital approach to capitalism as opposed to traditional capitalism's sole focus on fiscal capital.

In 2015, the United Nations adopted its global development goals, the UN SDGs, and the SBTi was launched. The UN SDGs, including SDG Goal 7: affordable and clean energy and SDG Goal 13: take urgent action to combat climate change and its impacts, have been a further stimulus for companies to provide voluntary disclosures about their positive or negative contributions to the transition to a net zero economy. As discussed in

Part III, many companies report on how their activities work to further the achievement of the UN SDGs and over 3,000 companies are voluntarily working with the SBTi to reduce their GHG emissions in line with climate science.

In 2018, the Sustainability Accounting Standards Board (SASB), a nonprofit formed in 2011 in the United States, released its market-developed standards for voluntary reporting in mainstream annual reports and regulatory filings (e.g., Form 10-Ks) about sustainability (a.k.a. ESG) issues, including climate change, that, in investors' eyes, may have a material financial impact on a company. The SASB standards were developed with versions applicable to companies in 77 industry sectors.

Eco-efficiency processes and systems to reduce GHG emissions by using and purchasing renewable energy, electrifying vehicle fleets, and heating, cooling, and powering facilities with carbon-free energy have their own reporting standards. The RE100 initiative, developed by the CDP and The Climate Group, has defined eight categories of electrical power in their guidance and technical criteria with details on each type of carbon-free energy option and the claims that can be made for each carbon-free energy source and zero-emission power category.[6] The RE100 does not include nuclear electric power as part of its standard. The U.S. Green Building Council LEED Zero energy standard requires measurement and reporting on total carbon-free energy generated on-site and possible clean power exported to the grid compared to all energy for building operations.[7]

THE CONSOLIDATION OF VOLUNTARY CLIMATE-RELATED DISCLOSURE INTO UNIVERSAL STANDARDS

In November 2015, at the time of the COP21 Paris meeting, Mark Carney, then Governor of the Bank of England and chair of the Financial Stability Board, announced the creation of a Task Force on Climate-Related Financial Disclosures (TFCD). The TFCD was created in response to institutional investors' frustration with a confusing "alphabet soup" of sustainability, ESG, and climate-reporting frameworks, guidelines, and self-styled standards as partially described in the previous section of this chapter. None of these standards addressed or satisfied investors' need to link corporate climate-related risks, strategies, or metrics with their present and future impacts on financial performance and enterprise value.

The TFCD was founded on the understanding that climate change is an existential issue that threatens the stability of global financial markets and capital markets need reliable, meaningful climate-related information from reporting by companies to enable sound investment decision-making, financial system stability, and prudent public policy decisions.

In 2017, the TFCD released its final *Recommendations* for voluntary climate-related financial disclosures by companies to provide investors with information about how climate change affects a company, and its business and financial condition. The *Recommendations* were developed before science-based emissions-reductions targets and net zero business models reached the prominence they enjoy today. The *Recommendations* have garnered sufficient global support in investor, corporate, and financial institution circles to be the likely starting point for development of future mandatory international climate-reporting standards. The disclosure recommendations from the TCFD seek enhanced disclosures for four segments of information: corporate governance, strategy, risk management, and targets.

There is also movement toward development of a universal approach to sustainability reporting. In 2021, the SASB and the International Integrated Reporting Council combined to form the Value Reporting Foundation. In 2022, the Value Reporting Foundation and the Climate Disclosure Standards Board became part of the International Sustainability Standards Board (ISSB), an investor-focused initiative of the International Financial Reporting Standards Foundation (the IFRS Foundation). In 2022, the GRI and the IFRS Foundation agreed to cooperate in their respective future standards setting programs, such as those of the ISSB.

In March 2022, the ISSB released Exposure drafts for two proposed sustainability reporting standards. The *Exposure Draft Sustainability Disclosure Standard* and the *Exposure Draft Climate-related Disclosures* were drafted with the intention of creating universal voluntary corporate sustainability reporting standards, which, like the International Accounting Standards Board's IFRS Accounting Standard for financial statements, could be adopted and made mandatory in any jurisdiction—a step supported by the International Organization of Securities Commissions.[8,9]

THE EVOLUTION OF MANDATORY CLIMATE-RELATED DISCLOSURE

While voluntary disclosure standards and frameworks were evolving, the U.S. Securities and Exchange Commission precipitated the first mandatory disclosure by U.S. registered issuers about climate-related business risks. In 2010, after much investor lobbying and a legal petition by Ceres, the SEC issued an interpretive release clarifying and confirming the requirement under existing SEC rules that companies must include disclosures about climate-related risks and uncertainties that would be deemed material to users in their annual reports.[10] This was the first move toward mandatory climate-related disclosure.

Now, voluntary disclosure is shifting to mandatory disclosure to bring consistency in how companies tell their net zero stories. Securities regulators around the world recognize the need to enhance and standardize existing corporate reporting practices and requirements about climate-related disclosure. There is a growing recognition that investors and other stakeholders need timely, reliable, decision-useful information about how a company is dealing with its GHG emissions and its transition to a net zero business model. This information must be more than mere data about GHG emissions and must include details about the company's business strategy to compete, business model design, and key transition points to net zero. This information would include management's estimates of the short-, medium- and long-term financial impacts of the transition to a net zero business model and information related to financial stress testing for potential carbon shocks.

Achieving net zero is becoming the corporate mantra. Since the Paris Agreement and the Glasgow COP26 meeting in 2021, an increasing worldwide chorus of companies, long-term investors, and financial institutions have made public pledges to achieve net zero by 2050 or sooner. Far less evident have been disclosures by such organizations of concrete, measurable plans, if any, to fulfil their pledges and transition to net zero. As will be discussed in Chapter 15, a company's pledge to achieve net zero that is not accompanied by a comprehensive and credible net zero transition plan may be misleading and amount to greenwashing.

The SEC recognizes the problem posed to investors by hollow pledges to achieve net zero and the lack of standardized disclosure. SEC Commissioner Caroline Crenshaw summed up the need for reliable disclosures concerning net zero pledges and how companies plan to fulfil them in December 2021:

> ". . . I noted, in particular, many public companies announcing net-zero emission pledges. In fact, recent data show a significant percentage of publicly traded companies around the world have committed to a net-zero strategy. This is, ostensibly, good news. Yet, when I dig a bit deeper, it is sometimes unclear to me how companies will achieve these goals. Nor is it clear that companies will provide investors with the information they need to assess the merits of these pledges and monitor their implementation over time."[11]

The SEC proposed new rules for climate change disclosures in March 2022.[12] It solicited comments on the proposed rules, which are expected to become effective with some revisions before this book is published in early 2023. With respect to an issuer's transition to a net zero business model, the proposed SEC regulations would require disclosure of its Scope 1 and Scope 2 GHG emissions. Disclosure of an issuer's Scope 3 emissions would be required if material or if the issuer has set GHG emissions-reduction targets that include Scope 3 emissions. Issuers would also be required to detail their net zero transition plans to comply with their disclosed net zero targets and timelines. Third-party assurance for emissions data would be phased in over time.

The SEC proposal notes that "Many commenters recommended that we require disclosure regarding a registrant's transition plan, stating that such a disclosure would help investors evaluate whether a registrant has an effective strategy to achieve its short -, medium-, or long-term climate related targets or goals."[13] In response, several institutional investor initiatives have emerged to prevail upon their investee companies to establish and disclose credible net zero transition plans.[14]

Under the proposed rules, issuers would file their first climate disclosures, including Scope 1 and 2 emissions data, in their annual reporting for fiscal 2023. Issuers would report on their Scope 3 emissions in their annual reporting for fiscal 2024. As PwC observed, the proposed disclosures send a strong signal that "All public companies must now quickly transition to investor grade reporting."[15]

The UK has enacted legislation to make climate reporting mandatory in 2022 for large companies. Beginning in April 2022, over 1,300 of the largest registered companies and financial institutions in the UK must disclose climate-related financial information on a mandatory basis. Companies subject to the new disclosure requirements include many of the UK's largest publicly listed companies, banks, and insurers, as well as private companies with over 500 employees and £500 million in turnover."[16] The definition of climate-related financial disclosures in the regulations includes emissions-reduction targets, performance indicators used to assess progress toward the targets, and the calculations upon which the key performance indicators are based.

Mandatory climate-related disclosures are also coming to the European Union. In 2021, the European Commission adopted the *Corporate Sustainability Reporting Directive (CRSD)* to strengthen the nature of ESG and sustainability reporting in the EU.[17] Associated regulations being developed are expected to require disclosures about companies' net zero transition plans in line with the Paris Agreement, overall GHG emissions, Scope 1, 2, and 3 emissions, and climate-related targets. The European Commission adopted the first reporting standards under the *CRSD* in

October 2022 with such standards applicable to companies for reports relating to their 2023 fiscal years.

The *CRSD* is part of the EU's goal to become an economy with net zero GHG emissions by 2050. To achieve this goal, the EU has set a target to reduce GHG emissions by at least 55% by 2030 from 1990 levels. The EU aspires to become the first climate-neutral continent and has outlined a strategic long-term vision for a prosperous, modern, competitive, and climate-neutral economy.[18]

It is expected that many jurisdictions around the world will enact a requirement for companies, investors, and financial institutions to prepare and issue climate-related disclosures as part of their annual financial reporting cycle by 2025. Mandatory periodic corporate reporting likely will require disclosures about climate change impacts on a company's business, its GHG emissions, its net zero transition plan, and the associated present and future financial impacts. Securities regulators issuing new reporting regulations, rules, directives, and statutes and stock exchanges revising their listing requirements will implement these new disclosure requirements.[19]

TELLING THE NET ZERO STORY BEFORE THE IMPLEMENTATION OF MANDATORY CLIMATE-RELATED DISCLOSURES

In the meantime, investors expect companies to provide quality climate-related disclosures. BlackRock, for example, "expects companies to have clear policies and action plans to manage climate risks and to realize opportunities presented by the global energy transition." Quality disclosures are necessary to help investors "analyze how climate risk is integrated into their long-term strategies and evaluate their preparedness to a low-carbon economy."[20] We conducted a detailed review of climate-related disclosures of companies with declared net zero aspirations to identify the key climate related-disclosures in addition to those called for by the leading climate-related disclosure standards. (See Exhibit 14.1 and Appendices

EXHIBIT 14.1 Summary table of key climate-related disclosure metrics

Net Zero Business Model Strategy Summary and Key Metrics	3-year Look-back LFY – 3	Current Performance LFY	2030 Target Range
Net Zero Business Model – Strategic Intent		Declared Net Zero Business Model	2030 % GHG reduction target
GHG tons Scope 1 and 2			
GHG tons Scope 3			
Total GHG emissions			
GHG tons Scope 1 and 2, target % reduction vs baseline year			
Carbon credits and offsets			
Tons CO_2e / $1 million revenue (Scope 1 and 2)			
Median CO_2e / $1 million for the comparative industry group			
Total enterprise MWh energy used			
% MWh - carbon-free energy consumed from power grid			
% MWh - carbon-free energy consumed total			
% MWh - fossil fuel energy			
Zero-emission SMART transportation fleet			
Zero-emission SMART sustainable buildings			
% revenues from product portfolio that are zero carbon products and services			
% revenues from product portfolio that are circular in design			
Carbon Adjusted Return on Capital stress test at $100 / ton CO_2e			
C-Suite – succession readiness rate for Net Zero Business Model transformation (ready now and ready in 5 years)			
Industry sector engagements to develop plans for industry and value chain(s) transformation to Net Zero industry sector			

Source: FutureZero

14.1, 14.2, and 14.3 for worksheets to benchmark carbon free energy, eco-efficiency, and innovation, and Appendix 14.4 for a gap analysis of net zero business model disclosures missing from guidance frameworks.) The climate-related disclosures on Exhibit 14.1 are also critical in designing incentive compensation aligned with a company's net zero transition plan by ensuring behavior is properly aligned with achieving its overall net zero strategy.

BlackRock and other institutional investors generally expect companies to make their climate-related disclosures in line with the reporting frameworks developed by the TCFD and the ISSB. The TCFD and ISSB frameworks address the physical, liability, and transition risks associated with climate change and provide guidance to companies about how to tell the story of their transition to a net zero business model with financially material and decision-useful information.

State Street Global Advisors, the world's fourth largest asset manager, is quite clear about its expectations about climate-related disclosure. It expects companies to align their disclosures with the TCFD recommendations. Such disclosure must include information about board oversight of climate-related risks and opportunities, GHG emissions, and targets for reducing GHG emissions. State Street warned that it will start "taking voting action against directors across applicable indices should companies not meet these disclosure expectations."[21] During 2022, State Street engaged with the most significant emitters of GHGs in its portfolio to encourage disclosures in alignment with its expectations for net zero transition plans. Starting in 2023, State Street "will hold companies and directors accountable for failing to meet those expectations."[22]

In Canada, CPP Investments, a global investment management organization that invests the assets of the Canada Pension Plan, developed a framework to measure companies' capacity to report and abate their emissions. CPP Investments hopes its framework will have a transformative impact by providing a common three-step approach to GHG reporting and abatement. The first step is to create a standardized assessment of each company's current Scope 1, 2, and 3 emissions. Companies should prioritize Scope 1 and 2 emissions as methods for assessing Scope 3 emissions continue to be developed. The second step is to assess the company's capacity to reduce its GHG emissions cost-effectively now. The third step is to report on the company's projected abatement capacity.[23] CPP Investments proposes that companies "use standardized carbon prices that are higher than current levels (e.g., US$100 and US$150 per tCO_2e)." In addition to these carbon prices, companies could also consider using internal shadow prices that based on their own unique situations. According to CPP Investments, this framework is a valuable complement to climate disclosure rules that have recently been proposed by national and international financial regulatory bodies.[24]

The Council of Institutional Investors supports the SEC proposal and further comments:

> . . . that a registrant describe the actual and potential impact of its material climate-related risks on its strategy, business model and outlook. We agree with commenters that have stated that many registrants have included largely boilerplate discussions about climate change risks and failed to provide meaningful analysis of the impacts of those risks on their business. There is inadequate information currently disclosed when climate risks would have material effect on impairment analysis, fair value calculations, or estimates of expected credit losses. We believe that disclosure of scope 3 emissions data could help investors understand transition risks and potential disruptions in a company's supply chain, business model and cashflows.[25]

The IFRS Foundation's *Exposure Draft Climate-related Disclosures* based on the TCFD Recommendations, presented detailed disclosure proposals formatted as future ISSB standards.[26] Institutional investors are likely to expect their portfolio companies' climate-related disclosures, including disclosures regarding net zero transition plans, GHG inventories, and emissions-reduction targets, to be aligned with this draft climate-related disclosure standard until it becomes mandatory by regulatory adoption in particular jurisdictions. Boards of directors should consider these issues regularly under the following eight categories and review them with management:

Governance. The draft standard expects issuers to disclose information to enable investors "to understand the governance processes, controls and procedures used to monitor and manage climate-related risks and opportunities."[27] It expects an issuer to identify the body responsible for oversight of climate-related risks and opportunities and its responsibilities, processes, and procedures.

Strategy. The draft standard expects issuers to provide information to enable investors "to understand an entity's strategy for addressing significant climate-related risks and opportunities."[28] It expects an issuer to describe the effects of such risks and opportunities on its strategy and decision-making, including its net zero transition plans.

Climate-related risks and opportunities. The draft standard expects issuers to disclose information to enable investors "to understand the significant climate-related risks and opportunities that could be reasonably expected to affect the entity's business model, strategy and cash flows over the short, medium or long term."[29] In particular, it expects an issuer to distinguish between physical risks and those pertaining to its net zero transition plans, including regulatory, technological, market, legal, or reputational risks.

Strategy and decision-making. The draft standard expects issuers to provide information to enable investors "to understand the effects of significant climate-related risks and opportunities on its strategy and decision making, including its transition plans."[30] It expects issuers to provide information about changes to their business model, such as those described in the Pathways in Part III of this book. Companies need to consider what investors need to understand about the Pathway they have chosen. The draft standard expects issuers to provide information about how they will finance their net zero transition plans and achieve their emissions-reduction targets. Issuers also are expected to articulate how much of such targets will be achieved through emissions reductions or carbon offsets.

Financial position, financial performance, and cash flows. The draft standard expects issuers to provide information to enable investors "to understand the effects of significant climate-related risks and opportunities on the company's financial position, financial performance and cash flows for the reporting period, and the anticipated effects over the short, medium and long term."[31] This information should show how these risks and opportunities are included in an issuer's financial planning and identify the sources of funding to implement its strategies, which would include implementing its net zero transition plan.

Climate resilience. The draft standard expects issuers to provide information to help investors "understand the resilience of the company's strategy (including its business model) to climate-related changes, developments or uncertainties."[32]

Risk management. The draft standard expects issuers to disclose information to enable investors to "understand the process, or processes, by which climate-related risks are identified, assessed and managed."[33]

Metrics and targets. The draft standard expects issuers to disclose information to enable investors "to understand how an entity measures, monitors and manages its significant climate-related risks and opportunities."[34] This would include information that allows investors to understand how the issuer assesses its progress toward meeting its eco-efficiency and GHG emissions-reduction targets.

OTHER KEY ROLES FOR DISCLOSURE PROCESS DEVELOPMENT

Responsibility of CFOs for internal control over climate-related disclosures. Although sustainability reporting has typically been the domain of corporate sustainability and CSR departments, mandatory reporting of information about climate-related and net zero business model transition risks needs to be the CFO's responsibility, with input from the legal department and other corporate functions and business units as necessary. Companies should transfer accountability for climate-related disclosures to the finance function, if they have not already done so, in anticipation of such disclosures becoming mandatory.

The CFO and the finance function are best suited to apply the concept, policies, and practices of internal control over financial information to climate-related disclosures. The CFO and the finance function are also best suited to deploy reliable data collection systems and processes comparable to standard corporate financial accounting systems and to implement appropriate disclosure controls and procedures.

The CFO and the finance function are well-suited to add reliable climate-related data to the information they normally provide for internal management decision-making and monitoring purposes. CFOs are accustomed to managing internal audit functions and the relationship with outside auditors and are, therefore, well-suited to manage the internal audit and external assurance of the integrity of climate-related data and related information systems. SEC Commissioner Crenshaw reminded companies about the importance of internal accounting controls in relation to ESG disclosures and, by extension, to climate-related financial information.[35]

Audit committee role. The audit committee of the board of directors is well-suited to review and approve external reporting to investors of climate-related disclosures and information about a company's transition to a net zero business model. The audit committee should approve how business model risks, opportunities, and net zero transition plans are integrated into the company's performance measurement processes and then further integrated into components of the annual report disclosure for shareholders. This oversight would include processes for stress testing for carbon shocks and related calculations of carbon adjusted net operating profit after tax and carbon adjusted return on capital. Lastly, the audit committee should ensure measurement processes are in place for consistency with other nonfinancial information included not only in mandatory periodic financial reporting and filings, but also in other ESG and sustainability reporting.

External assurance. Many companies, such as Nestlé, already obtain and disclose independent external assurance over aspects of their sustainability and climate-related reports or parts thereof, such as GHG emissions data. Expectations for independent external assurance of climate-related disclosures to investors likely will increase in the future, even if not expressly called for by regulation, to enhance investor confidence in climate-related disclosures.

Placement of climate-related disclosures in corporate reporting documents. Climate-related disclosures help investors understand the present and future financial impacts of climate-related risks and opportunities, and in particular the financial implications of net zero transition plans. Companies can present climate-related disclosures alongside financial statements to provide additional and forward-looking context for what the financial statements disclose, preferably within or alongside disclosures such as descriptions of the company's business or management's discussion and analysis of operations and results. Companies also may choose to provide stand-alone sustainability or climate reports, released soon after, if not at the same time as, their other financial filings.

SUMMARY

Companies are on the brink of a new era in corporate sustainability related reporting that will mandate reliable climate-related disclosure for investors. Reporting on companies' Pathways to net zero, net zero transition plans, and progress toward declared net zero targets will be integrated with traditional reporting. This new dimension of corporate transparency will make it easier for investors to hold boards of directors accountable to achieving net zero and identify the winners in the race to net zero in their portfolios.

ISSB standards likely will be adopted as the basis of corporate reporting requirements for investor purposes in most jurisdictions around the world. ISSB issued standards for climate-related disclosures to investors likely are to be followed by standardized disclosures about other environmental and social factors and governance thereof (ESG) that have significant business and financial implications for a company. It remains to be seen how closely aligned future SEC sustainability and climate-related disclosure requirements will be with ISSB standards.

Reporting companies should prepare themselves now for mandatory climate-related disclosure by inventorying their Scope 1, 2, and 3 emissions using the *GHG Protocol*, setting science-based near-term and long-term GHG emissions-reduction targets using the SBTi framework, choosing a Pathway, and creating a comprehensive net zero transition plan. Companies should put in place a data analytics strategy and adopt appropriate governance architecture to support their transition plans. Companies should consider making climate-related disclosures using some of the approaches discussed in this chapter. Companies that start making voluntary climate-related disclosure now will have the systems in place and will have developed the skills to handle mandatory climate-related disclosures when they go into effect in 2024 or 2025.

NOTES

1. Massoud, M. (2021). A call to action: an interview with Mark Carney. *Pivot* (November/December): 22–28. https://www.cpacanada.ca/en/news/pivot-magazine/archives.

2. The Glasgow Financial Alliance for Net Zero, the International Corporate Governance Network, the Climate Action 100, and the Council of Institutional Investors represent $130 trillion, $70 trillion, $68 trillion, and $4 trillion of assets under management, respectively.

3. Massoud, M. (2021). A call to action: an interview with Mark Carney.

4. Global Reporting Initiative. (n.d.). *GRI Standards*. https://www.globalreporting.org/how-to-use-the-gri-standards/gri-standards-english-language/ (accessed 22 August 2022).

5. UN Principles for Responsible Investment. (n.d.). Investment tools. https://www.unpri.org/investment-tools.

6. RE 100. www.there100.org (accessed 22 August 2022).

7. U.S. Green Building Council. (2020). LEED Zero Program Guide (April). https://www.usgbc.org/sites/default/files/2020-04/LEED_Zero_Program%20Guide_April%202020.pdf.

8. International Sustainability Standards Board. (2022). Exposure Draft: IFRS Sustainability Disclosure Standard: [Draft] IFRS S1 General Requirements for Disclosure of Sustainability-related Financial Information. IFRS Sustainability (March). https://www.ifrs.org/content/dam/ifrs/project/general-sustainability-related-disclosures/exposure-draft-ifrs-s1-general-requirements-for-disclosure-of-sustainability-related-financial-information.pdf.

9. International Sustainability Standards Board. (2022). Exposure Draft: IFRS Sustainability Disclosure Standard: [Draft] IFRS S2 Climate-related Disclosures. IFRS Sustainability (March). https://www.ifrs.org/content/dam/ifrs/project/climate-related-disclosures/issb-exposure-draft-2022-2-climate-related-disclosures.pdf.

10. U.S. Securities and Exchange Commission. (2010). Commission guidance regarding disclosure related to climate change (8 February). https://www.sec.gov/rules/interp/2010/33-9106.pdf.

11. Crenshaw, C. (2021). Virtual remarks at the Center for American Progress and Sierra Club: down the rabbit hole of climate pledges. U.S. Securities and Exchange Commission (14 December). https://www.sec.gov/news/speech/crenshaw-cap-sierra-club-20211214.

12. U.S. Securities and Exchange Commission. (2022). The enhancement and standardization of climate-related disclosures for investors (21 March). https://www.sec.gov/rules/proposed/2022/33-11042.pdf.

13. U.S. Securities and Exchange Commission. (2022). SEC proposes rules to enhance and standardize climate-related disclosures for investors. Press release (21 March). https://www.sec.gov/news/press-release/2022-46.

14. International Corporate Governance Network. (2022). US – SEC: Climate change disclosure. https://www.icgn.org/us-sec-climate-change-disclosure (20 June); Ceres. (2022). Public input on climate change disclosures. Letter to U.S. Securities and Exchange Commission (10 June). https://www.ceres.org/sites/default/files/6-10-21%20Ceres%20Letter%20to%20SEC%20-%20Final.pdf.

15. PwC. (n.d.). SEC climate disclosures and your company. www.pwc.com/us/en/services/esg/library/sec-climate-disclosures.html (accessed 22 August 2022).

16. UK Department for Business, Energy & Industrial Strategy. (2021). UK to enshrine mandatory climate disclosure for largest companies in law. Press release (29 October). https://www.gov.uk/government/news/uk-to-enshrine-mandatory-climate-disclosures-for-largest-companies-in-law.

17. EUR-Lex. (2022). Proposal for a Directive of the European Parliament and of the Council amending Directive 2013/34/EU, Directive 2004/109/EC, Directive 2006/43/EC and Regulation (EU) No 537/2014, as regards corporate sustainability reporting. European Commission (21 April). https://eur-lex.europa.eu/legal-content/EN/TXT/?uri=CELEX:52021PC0189.

18. EUR-Lex. 28 November (2018). A clean planet for all: A European strategic long-term vision for a prosperous, modern, competitive, and climate neutral economy. European Commission (28 November). https://eur-lex.europa.eu/legal-content/EN/TXT/?uri=CELEX:52018DC0773.

19. Eccles, R. and Mirchandani, B. (2022). We need universal ESG accounting standards. *Harvard Business Review* (15 February). https://hbr.org/2022/02/we-need-universal-esg-accounting-standards.

20. BlackRock, Inc. (2022). Climate risk and the global energy transition (February). https://www.blackrock.com/corporate/literature/publication/blk-commentary-climate-risk-and-energy-transition.pdf.

21. State Street Global Advisors. (2022). CEO's letter on our 2022 proxy voting agenda (12 January). https://www.ssga.com/international/en/institutional/ic/insights/ceo-letter-2022-proxy-voting-agenda.

22. Ibid.

23. CPP Investments Insights Institute, 2 November 2022. The Decarbonization Imperative. https://www.cppinvestments.com/insights-institute/the-decarbonization-imperative (Accessed 15 November 2022).

24. Ibid.

25. Council of Institutional Investors. (2022). Comment letter to the U.S. Securities and Exchange Commission (19 May). https://www.cii.org/correspondence.

26. International Sustainability Standards Board. (2022). Exposure Draft: IFRS Sustainability Disclosure Standard: [Draft] IFRS S2 Climate-related Disclosures.

27. Ibid.

28. Ibid.

29. Ibid.

30. Ibid.

31. Ibid.

32. Ibid.

33. Ibid.

34. Ibid.

35. Crenshaw, C. (2021). Remarks at the PepsiCo-PwC CPE Conference: Controlling internal controls. U.S. Securities and Exchange Commission (16 November). https://www.sec.gov/news/speech/crenshaw-controlling-internal-controls-20211116.

15

OBSTACLES TO NET ZERO

"As net zero intent gets translated into action, it will become increasingly costly to be part of the problem and—we believe—increasingly profitable to be part of the solution."[1]

—Rolls-Royce website

The idea that humanity needs a net zero economy has entered the mainstream. Achieving a net zero economy is no longer perceived as a fringe idea. Using Geoffrey Moore's model for the adoption of disruptive technologies, the economy is probably "crossing the chasm."[2] This is the point at which enough pioneers and early adaptors have committed to net zero and proven that it is possible to reduce GHG emissions and be successful commercially. Even companies with high carbon intensity can decarbonize and conform their business models to a net zero economy. Companies can follow safely the pioneers and early adopters that have paved the way to net zero.

The reality is, however, there is still a lot of resistance to creating a net zero emissions economy and to conform business models to it. The resistance comes in many forms and occurs at many points in the transformation process. According to Being First, identifying as many of the obstacles to a transformation as possible and neutralizing them helps optimize its probability of success.[3] This chapter highlights some of the common obstacles on the path to net zero, including obstacles relating to people's mindsets that are encountered in transformations of any kind.

MENTAL OBSTACLES

The difficulty of behavior change. The subconscious mind intuitively recognizes that conforming a business model to a net zero economy requires a significant amount of change. The sheer magnitude of the tasks of inventorying GHG emissions, setting science-based emissions-reductions targets, creating a net zero transition plan, and then reducing emissions can create resistance. Naming this resistance helps to discharge it.

It helps to understand it is difficult for humans to change their behavior. Only about one in nine people can change their behavior without help. This is because the need to change behavior triggers a flight-or-fight response in the brain that releases cortisol and adrenaline, which create resistance to change. The larger the change, the more resistance.

A company's transition to net zero is a huge undertaking that will trigger resistance, but there are proven techniques for overcoming that resistance. The Center for Creative Leadership, for example, has found the act of writing down an action and sharing it with another person largely transcends this resistance. In the context of the transition to net zero, this is the hidden power of a transition plan with clear SMART goals.[4] Companies that publish credible net zero transition plans and ask their stakeholders to hold them accountable to fulfilling them optimize the probability of achieving net zero.

Lack of capacity to change. Otto Scharmer, Senior Lecturer at the MIT Sloan School of Management and co-founder of the Presencing Institute, observes that humanity suffers from a massive failure of capacity to face disruption. To better lean into a disruptive future requires the expansion of three core capacities: curiosity, which means having an open mind, compassion, which means having an open heart, and courage, which means having an open will.[5]

Ray Anderson, the founder and former CEO of Interface, Inc., a carpet manufacturer, modeled what it takes to open the minds, hearts, and wills of directors and officers to a net zero future. In the early 1990s, customers started asking about what his company was doing for the environment. He had no answer. He had never given a thought about what his company was doing to the Earth. He read *The Ecology of Commerce* by Paul Hawkins and wept.[6] Anderson called this his "spear in the chest" moment because he realized environmental problems were products of "an industry system, of which his company, his third child, was an integral part."[7] From that moment almost 30 years ago, Interface has been on a path to sustainability. Today, the company is committed to become carbon negative by 2040.[8]

It is possible to expand the capacity to change. Eco-efficiency processes and systems are a great way to build capacity to change that will accelerate a transition to net zero. Most companies save money when they apply eco-efficiency processes and systems. This gives them an easy, money-saving win that builds confidence and develops an emissions-reduction mindset.

Complacency. Many companies are happy with their profitable, high-carbon business models and have little interest or incentive to conform their business models to a net zero emissions economy. The fossil fuel economy works well for Saudi Aramco, for example, which has the world's second largest proven crude oil reserves. At $100 per barrel, its 270 billion barrels of reserves represent $27 trillion dollars of potential revenue.[9] With estimated fully loaded costs of $40 per barrel, this represents about $16 trillion of profit at a market price of $100 per barrel of crude oil.[10] Saudi Aramco has little financial incentive to conform its business model to a net zero economy. There is simply too much money to be made. If combusted, these reserves would generate approximately 117 billion metric tons of CO_2.

Complacency affects individuals, too. Many executives and directors are close to retirement age and are focused on the relative short-term horizon until their retirement. The journey to net zero takes years, if not decades, and involves an enterprise-wide commitment and lots of work. Some CEOs understand the urgency of the climate situation but simply are not interested in moving toward net zero during the remainder of their tenures. Their companies will not make meaningful progress toward net zero until such officers and directors retire or are replaced.

Ignorance. Many companies still are not aware there is a movement afoot to create a net zero economy. Most companies have not inventoried their GHG emissions or have only completed a partial inventory. These companies have not developed plans to conform their business models to a net zero economy.

A recent KPMG poll revealed most boards of directors do not consider the impact of climate change in their oversight of strategy or only consider it to a limited extent.[11] Many boards put their companies' net zero goals in the category of ESG and fail to see the strategic and financial implications to their companies and their business models.

About 9% of companies have inventoried their GHG emissions, set emissions-reduction targets, reduced their GHG emissions, and developed plans to conform their business models to a net zero economy.[12] These companies demonstrate it is possible to inventory all GHG emissions, including Scope 3 emissions, set science-based emissions-reduction targets, reduce emissions, and be successful commercially.

Fear. Many officers and directors are afraid of facing the carbon intensity of their business models and doing something about it. Creating a new business model may involve creative destruction. A company may have to cannibalize its existing products and business model to create new products and a new business model aligned with a net zero economy. As General Motors illustrated in Chapter 8, this can be a major undertaking. Fear of the process may hold them back.

Often, management is wary of the cost of the transition to net zero and afraid of making less money. Eco-efficiency processes and systems will save most companies money and customers may be able to absorb some of the net zero transition costs.

Other common fears include the fear of doing something new, the fear of doing it wrong, and the fear of looking foolish doing it. The stories of the companies profiled in Part III may assuage these fears and make officers and directors feel safe committing their companies to achieve net zero.

Belief and denial. Many companies are led by people who do not believe the scientific consensus that the Earth's temperature is rising due to GHG emissions or choose to ignore it. These companies are unlikely to work to achieve net zero unless their leaders have a change of heart, or government regulations force them to.

GREENWASHING

Many companies greenwash their net zero efforts. Greenwashing in the context of net zero occurs when a company pays more attention to marketing itself as environmentally friendly than on reducing its greenhouse gas emissions. In a recent survey of 1,491 executives in different industries around the world, 58% admitted their companies were engaged in greenwashing.[13] A full two-thirds of the surveyed executives were unsure whether their companies' sustainability efforts are genuine.[14] The most common greenwashing techniques include:

The hollow pledge. Most companies have set 2050 as their target date to achieve net zero or carbon neutrality but fewer than 10% of them also have set interim targets.[15] The 2050 target date sounds good because it is in alignment with the Paris Agreement and the desire to limit global warming to 1.5°C by 2050, but looking beyond the company's press release, there is not much substance to the pledge. The pledge may lack near-term emissions-reduction targets and any plan to achieve net zero emissions. In short, the pledge sounds noble but is hollow.

The fractional pledge. A company may have pledged to achieve net zero by 2050, but the pledge is limited to its Scope 1 and 2 emissions and ignores its Scope 3 emissions, which usually represent most of its GHG emissions. Among financial institutions, such as global asset managers, asset owners, insurers, and banks, for example, Scope 3, category 15 (investments) emissions average 700 times larger than their Scope 1 and 2 emissions.[16] In short, a pledge to achieve net zero without including a company's Scope 3 emissions is hollow and incomplete.

Companies that choose not to inventory their Scope 3 emissions have many excuses. Some companies, such as Exxon Mobil, may claim Scope 3 data is not available. As discussed in Chapter 2, most Scope 3 data comes from a company's value chain and requires collaboration with partners, customers, and suppliers to obtain. This requires some effort, but that does not mean the information is not available as Walmart has demonstrated by getting over 4,500 of its suppliers to sign up for its Project Gigaton.

Furthermore, data from two categories of Scope 3 emissions—category 7 (employee commuting) and category 6 (business travel)—are readily available. Companies can extrapolate their employee travel emissions easily from their employees travel expense reports. Companies also can extrapolate their employee commuting emissions by calculating the distance between their employees' homes, which they know from their personnel records, and their offices and applying the appropriate mileage emissions factor.

Other companies complain that Scope 3 emissions data is misleading or flawed because it can result in double counting of emissions. As discussed in Chapter 2, Scope 3 emissions recognize the interdependency of emissions in the supply chain and encourage collaboration to reduce them. Most companies that complain about the unavailability of Scope 3 emissions data have not started collaborating with their supply chains to collect the data.

A company may have pledged to achieve net zero by 2050, but its pledge only applies to its CO_2 emissions and not its emissions of other GHGs covered by the *GHG Protocol*. About 25% of warming from greenhouse gases comes from gases other than CO_2.[17] Methane is at least 25 times more effective than CO_2 at trapping heat in the atmosphere. A net zero pledge of an oil and gas company with high methane emissions, for example, may be subject to claims of greenwashing if its pledge does not include achieving net zero across all types of GHGs, including methane.

The offsets and carbon capture–based pledge. The SBTi recognizes some emissions are unavoidable and suggests science-based targets use carbon offsets and carbon capture to offset such unavoidable emissions that remain after eliminating all other emissions. As discussed in Chapter 4, offsets are problematic and insufficient by themselves to offset the magnitude of global emissions. Carbon capture technologies cannot be relied on because they are nascent, expensive, and nowhere near being ready to scale. A pledge that relies primarily on offsets and carbon capture to offset its emissions without a credible plan to reduce and eliminate a company's own emissions is suspect inherently.

The creative pledge. Many companies make net zero pledges but are not part of an initiative whose standards are aligned with the UN Race to Zero, SBTi, or similar initiatives that use science-based criteria to guide emissions-reduction targets. The 450 financial institutions that are members of the Glasgow Financial Alliance for Net Zero (GFANZ) represent more than $130 trillion in assets under management. All members of GFANZ, for example, are committed to the Race to Zero's goal of halving their emissions by 2030 and to use science-based targets to reach net zero across all scopes of emissions by 2050. GFANZ members must set interim 2030 emissions-reduction targets and commit to transparent reporting and accounting.[18]

Although it is possible for companies to use their own criteria to set credible independent emissions-reduction targets, it is generally a red flag if they are not also part of a net zero initiative. Joining such an initiative has many advantages, in addition to having established frameworks and methodologies for setting science-based targets. Such initiatives enable their members to collaborate and share best practices. The GFANZ, for example, offers many useful publications downloadable on its website, including "Recommendations and Guidance on Net-zero Transition Plans," to help members design their own net zero transition plans.[19]

The pledge with an asterisk. As discussed in Chapter 1, one of the obstacles to net zero is the lack of universally accepted terminology. Companies often express their emissions-reduction targets using language that sounds confusingly like a net zero pledge, such as "climate neutral" or "carbon neutral." Companies also celebrate reductions in their carbon intensity while their absolute GHG emissions continue to rise.

For example, some companies have committed to become climate neutral by 2050, which is a worthy goal but not as stringent as a net zero pledge. Under UN Race to Zero criteria, a company's remaining difficult-to-abate emissions need to be offset by "like-for-like" removals, which means the source of the emissions and the sink for removing emissions are equivalent in durability and duration. Since crude oil is permanent and stable underground, a "like-for-like" removal for emissions from combusting oil in a net zero pledge would need to be equivalent in permanence and stability.

Climate-neutral pledges do contribute to achieving a net zero economy. Climate Neutral, for example, is a nonprofit organization working to eliminate GHG emissions. Like Walmart's Project Gigaton, Climate Neutral aims to eliminate 1 billion metric tons of GHG emissions by 2030 by getting brands to commit to being climate neutral.[20] To date, 294 consumer brands have committed to become Climate Neutral Certified, which requires a brand to measure its emissions, offset all emissions with carbon credits, and develop and implement plans to reduce future emissions. Climate Neutral Certified brands with over $100 million in revenue are required to set "science-aligned" targets to reduce their emissions by 50% by 2030 but are not required to set long-term science-based targets to achieve net zero.[21]

Products of Climate Neutral Certified brands may carry labels identifying them to consumers as "Climate Neutral," but this inadvertently may sow confusion if consumers conflate "climate neutral" with "net zero." Climate Neutral may achieve its goal of eliminating 1 billion metric tons of GHG emissions without the companies behind the certified brands eliminating their remaining emissions by committing to net zero.

The equivocated pledge. Many companies talk a good game about their commitment to net zero but do not always walk their talk. Black-Rock, for example, as a member of the GFANZ has committed to achieve net zero by 2050 under the UN Race to Zero criteria. BlackRock was a founding member of the TCFD and a signatory of the Net Zero Asset Managers Initiative and has joined the Climate Action 100. BlackRock expects its portfolio companies to develop plans to conform their business models to a net zero economy but has been slow to set its own near-term and long-term science-based targets.

BlackRock's Chairman and CEO declared recently "We are not going to support Scope 3 at this time. . . . I have no problem in doing Scope 1 and Scope 2, but we've always said Scope 3 is forcing big companies, banks, and asset managers to be the environmental police. I've been loud about this and spoken about this in COP26. I'm against it."[22] As the world's largest asset manager, BlackRock has used its market position to get business engaged in the net zero transition. BlackRock could be even more of a transformational leader in the transition to a net zero economy if it proactively supported reporting on and reducing Scope 3 emissions and set near-term and long-term science-based emissions-reduction targets.

London-based think tank InfluenceMap recently reported that the world's 30 largest listed financial institutions undermine their net zero goals by lobbying to weaken sustainable finance policies and by continuing to provide project financing for fossil fuel expansion. All but one of these institutions are members of GFANZ, which requires them to commit to set near-term and long-term emissions-reduction targets to achieve net zero by 2050. All these institutions are members of industry groups, such as the U.S. Chamber of Commerce and the American Gas Association, that lobby against climate policies.[23]

InfluenceMap found that their actions are contrary to their net zero commitments. During 2020 and 2021, these institutions facilitated over $697 billion of financing for oil and gas production and $42 billion for coal production.[24] JPMorgan, for example, increased its financing of coal production from $1.28 billion in 2020 to $3.08 billion in 2021, despite having set a near-term target to reduce power sector emissions by 2030.[25] To get in alignment with the International Energy Agency (IEA) roadmap to net zero, which contemplates no new oil and gas fields and no new coal mines or extensions after 2021, these financial institutions could be more aligned with net zero if they stop facilitating new fossil fuel production.[26]

Brown-spinning. State Street Global Advisors coined the term "brown-spinning" to describe public companies that sell off assets with high carbon intensity to private equity and other buyers at a discount.[27] The sale of assets allows the public company to reduce its emissions and appear greener but there is no overall reduction in GHG emissions because the buyer continues to operate the high GHG-emitting assets.

If a public company is not transparent about its net zero pledge, its shareholders can make a shareholder proposal seeking greater transparency or propose candidates for the board of directors. When a public company transfers high carbon intensity assets to a private party, however, such assets disappear from public view and continue to operate without transparency and accountability. A public company may boast it has reduced its emissions, but it has just offloaded those emissions onto another party.

HIDDEN OBSTACLES

Many of the obstacles to net zero are hidden in the guiding principles of the prevailing economic system and its component parts. These guiding principles are so embedded in the economic system, by law or custom, that they largely have become invisible. These guiding principles, however, often determine corporate behavior and have unwittingly contributed to the circumstances that require humanity to take action to limit global warming.

Shareholder primacy. Since New York State combined the concept of limited liability with free incorporation in 1811, the limited liability corporation has become the prevailing corporate vehicle in the global economy. By eliminating the need for an act of legislation to charter a corporation and by eliminating the joint and several liability of shareholders for the debts and liabilities of the corporation, capital could flow quickly and easily into corporations. This invention greatly facilitated the economic development of the last 200 years.

By reducing incorporation to a rote process and severely limiting the sovereign's ability to revoke a corporate charter, however, the corporation lost its primitive external conscience. Under prevailing Anglo-Saxon common law, the modern corporation has only a limited internal conscience, which is expressed in the doctrine of shareholder primacy. The sole legitimate purpose of the modern corporation is to maximize stockholder welfare and the fiduciary duties of a corporation's directors flow exclusively to its shareholders.[28] The doctrine of shareholder primacy has normalized the corporate practice of externalizing as many as possible of the negative costs of corporate action onto society and the environment.

On the environmental front, the corporate practice of externalizing such costs contributed to air and water pollution, which spawned legislation like the Clean Air Act and the creation of administrative bodies to protect the environment such as the U.S. Environmental Protection Agency. Much progress has been made in reducing particulate matter pollution, but greenhouse gases have been harder to regulate because they are invisible and their negative consequences compound over time.

Many businesses that have played by the rules of shareholder primacy are reluctant to change the rules of engagement and hold themselves accountable for the externality of their GHG emissions. For decades, corporations have been able to freely emit GHGs without having to worry about, or take responsibility for, the consequences. Their primary obligation is to maximize profit for shareholders, not protect the environment. It is natural for corporations, especially those in high carbon intensity businesses such as energy and oil and gas, to resist having to be accountable for their GHG emissions.

The benefit corporation is a relatively new for-profit corporate form better aligned with the transition to a net zero economy than the traditional shareholder primacy-based corporate form. The benefit corporation endows the corporation with a social and environmental conscience that complements the pecuniary conscience of the traditional corporation.

In a benefit corporation, directors' fiduciary duties flow to all its stake-holders, including society and the environment. This relatively new corporate form is better aligned with stakeholder capitalism than the traditional corporation. Since the adoption of the first benefit corporation statute in 2010, the form has been adopted by 50 jurisdictions around the world.

Financial accounting standards and practices. Just as the doctrine of shareholder primacy unwittingly encourages companies to foist their negative externalities, such as their GHG emissions, on society and the environment, financial accounting standards and practices may have the same impact. There are two reasons for this.

First, since there is currently no cost associated with GHG emissions in most jurisdictions, there are no costs to be recorded and nothing to account for in a company's financial statements. In financial accounting there is often little or no cost for pollution. This defect could be mitigated or fixed if a global system of carbon pricing were adopted.

Second, financial accounting standards are based on several fundamental principles, one of which is a company's revenues must be recognized appropriately, all the costs incurred in the period must be recorded, and the shareholder's capital must be maintained before a profit can be reported.

Unfortunately, this principle tends to make companies focus almost exclusively on the maintenance of their shareholder's capital and measuring the returns being earned on this capital and discourages them from measuring and accounting for their other forms of capital such as built, intellectual, human, social and relationship, and natural. Consequently, companies can mismanage and undervalue these other forms of capital unintentionally because they do not measure or account for them with the same rigor they measure and account for shareholder's capital in the financial statements currently required by securities regulations.

This can result in companies not paying attention to, and being blind to, the effect their businesses have on their own stores of these capitals and on those shared in the commons. Also, companies may not pay attention to the risk that mismanagement of these other capitals can in the long term impair their shareholder's capital.

As discussed in Chapter 14, the *Integrated Reporting Framework* helps companies account for and manage their broad base of capitals. There are new multicapital accounting systems that complement the *Integrated Reporting Framework*, such as the *MultiCapital Scorecard* (MCS) that provides an integrated measurement, management, and reporting system that enables companies to manage impacts on all their capitals. The MCS is a free and open-source management tool that allows companies to assess how well they are meeting their obligations to their stakeholders, including society and the environment.[29] The theory behind the MCS is that to be successful, a company must not put at risk either the sufficiency of its vital capitals or the well-being of its stakeholders who depend on them.

Modern portfolio theory. Modern investors generally do not own individual stocks but mutual funds, index funds, and other diversified portfolios of assets. This approach follows modern portfolio theory, which is based on the premise that a portfolio's total return and risk profile is more important than the return and risk profile of any individual investment. As a result, today's typical shareholder invests in the market, not in individual stocks.

The blind spot in modern portfolio theory is that it does not account for the effect that individual investments make on the market. Modern portfolio theory ignores how companies' externalities, such as their GHG emissions, affect their shareholders by reducing the value of other assets in their portfolios. Since public companies are not required to report on their externalities, their shareholders cannot determine the full impact they have on their overall portfolio return. Several highly profitable multinational oil and gas companies, for example, have Scope 3 GHG emissions representing more than 1% of total global GHG emissions but do not report their Scope 3 emissions. Because modern portfolio theory does not account for the effect of externalities on overall market return, the implication is such externalities are not important and can be ignored.

Neoliberal economic theory. Today's global, free-market economic system, commonly known as neoliberal economics, has its origins in the Statement of Aims of the Mont Pelerin Society.

In 1947, perceiving that "the central values of civilization are in danger," a group of economists, historians, philosophers, and students of public affairs from the United States and Europe met in Mont Pelerin, Switzerland, to address the struggle between the totalitarian and the liberal orders. The assembled group was particularly worried about "a decline of belief in private property and the competitive market."[30]

Those gathered also described this struggle as a moral crisis with the rival totalitarian order having a "view of history which denies all absolute moral standards."[31] The group conflated a free global market regulated by the rule of law and the values of those of the Greatest Generation who sacrificed everything to win the war with the core principles of the democratic West in its ideological struggle with the state-run, centrally planned economy of the Soviet Union. This conflation of neoliberal economics with patriotism often still carries the emotional charge of the Cold War. Often, criticism of neoliberal economics or free market capitalism triggers a spirited defense in which the critic is labelled unpatriotic, communist, socialist, or woke.

Neoliberal economics posits governments should stay out of the way of the market. Government's function is to create a favorable environment for the market to operate freely and not interfere by regulating GHG emissions, for example.

The blind spot in neoliberal economics is that it fails to recognize that the free market is not a stand-alone system but is an interdependent system that interoperates with society and the environment. Economist Kate Raworth, in her book *Doughnut Economics*, paraphrases the blind spot in her description of two core beliefs of neoliberal economics: "the earth, which is inexhaustible, so take all you want" and "society, which is nonexistent, so ignore it."[32] Since neoliberal economics focuses on the primacy of the free market, it tends to ignore the effects of that free market, such as GHG emissions, on society and the environment.

Short-term thinking. Publicly listed companies are often stuck in short-term thinking where their strategic horizon tends to be limited to concerns about the next quarter's financial results. As soon as a company releases its quarterly results, its focus shifts to making the next quarter's numbers. Long-term planning horizons in most companies tend to be limited to a range of three to five years.

Setting near-term and long-term science-based net zero emissions targets exceeds the horizon planning capacity of most companies because the near-term target is generally 2030, which is several years away, and the long-term target is 2050, 20 years after the near-term target. Companies and their directors and executive management have to significantly extend their long-term strategic planning horizons to achieve net zero business models. This will be challenging in a market that is focused on an immediate, short-term horizon.

FOSSIL FUELS AND THE DEVELOPING WORLD

Underlying the transition to a net zero economy is the reality that many of those in control of the world's fossil fuel reserves would rather realize the revenue from those reserves than keep them in the ground. This reality presages a major conflict between forces that aim to preserve the planet for future generations by achieving a net zero economy and the forces that control the fossil fuels and wish to monetize them.

In 2018, the world had proven oil reserves of approximately 1.73 trillion barrels.[33] Petrostates whose economies are heavily dependent on the extraction and export of oil and natural gas include Venezuela, Saudi Arabia, Iran, Iraq, Kuwait, the United Arab Emirates, and Russia. These countries control most of these reserves. At today's price of about $100 per barrel, this represents about $173 trillion of revenue. At such prices, petrostates and the major oil and gas producing companies have little financial incentive to sell less oil and gas to avoid the approximately 748 billion metric tons of GHG emissions such reserves would emit.

The developed economies in Europe and North America are committed to transitioning to electric vehicles and clean grids but the developing world is dependent on fossil fuels to maintain economic growth and lift their populations out of poverty. China and India, for example, will not stop using fossil fuels, including coal, to grow their economies unless there are cheaper clean and green energy sources available. *Foreign Affairs* estimates there are 20 developing economies poised to greatly expand their use of fossil fuels unless they receive economic assistance from the developed countries to pursue low-carbon development.[34] Countries such as India, with a strong domestic coal industry, are inclined naturally to follow the "develop now, clean up later" approach that Europe, North America, and East Asia pursued in their economic development.

Solving this conflict must start with acknowledging the inequities of the situation. From the point of view of the developing world, the developed world, which is responsible for the historical GHGs causing global warming, appears to be asking the developing world to avoid emissions and keep their people in poverty. Rich nations—the United States, Canada, Japan, and Western Europe—account for 12% of the world's population but are responsible for 50% of historical GHG emissions. The less-wealthy countries bear a disproportionate share of the effects of climate change.[35] The rich nations have a credibility problem, however, because they reneged on their promise delivered at COP15 in 2009 to provide $100 billion a year in assistance by 2020 to help less-wealthy countries adapt to climate change and mitigate further rises in temperature.

There is hope in forging a solution by emulating how the developing world skipped landline telephony and leapfrogged into smart phones and wireless communication. The developing world could skip the need to clean up later if it developed now with clean and renewable energy, but this will require financial assistance and the developed world will need to stop selling fossil fuel power plants to the developing world. Between 2018 and 2020, 52% of new power plants financed in the developing world are inconsistent with the goals of the Paris Agreement.[36] Most of these new plants run on natural gas, which may emit less GHG emissions than coal-fired power plants but will be significant emitters of GHGs for decades to come.

Companies in developed countries working to reduce their Scope 3 emissions may help move the developing world more quickly to renewables.

Since the developed world has outsourced much of its manufacturing to Asia and the developing world, it has also outsourced much of its Scope 3 emissions there, too. Achieving net zero requires partners in the developing world to reduce their carbon footprint and help spur demand for clean and renewable energy.

In the meantime, however, petrostates and multinational oil companies will look for new customers to replace sagging demand in North America and Europe. The European boycott of Russian oil, gas, and coal in response to Russia's invasion of the Ukraine already has sent Russian fossil fuels to India and China. Developing markets look promising to petrostates and multinational oil and gas companies. In addition, the Russia-Ukraine war, which revealed Europe's dependency on Russian oil, reinvigorated the fossil fuel industry and triggered calls for more exploration for, and production of, fossil fuels in the interests of national security.

Some commentators have expressed concern that the oil and gas industry will follow the playbook of the tobacco industry.[37] When tobacco was regulated in North America and Europe, tobacco companies found replacement markets in the developing world. Conditions are ripe for oil companies to pursue a similar strategy because the IEA predicts that through 2030, fossil fuel demand will decline in North America, Europe, and Japan but increase everywhere else.[38] If the oil and gas industry follows the playbook of the tobacco industry, it may ramp up exports to the developing world, greenwash at home, and engage in share buybacks and pay dividends rather than invest in renewable energy.[39]

FICKLE POLITICAL SUPPORT

Although 194 nations and the European Union have signed the Paris Agreement, maintaining the political will within individual nation-states to achieve their net zero commitments is challenging. The Trump Administration in the United States, for example, withdrew from the Paris Agreement. Although the subsequent Biden Administration rejoined the Paris Agreement, the fragility of the agreement and the commitments of individual signatories is evident. The Biden Administration, with a razor thin majority in the U.S. Senate, was unable to pass any climate-related legislation until August 2022 due to the lack of support of one Democratic senator from a coal-producing state.[40]

While the need to address climate change has moved up the political agenda, the need to achieve a net zero economy is a long-term issue that competes with more immediate issues for political support. The Tony Blair Institute for Global Change found that although there is "strong and sustained desire for climate action" there is increasing political polarity that threatens the development of a long-term political coalition to support the actions necessary to achieve a net zero economy.[41] In other words, political support for net zero in Western democracies may be fickle and somewhat unstable.

The political winds can, however, shift quickly in Western democracies, especially in the face of a crisis. The Western democracies responded quickly to the Covid-19 pandemic and coalesced quickly to support Ukraine in its war with Russia. A particularly devastating climate disaster could precipitate a similar, rapid coordinated response. A heat wave that kills 20 million people, like the fictional disaster that stirs the world into climate action in *The Ministry of the Future* by Kim Stanley Robinson, could be the precipitating event that compels a more concerted and serious political response to climate change. In their scenario planning for a potential carbon shock stemming from a carbon tax, companies should anticipate a sudden shift in net zero–related policies.[42]

SUMMARY

Achieving a net zero economy faces many obstacles. The collection of obstacles discussed in this chapter is by no means complete or exhaustive but is intended to help companies identify the plethora of obstacles they may face on their Pathway to net zero and develop strategies to neutralize them.

NOTES

1. Rolls-Royce plc. www.rolls-royce.com (accessed 19 August 2022).
2. Moore, G. (1991). *Crossing the Chasm: Marketing and Selling Disruptive Products to Mainstream Customers.* New York: HarperCollins.
3. Anderson, D. and Anderson, L. (2010). *Beyond Change Management: How to Achieve Breakthrough Results Through Conscious Change Leadership.* San Francisco: Pfeiffer.
4. SMART is an acronym that stands for Smart, Measurable, Achievable, Relevant, and Time-based.
5. Scharmer, O. (2020). Turning toward our blind spot: seeing the shadow as a source for transformation. Field of the Future Blog (28 June). https://medium.com/presencing-institute-blog/turning-toward-our-blind-spot-seeing-the-shadow-as-a-source-for-transformation-aff23d480a55.
6. Hawkins, P. (1993). *The Ecology of Commerce: A Declaration of Sustainability.* New York: HarperCollins.
7. The Ray C. Anderson Foundation. https://www.raycandersonfoundation.org/rays-life/ (accessed 22 August 2022).
8. Interface Inc. (2020). Redefining carbon metrics for a carbon negative future. Interface blog (2 October). https://blog.interface.com/redefining-metrics-carbon-negative-future/.
9. Organization of Petroleum Exporting Countries. (2018). OPEC annual statistical bulletin (21 August). https://www.opec.org/opec_web/static_files_project/media/downloads/publications/ASB%202018.pdf.
10. Rapier, R. (2019). Saudi Aramco's breakeven oil price is higher than expected. Forbes.com (1 April). https://www.forbes.com/sites/rrapier/2019/04/01/saudi-aramcos-breakeven-oil-price-is-higher-than-expected/.
11. Angele, S. (2021). Seeing climate as a critical business issue for the board. KPMG, LLP, Board Leadership Center (September). https://boardleadership.kpmg.us/relevant-topics/articles/2022/seeing-climate-as-critical-business-issue-for-board.html.
12. World Economic Forum in collaboration with the Boston Consulting Group. (2022). Winning the Race to Net Zero: The CEO Guide to Climate Advantage. World Economic Forum (January). https://www3.weforum.org/docs/WEF_Winning_the_Race_to_Net_Zero_2022.pdf.

13. Peters, A. (2022). 68% of U.S. execs admit their companies are guilty of greenwashing. *Fast Company* (13 April). https://www.fastcompany.com/90740501/68-of-u-s-execs-admit-their-companies-are-guilty-of-greenwashing.

14. Ibid.

15. Peters, A. (2022). How to tell if a company's 'net zero' goals are serious—or just greenwashing. *Fast Company* (2 February). https://www.fastcompany.com/90588882/how-to-tell-if-a-companys-net-zero-goals-are-serious-or-just-greenwashing.

16. Climate Disclosure Project. (2022). Finance sector's funded emissions over 700 times greater than its own (28 April). https://www.cdp.net/en/articles/media/finance-sectors-funded-emissions-over-700-times-greater-than-its-own.

17. Ritchie, H. and Roser, M. (n.d.). Greenhouse gas emissions. Our World in Data. https://ourworldindata.org/greenhouse-gas-emissions (accessed 19 August 2022).

18. Glasgow Financial Alliance for Net Zero. www.gfanzero.com/ (accessed 22 August 2022).

19. Glasgow Financial Alliance for Net Zero. (2022). Financial institution net-zero transition plans (June). https://assets.bbhub.io/company/sites/63/2022/06/GFANZ_Recommendations-and-Guidance-on-Net-zero-Transition-Plans-for-the-Financial-Sector_June2022.pdf.

20. Climate Neutral. www.climateneutral.org/ (accessed 22 August 2022).

21. Ibid.

22. Brush, S. and Massa, A. (2022). Fink says BlackRock doesn't want to be environmental police. Bloomberg (2 June). https://www.bloomberg.com/news/articles/2022-06-02/fink-says-blackrock-doesn-t-want-to-be-environmental-police.

23. InfluenceMap. 25 March (2022). World's largest financial institutions undermine own net zero targets. Press release (25 March). https://influencemap.org/site/data/000/018/2022_-_03_Climate_and_finance_report.pdf.

24. Ibid.

25. Ibid.

26. International Energy Agency. (2021). Net zero by 2050 (May). https://www.iea.org/reports/net-zero-by-2050.

27. State Street Global Advisors. (2022). CEO's Letter on Our 2022 Proxy Voting Agenda.

28. Strine, L.E., Jr. (2015). The dangers of denial: the need for a clear-eyed understanding of the power and accountability structure established by the Delaware General Corporation Law. *Wake Forest Law Review* 50: 761; University of Pennsylvania Institute for Law and Economics Research paper no. 15-08. https://papers.ssrn.com/sol3/papers.cfm?abstract_id=2576389.

29. MultiCapital Scorecard. (n.d.). About MultiCapital Scorecard™. https://www.multicapitalscorecard.com/multicapital-scorecard/ (accessed 22 August 2022).

30. Eaton, A. (2021). The club that changed the world [Mont Pelerin Society Statement of Aims quoted within]. Share the Wealth (21 July). https://medium.com/share-the-wealth/the-club-that-changed-the-world-2d78d9f34b22.

31. Ibid

32. Raworth, K. (2017). *Doughnut Economics: 7 Ways to Think Like a 21st Century Economist.* White River Junction, VT: Chelsea Green (pp. 60–61).

33. BP plc. (2020). Statistical Review of World Energy 2020 (June). https://www.bp.com/content/dam/bp/business-sites/en/global/corporate/pdfs/energy-economics/statistical-review/bp-stats-review-2020-full-report.pdf.

34. Gallagher, K. (2022). The coming carbon tsunami: developing countries need a new growth model—before it's too late. *Foreign Affairs* (January/February). https://www.foreignaffairs.com/articles/world/2021-12-14/coming-carbon-tsunami.

35. Popovich, N. and Plumer, B. (2021). Who has the most historical responsibility for climate change? *The New York Times* (12 November). https://www.nytimes.com/interactive/2021/11/12/climate/cop26-emissions-compensation.html?referringSource=articleShare.

36. Ball, J. (2021). The climate fight isn't about morality. it's about cold, hard cash. *The New York Times* (9 November). https://www.nytimes.com/2021/11/09/opinion/climate-emissions-developing-countries.html?referringSource=articleShare.

37. Van Lierop, W. (2022). Big oil's strategy is stalling the energy transition. *Forbes* (28 January). https://www.forbes.com/sites/walvanlierop/2022/01/28/big-oils-strategy-is-stalling-the-energy-transition/?sh=6fafaf8447e8.

38. World Energy Outlook 2020. (2020). Outlook for energy demand. International Energy Agency. https://www.iea.org/reports/world-energy-outlook-2020/outlook-for-energy-demand (accessed 22 August 2022).

39. Van Lierop, W. (2022). Big oil's strategy is stalling the energy transition.

40. Weisman, J. and Friedman, L. (2021). Behind Manchin's opposition, a long history of fighting climate measures. *The New York Times* (20 December). https://www.nytimes.com/2021/12/20/us/politics/manchin-climate-change-coal.html?referringSource=articleShare.

41. Lord, T., Meyer, B., and Mulheirn, I. (2021). Polls apart? Mapping the politics of net zero. Tony Blair Institute for Global Change (22 March). https://institute.global/policy/polls-apart-mapping-politics-net-zero.

42. Robinson, K. (2020). *The Ministry of the Future*. New York: Orbit.

Part V

Beyond Net Zero: Systems Change

16

EPILOGUE: TOWARD A NET ZERO CIVILIZATION

"Love Your Home."[1]

—Title of Ørsted video

Achieving a net zero economy is predicated upon the convergence of the energy transformation and the digital transformation that will support the infrastructure of the net zero economy. Smart cars, smart homes, smart buildings, and a smart planet using artificial intelligence and data analytics will enable eco-efficiency processes and systems at scale by empowering everyone to intelligently monitor and manage their energy usage.

THE SHIFT TO STAKEHOLDER CAPITALISM

These two transformational societal trends are converging with a third trend to transform the theoretical basis of capitalism from shareholder capitalism to stakeholder capitalism. There is growing acknowledgement that capitalism as we know it is broken, as evidenced by climate change. Marc Benioff, the CEO and founder of Salesforce, declared in a *New York Times* editorial ". . . as a capitalist, I believe it's time to say out loud what we all know to be true: Capitalism, as we know it, is dead."[2] Mr. Benioff was also one of 181 public company CEOs who signed a Business Roundtable letter advocating a shift to stakeholder capitalism.[3]

The World Economic Forum also has advocated a shift to stakeholder capitalism, "a form of capitalism in which companies do not only optimize short-term profits for shareholders, but seek long term value creation, by taking into account the needs of all their stakeholders, and society at large."[4] Stakeholder capitalism recognizes that two of the primary stakeholders are the planet and its people. Corporate externalities, such as GHG emissions, need to "be incorporated or internalized in the operations of every . . . company."[5] At the center of the global economic system are the planet and its people. Stakeholder capitalism recognizes the planet's "health should be optimized in the decisions made by all other stakeholders" and the well-being of all people should be optimized as well.[6]

From a purely financial perspective, stakeholder capitalism has advantages over shareholder capitalism. The economic data suggests companies that adopt a multiple stakeholder model outperform their conventional peers in terms of economic performance. Professor Raj Sisodia and his co-authors in the second edition of *Firms of Endearment* showed that public companies that follow a multiple stakeholder model provide a 3x greater return to investors over a 10-year period than their conventional peers, as adjusted to reflect the effects of the 2008 downturn.[7]

Doing business in the planet-healthy way embedded in stakeholder capitalism also may provide a greater rate of return to investors. Robert Eccles and his colleagues' research at Harvard Business School suggests businesses that adopt principles of sustainability, such as, by extension, those embraced by a company committed to achieve net zero, provide a 5% greater IRR to investors than their conventional peers.[8]

THE INFRASTRUCTURE OF STAKEHOLDER CAPITALISM AND SYSTEMS CHANGE

Jay Coen Gilbert, the CEO of Imperative 21 and one of the founders of B Lab, says the two preconditions necessary for systems change of the economic system are now present. First, there is acknowledgment that the current fossil fuel–based system of shareholder capitalism is broken. Second, for a system of capitalism to change, there must be a viable alternative, otherwise the rhetoric advocating stakeholder capitalism risks becoming just another form of greenwashing.[9]

Much of the necessary infrastructure for the viable alternative of stakeholder capitalism is already in place. Such infrastructure also supports the transition to a net zero economy and a more just, sustainable, and regenerative economic system as envisioned by the UN SDGs. The three transformational trends—digitization, decarbonization, and stakeholder capitalism—already have changed the guiding principles of the economic system and have converged to create a viable alternative to shareholder primacy–based capitalism.

Stakeholder capitalism espoused by the Business Roundtable, the World Economic Forum, and asset managers like BlackRock conflicts with much of the established infrastructure of shareholder capitalism. As discussed in Chapter 15, the traditional limited liability corporation, for example, has a single-stakeholder model in which directors' fiduciary duties flow exclusively to stockholders. Under prevailing Delaware law, the sole purpose of the traditional corporation is to "maximize stockholder welfare."[10] This makes it problematic for directors to look out for the interests of all the corporation's stakeholders.

BENEFIT CORPORATION GOVERNANCE

The benefit corporation, as discussed in Chapter 15, is well-aligned with stakeholder capitalism because it expressly authorizes a multiple stakeholder corporate model. In a benefit corporation, the directors' fiduciary duties flow not only to stockholders as usual but also to all the corporation's other stakeholders, including employees, society, and the environment. In other words, the benefit corporation legitimizes a multiple stakeholder approach to business that is aligned with stakeholder capitalism. The benefit corporation puts the power of law behind the rhetoric of stakeholder capitalism.

The benefit corporation also provides more suitable governance architecture for companies on the path to net zero. The Delaware version of the benefit corporation requires companies to operate in "a responsible and sustainable manner" and "balance the pecuniary interests of the corporation, the interests of those affected by corporate behavior (its stakeholders) and the special benefit purpose of the company."[11] The version of the benefit corporation adopted by most jurisdictions requires companies to provide "a material positive impact on society and the environment."[12]

The benefit corporation demonstrates one of the key principles of systems change: identify and make the smallest possible changes necessary to change the entire system. The benefit corporation is identical to the traditional corporation but for two small changes to the corporate code. The benefit corporation extends the fiduciary duties of directors to all the corporation's stakeholders and has an additional public purpose of creating a material positive impact on society and the environment. These changes endow the benefit corporation with a social and environmental conscience that transcends and includes the usual pecuniary one limited to protecting the interests of stockholders.

The benefit corporation is not available in all jurisdictions, but the form is spreading globally. Since the state of Maryland adopted the first benefit corporation legislation in 2010, the form has been adopted in more than 40 states in the United States, the District of Columbia, and Puerto Rico as well as in Canada, Italy, France, Rwanda, Columbia, Peru, Ecuador, and Uruguay.[13] The proposed Better Business Act in the UK would create a default/mandatory benefit corporation form for every business in the country.[14]

MULTICAPITAL ACCOUNTING

Stakeholder capitalism requires a rethinking of accounting systems and various forms of capital. Just as lawyers have reimagined the corporation, accountants are transforming accounting. As discussed in Chapter 15, to supplement traditional double-entry accounting systems that only account for fiscal capital, there are new multicapital accounting systems that complement the *IR Framework*, such as the *MultiCapital Scorecard,* which measure a business's natural, built, intellectual, and relational capital.

DOUGHNUT ECONOMICS

Stakeholder capitalism requires a rethinking of the fundamental principles of neoliberal economics. Economist Kate Raworth, in her book *Doughnut Economics*, identifies the 11 underlying beliefs of neoliberal economics.[15] To transform the economic system so it is more just, sustainable, and regenerative, Ms. Raworth suggests 11 replacement beliefs. She suggests replacing the prevailing beliefs about the Earth and society, discussed in Chapter 15, with "the earth—which is life giving—so respect its boundaries" and "society—which is foundational—so nurture its connections." In the viable alternative of stakeholder capitalism, the free market is embedded responsibly within society and respects, and operates within, the ecological boundaries of the biosphere (see Exhibit 16.1).

EXHIBIT 16.1 **The doughnut and social and planetary boundaries**

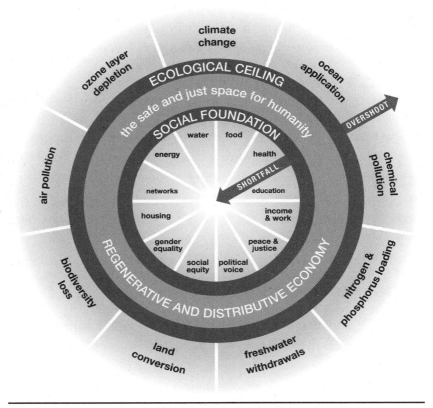

Source: Raworth, K. (2017). *Doughnut Economics: 7 Ways to Think Like a 21st Century Economist.* White River Junction, VT: Chelsea Green. Credit: Kate Raworth and Christian Guthier. CC-BY-SA 4.0.

The UN Sustainable Development Goals, which were adopted by all UN member states in 2015, provide a vision of the kind of world stakeholder capitalism can help manifest. The 17 SDGs provide a blueprint for peace and prosperity. Many of the companies discussed in this book are working to fulfill the UN SDGs, set SDG-related goals, and report on their progress toward them.

HEART-BASED LEADERSHIP

Stakeholder capitalism also requires an expanded concept of leadership that enables corporate leaders to care for all their corporations' stakeholders, including society and the planet, not just shareholders. Bob Chapman, CEO of Barry Wehmiller, a St. Louis-based manufacturing company, had an epiphany that every one of his employees was someone's precious child. He realized that everybody matters. His leadership style is now based on care. Mr. Chapman calls leading from the heart in this way "Truly Human Leadership."[16]

Stakeholder capitalism calls for leaders who lead from the heart not only to care for the welfare of their businesses but also for the well-being of society and the planet. Leading from the heart is one aspect of the "teal" leadership that Frederic Laloux describes in *Reinventing Organizations*.[17] The leaders Laloux profiles in his book engage their employees by leading from the heart. Such leaders create workplaces that run on trust by empowering their employees to do their jobs rather than use their positional power over them to get things done. Having love for one's stakeholders makes for an excellent leadership system but in a business context, words like "care" and "trust" are used instead to describe leading from the heart because the "L" word is loaded.

Trust-based businesses also may be more profitable because they increase employee engagement, satisfaction, and productivity and reduce employee turnover. Dr. Paul Zak, a neuro-economist at the Claremont Graduate Institute, found that workers at high-trust businesses are 76% more engaged at work, 50% more productive, and 60% enjoyed their jobs more than workers whose firms were in the bottom quartile as measured for trust. In addition, workers at high-trust workplaces were 50% more likely not to switch jobs over the next year than workers in low-trust workplaces.[18] By contrast, according to Gallup, only 21% of American workers are engaged at work.[19]

Leading from the heart, however, may be a challenge in a traditional corporation because the doctrine of shareholder primacy requires its directors to put the interests of its stockholders ahead of those of its employees and other stakeholders. The benefit corporation's multiple stakeholder model of governance is well-suited to heart-based leadership because the law requires directors to extend their fiduciary responsibilities to all stakeholders.

Many of the winners in the net zero economy will have leaders who lead from the heart with the global systems-thinking capacities described in Chapter 13 in companies with multiple stakeholder governance architecture like the benefit corporation. In the field of developmental psychology, there are many systems of constructive developmental theory that posit that adults move through distinct stages of development. In such models, global systems thinking tends to be characteristic of later stages of development.

This process is called vertical development. The core concept of vertical development is that life experiences pull us up the developmental ladder just as ever-more complex job assignments cultivate the development of systems-thinking capacities, as discussed in Chapter 13. Each successive stage takes a bigger perspective that generates a broader overall perspective. The developmental arc generally takes adults from being egocentric, to being concerned also for their family and tribes, to being concerned also for their communities, to being concerned also for their nations, to being concerned also for the world.

David Rooke and William Torbert call the perspective associated with a particular stage of development its "action logic."[20] In their seven-level developmental framework, global systems thinking is characteristic of the two latest stages of development: the strategist and the alchemist. These two stages differ from the prior five stages because they are concerned about the health of the whole system and look to find win-win solutions that benefit all stakeholders. Rooke and Torbert call these stages second tier because of their holistic perspective. The five prior stages are called first tier because they tend to look out for the health of a part of a system and tend to promote win-lose solutions.

Strategists and alchemists are particularly well-suited to lead transformations. Like the U.S. Armed Forces' findings discussed in Chapter 13,

Rooke and Torbert's research indicates leaders with global systems thinking are relatively rare, with only about 4% of adults operating as strategists and fewer than 1% operating as alchemists.

The strategist's action logic is comfortable with the emergent process of a transformation. The strategist is good at creating an overarching vision and recognizes that transformations entail an "iterative developmental process."[21] The alchemist has "an extraordinary capacity to deal simultaneously with many situations at multiple levels. The alchemist can talk with both kings and commoners. He can deal with immediate priorities yet never lose sight of long-term goals."[22] Alchemists often are involved in multiple organizations and able to deal effectively with the issues of each.

Frederic Laloux calls companies with strategist and alchemist (teal) leaders self-organizing organizations. Such organizations empower individuals (self-management), create a safe environment that encourages people to show up fully at work (wholeness), and have an evolutionary purpose, such as contributing to the creation of a net zero economy that transcends and includes just making money. Self-organizing corporations require a strategist or alchemist leader and a supportive board of directors.[23]

According to Laloux, the two key roles of a strategist or alchemist leader are "holding the space" and "role modeling behaviors."[24] Fulfilling these roles ensures the workplace remains a safe place where everyone is safe to show up fully as who they are and are becoming. In short, the leader's state of being emanates the field of consciousness within the workplace. A strategist or alchemist has generally transcended the reactivity of the limbic system so as not to be victimized constantly by fear. This enables the leader's brain to stay centered out of the amygdala in the frontal cortex or heart and produce more positive neurotransmitters—oxytocin for bonding and dopamine for feeling good. In a VUCA world, this level of self-mastery will become an increasingly critical leadership skill. At their best, strategist and alchemist leaders also can facilitate collective flow states that are endemic of peak performance.

The essential point is that the CEO is the ultimate instrument of change on a company's chosen Pathway to net zero. Everything flows from the leader's state of being. How a CEO is on the inside is foundational to how he or she shows up at work. Mastering the limbic system enables a leader to stay centered and present. This self-mastery allows a strategist or alchemist leader to "sense and respond" to situations as they unfold.[25]

Being First has identified five key skills of strategists and alchemists. In addition to self-mastery of the limbic system, a second-tier leader can set a holistic context for a complex problem so others can see the relationships and interdependencies among the parts. In other words, a second-tier leader has the global systems-thinking capacities to see the whole and help make the invisible visible by identifying and connecting all the dots. A second-tier leader has an open mind and is genuinely curious, seeking multiple perspectives with the knowledge that multiple heads are better than one. A second-tier leader not only seeks the ideas and perspectives of others but also can take on their perspectives by trying them on. Finally, a second-tier leader not only holds the space, but also holds it open to allow the integration of various perspectives and permit the solution to emerge. This ability to hold open the field of possibilities is counterintuitive because the ego wants to come to a solution and implement it as quickly as possible.

The leader's ability to hold open the field of possibilities is the key to sensing and responding to the future as it emerges. The net zero economy is emergent as are the smart electric vehicle industry, the smart and clean grid, and the green hydrogen industry. Even Pathway One, Pathway Two, Pathway Three, and Pathway Four are emergent in that transition plans will adjust as larger systems evolve and new technologies emerge.

In Otto Scharmer's Theory U, the key to leading from the future as it emerges is the ability to transcend fear, which tends to close the mind, stifle the heart, and thwart the will. The key to leading from the future as it emerges is for leaders to be able to maintain an open mind, an open heart, and an open will. This allows them to lead confidently with a curious mind, a compassionate heart, and a courageous will. The curiosity of open minds, the compassion of open hearts, and the courage of open wills will be needed for the global economy to achieve net zero.[26]

CONCLUSION

Every Pathway One, Pathway Two, Pathway Three, and Pathway Four company should align its net zero transition strategy with the three transformational trends. These three trends may have a collective flywheel effect (see Exhibit 16.2) like Walmart's project Gigaton. Companies that align their net zero strategy with these three trends can leverage their momentum. Companies that do not align with these trends risk being left behind.

Globalization has made it clear that we are one human family sharing one fragile planetary home. Stakeholder capitalism and the drive to create a net zero economy are part of a global movement that recognizes that business can be a force for good. This global movement is a response to the profound spiritual crisis facing humanity in which the survival of our civilization is threatened by existential threats like global warming.

EXHIBIT 16.2 The net zero sweet spot and the three transformational trends

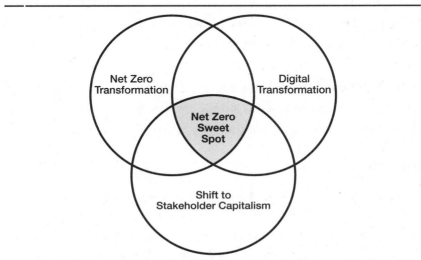

This crisis is fueled by a hidden conflict between two incompatible moral systems. The moral compass for individual citizens around the world is each of our spiritual traditions' equivalent of the Golden Rule—do unto others as you would have them do unto you. The moral compass for corporations and those who run them, however, is the doctrine of shareholder primacy, which by law or custom, maximizes profit for shareholders while externalizing the negative costs of corporate behavior onto society and the environment.

This conflict is at the root of the spiritual crisis facing humanity today. Today the struggle is not between the totalitarian and liberal orders but between the rule of gold and the Golden Rule. Neoliberal economics, which were the solution to the post-World War II crisis, have unwittingly become one of the contributors to our current spiritual crisis. The infrastructure of stakeholder capitalism begins to address the conflict in moral systems because it is more in alignment with the Golden Rule. These changes make stakeholder capitalism more prone to altruistic behavior rather than behavior that is unwittingly prone to be sociopathic and destructive to the environment.

To transform the prevailing free market economic system into a net zero economy that is also more just, sustainable, and regenerative requires changing its foundational beliefs to promote the well-being of people and planet. To paraphrase the World Economic Forum, we need to take better care of each other and our planet. In other words, we need to love our global family and our precious planetary home. Love is the ultimate force for good. If we can awaken this force, we will achieve a net zero economy faster than we can possibly imagine.

NOTES

1. Ørsted. (2018). Love Your Home. Video (2 February). https://www.youtube .com/watch?v=NYpsASj2pto.
2. Benioff, M. (2019). We need a new capitalism. *The New York Times* (14 October). https://www.nytimes.com/2019/10/14/opinion/benioff-salesforce-capitalism .html.

3. Business Roundtable. (2019). Statement on the purpose of a corporation (19 August; updated May 2022). https://s3.amazonaws.com/brt.org/2022.06.01-BRTStatementonthePurposeofaCorporationwithSignatures.pdf.

4. Schwab, K. and Vanham, P. (2021). What is stakeholder capitalism? World Economic Forum (22 Jannuary). https://www.weforum.org/agenda/2021/01/klaus-schwab-on-what-is-stakeholder-capitalism-history-relevance/.

5. Ibid.

6. Ibid.

7. Sisodia, R., Sheth, J., and Wolf, D. (2003). *Firms of Endearment: How World-Class Companies Profit from Passion and Purpose.* Upper Saddle River, NJ: Pearson Education.

8. Eccles, R., Ioannou, I., and Serafeim, G. (2014). The impact of corporate sustainability on organizational process and performance. *Management Science* 60 (11): 2835–2847. https://www.hbs.edu/faculty/Pages/item.aspx?num=47307.

9. Gilbert, J.C. (2019). Keynote speech on systems change. B Corp Summit in Amsterdam (23 October). https://www.youtube.com/watch?v=YuyffQ9ekq4.

10. Strine, L. (2015). The dangers of denial: the need for a clear-eyed understanding of the power and accountability structure established by the Delaware General Corporation Law. *Wake Forest Law Review* 50: 761; University of Pennsylvania Institute for Law & Economic Research paper no. 15-08. https://papers.ssrn.com/sol3/papers.cfm?abstract_id=2576389.

11. The Delaware Code Online. (n.d.). Title 8 Corporations, Chapter 1 General Corporation Law, Subchapter XV Public Benefit Corporations. https://delcode.delaware.gov/title8/c001/sc15/.

12. Clark, W.C., Vranka, L. et al. (2013). White Paper: The need and rationale for the benefit corporation: why it is the legal form that best addresses the needs of social entrepreneurs, investors, and, ultimately, the public. White paper (18 January).

13. Fukayama, M. (2022). The policy #BehindtheB: how we're creating new rules for the global economic system. B Lab Global (16 March). https://www.bcorporation.net/en-us/news/blog/behind-the-b-inside-policy-at-b-lab.

14. Turner, C. (2022). The U.K. has the chance to build better capitalism. Bloomberg US Edition (27 January). https://www.bloomberg.com/opinion/

articles/2022-01-28/the-u-k-s-better-business-act-can-build-a-better-capitalism.

15. Raworth, K. (2017) *Doughnut Economics: 7 Ways to Think Like a 21st Century Economist*. White River Junction, VT: Chelsea Green (pp. 62–63).

16. Chapman, B. and Sisodia, R. (2015) *Everybody Matters: The Extraordinary Power of Caring for Your People like Family*. New York: Portfolio/Penguin.

17. Laloux, F. (2014). *Reinventing Organizations: A Guide to Creating Organizations Inspired by the Next Stage of Human Consciousness*. Brussels: Nelson Parker.

18. Zak, P. (2017). The neuroscience of trust, management behaviors that foster engagement. *Harvard Business Review* (January-February). https://hbr.org/2017/01/the-neuroscience-of-trust.

19. Gallup. (2022). State of the global workplace: 2022 report. https://www.gallup.com/workplace/349484/state-of-the-global-workplace.aspx?utm_source=google&utm_medium=cpc&utm_campaign=gallup_access_branded&utm_term=&gclid=Cj0KCQjw_7KXBhCoARIsAPdPTfjwgOfLW__zGmG7KZDpHKRopFUP0tADqUsuaadSJS0mgjve8pw2rHMaAqdDEALw_wcB.

20. Rooke, D. and Torbert, W. (2005). Seven transformations of leadership. *Harvard Business Review* (April). https://hbr.org/2005/04/seven-transformations-of-leadership.

21. Ibid.

22. Ibid.

23. Laloux, F. (2014). *Reinventing Organizations*.

24. Ibid.

25. Ibid.

26. Scharmer, O. (2013). *Leading from the Emerging Future: From Ego-System to Eco-System Economies*. Oakland, CA: Berrett Koehler Publishers.

APPENDICES

Target Companies with Best Climate-Related Disclosure Practices

IKEA Group	Intel	PACCAR	NEXTera Energy
Unilever	Taiwan Semiconductor	Maersk	Iberdrola
Nestle	Samsung Electronics	Honeywell	Southern California Edison
Coca-Cola	ASML	Johnson Controls	Ørsted
Nike	Microsoft	Schneider Electric	Vattenfall
Mitsubishi Heavy Industries	Cisco	Signify	Royal DSM
BASF	Alphabet / Google	Cummins	Schlumberger
BHP	Toyota	Siemens	Shell
Rio Tinto	BMW Group	Deere & Co	SASOL
Anglo American	Tesla	Weyerhaeuser	Brookfield Asset Management

Source: FutureZero.

APPENDIX 1.1 **NextEra's Three Transformations**

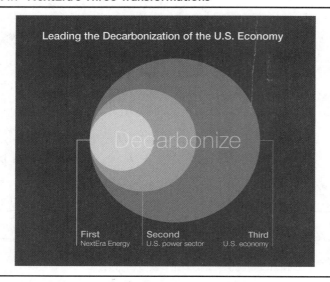

Leading the Decarbonization of the U.S. Economy

Decarbonize

| First | Second | Third |
| NextEra Energy | U.S. power sector | U.S. economy |

APPENDIX 1.2 **The Nine Planetary Boundaries**

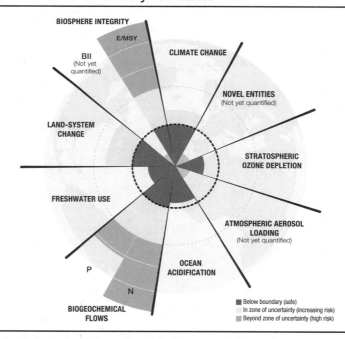

Source: Stockholm Resilience Centre, Stockholm University. Credit: J. Lokrantz/Azote based on Steffen et al. 2015. CC-BY-SA 4.0.

322

APPENDIX 1.3 The 17 UN Sustainable Development Goals

APPENDIX 2.1 Google's Carbon-Free Energy

Regional Grid	Data Center Location	2021 Grid CFE %	2021 Google CFE %
Energy Market Authority of Singapore	Singapore	3%	4%
Taiwan Power Company, Taiwan	Chaughua County	17%	17%
Tennet, Netherlands	Eemshaven	35%	53%
Sistema Interconectado, Chile	Quilicura	43%	69%
Pennsylvania, Jersey, Maryland, Power Pool (PJM)	Loudoun, VA & New Albany Ohio	40%	40%
Midcontinental ISO (MISO)	Council Bluffs, IA	33%	97%
Duke Energy Carolinas	Lenoir, NC	60%	65%
Southwest Power Pool (SPP)	Mayes County, OK	46%	88%
Bonneville Power Administration	The Dalles, OR	88%	88%
Electric Reliability Council of Texas, ERCOT	Midlothian, Texas	40%	40%
Nevada Energy	Henderson, NV	21%	21%

Note: Our carbon-free energy (CFE) percentage measures the degree to which our electricity consumption on a given regional grid is matched with CFE on an hourly basis. This is calculated using both CFE under contract by Google as well as CFE coming from the overall grid mix. CFE coming from the overall grid mix is based on data obtained from a third-party, ElectricityMap, and has not been assured.

Source: Google Carbon-Free Energy Performance Report

APPENDIX 2.2 Resources About Calculating Greenhouse Gas Emissions

To become familiar with Scope 1, 2, and 3 emissions in general, review:

Greenhouse Gas Protocol
Corporate Accounting and Reporting Standard

For detailed instructions on how to calculate Scope 1, 2, and 3 emissions, including all 15 categories of Scope 3 emissions, review:

U.S, EPA Greenhouse Gas Inventory Guidance: Direct Emissions from Stationary Combustion Sources

U.S. EPA Greenhouse Gas Inventory Guidance: Direct Emissions from Mobile Combustion Source

U.S. EPA Greenhouse Gas Inventory Guidance: Indirect Emissions from Purchased Electricity

U.S. EPA Greenhouse Gas Inventory Guidance: Direct Fugitive Emissions from Refrigeration, Air Conditioning, Fire Suppression, and Industrial Gases

Greenhouse Gas Protocol Scope 3 Guides:

Category 1 Purchased Goods and Services

Category 2 Capital Goods

Category 3 Fuel and Energy Related Activities Not Included in Scope 1 or Scope 2

Category 4 Upstream Transportation and Distribution

Category 5 Waste Generated in Operations

Category 6 Business Travel

Category 7 Employee Commuting

Category 8 Upstream Leased Assets

Category 9 Downstream Transportation and Distribution

Category 10 Processing of Sold Products

Category 11 Use of Sold Products

Category 12 End of Life Treatment of Sold Products

Category 13 Downstream Leased Assets

Category 14 Franchises

Category 15 Investments

APPENDIX 3.1 **The Effect of a $100 per Ton Carbon Tax on Return on Capital, after Cost of Capital and Cost of Carbon, on over 18,000 Publicly Traded Companies**

> A complete transformation of the global economy not just a transition

4-year Median CAPS: 2016-2019						
	95th	80th	Median	Average	20th	5th
Utilities	3.0	−1.0	−4.9	−8.2	−8.3	−37.7
Energy	2.6	−2.5	−6.1	−9.2	−10.2	−22.7
Materials	6.0	−0.8	−5.1	−7.7	−10.9	−32.7
Consumer Staples	17.3	5.1	−1.9	0.3	−5.6	−9.4
Telecommunication	17.8	5.3	−2.2	0.3	−5.7	−8.7
Industrials	12.4	3.6	−2.4	−1.4	−6.2	−11.8
Consumer Discretionary	12.0	3.3	−2.9	−1.2	−6.2	−9.2
Healthcare	14.2	4.9	−2.5	−1.9	−6.3	−20.1
Information Technology	16.6	5.3	−2.2	−0.4	−5.8	−11.3
Financials	16.7	5.5	−0.7	0.7	−6.0	−10.2
TOTAL	12.9	3.4	−2.7	−1.9	−6.4	−14.1

All industry sectors for the world negative Carbon-Adjusted Performance Spread (CAPS) @ median = Carbon-Adjusted Return on Capital (CAROC) = after cost of capital and cost of carbon @ $100 / ton – Scope 1 and 2

Source: FutureZero.

**APPENDIX 4.1 Resources About Setting Science-Based Emissions
Reduction Targets**

SBTi website: sciencebasedtargets.org/

> SBTi Corporate Net Zero Standard: https://sciencebasedtargets.org/resources/files/Net-Zero-Standard.pdf
>
> Small and Medium-Sized Enterprises (SMEs) FAQs: https://sciencebasedtargets.org/resources/files/FAQs-for-SMEs.pdf
>
> Private Equity Sector Science-Based Target Guidance: https://sciencebasedtargets.org/resources/files/SBTi-Private-Equity-Sector-Guidance.pdf
>
> Foundations for Science-Based Net-Zero Target Setting in the Corporate Sector: https://sciencebasedtargets.org/resources/files/foundations-for-net-zero-full-paper.pdf
>
> How-to Guide for Setting Near-Term Targets: https://sciencebasedtargets.org/resources/files/SBTi-How-To-Guide.pdf
>
> Target Validation Protocol for Near-Term Targets: https://sciencebasedtargets.org/resources/files/Target-Validation-Protocol.pdf
>
> SBTi Corporate Manual: https://sciencebasedtargets.org/resources/files/SBTi-Corporate-Manual.pdf
>
> SBTi Criteria and Recommendations: https://sciencebasedtargets.org/resources/files/SBTi-criteria.pdf
>
> Getting Started Guide for the SBTi Net-Zero Standard: https://sciencebasedtargets.org/resources/files/Net-Zero-Getting-Started-Guide.pdf
>
> Pathways to Net-Zero: SBTi Technical Summary: https://sciencebasedtargets.org/resources/files/Pathway-to-Net-Zero.pdf

The SBTi has published or plans to publish (in **bold**) guides for the following sectors:

> Forests, Land, and Agriculture (FLAG)
>
> FLAG (commodity pathway)

Buildings

Iron and Steel

Cement

Chemicals

Road and Rail Transport

Aviation

Oil and Gas

Power Generation

Apparel and Footwear

Information and Computer Technology

Automotive

Financial Services

APPENDIX 5.1 Intel's Three Domains of Innovation and Transformation

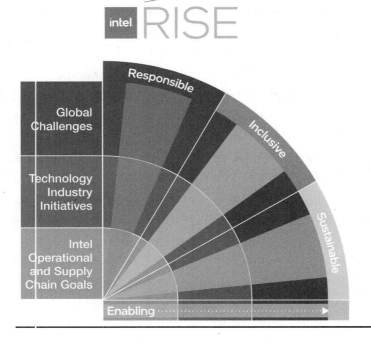

APPENDIX 6.1   Some Questions Pathway One Company Directors and Investors Might Ask and for Management to Consider

Note: These draft questions assume the company will have done a comprehensive carbon footprint assessment and analysis, including process maps of the activities, inputs, and outputs that generate the company's Scope 1, 2, and 3 carbon emissions and exposures.

Vision and Responsibilities

- What are the scope and quality of the company's current state carbon footprint and emissions analysis, and the findings from it?
- What process was followed by the board and management to determine the company's future state aspirations and responsibilities for dealing with climate change, including the role of the company in helping achieve the goals set forth in the Paris Agreement, at COP26, in SDG 13, and in government commitments?
- Which stakeholders were considered and/or consulted in determining the company's future state aspirations and responsibilities? What are their climate change assumptions and expectations?
- How have the company's future state and climate change aspirations and responsibilities been communicated internally, to supply chain partners, to customers, to investors, and to the public?

Strategy for Success (Transition to Net Zero *and* Commercial Success)

- What is management's assessment of the evolution of climate change laws and regulations, including escalations in the price of carbon, over the net zero planning horizon (e.g., 2030, 2040, 2050)?
- What is the size of the gap between the company's current state (carbon footprint/emissions exposure) and the desired future

state? How does this gap change over the planning horizon (e.g., 2030, 2040, 2050)?

- What data analytics and methodologies are being used to track and understand changing customer expectations with respect to climate change and demand for the company's products and market size? What are these analytics telling us?
- What engagement tools and methodologies are being used to track and understand employee expectations with respect to climate change and the company's net zero targets and plans? What are these analytics telling us?

Competitors

- What are our major competitors' climate change strategies and transition pathways? What threats do these strategies pose now and over the planning horizon (e.g., 2030, 2040, 2050)? Are the company's climate strategies leading or lagging in the industry?
- What is the potential for "disruptors" with new products and business models to enter the company's markets and capture market share?

Business Model Alignment

- Has management stress-tested the business model against various carbon price escalation levels and changing regulatory scenarios?
- What are the stress-test impacts on key metrics like total emissions, emissions tons/revenue, GAAP earnings, economic income, return on invested capital, and free cash flow?
- At what point will carbon price escalations and regulatory changes start to impair the ability of management to support the current business model through mitigation strategies like purchasing carbon credits or carbon capture?

- At what point does the current business model cease to be successful commercially?
- What factors or metrics would indicate that management and the board need to abandon the Pathway One transition approach and "level shift" to another transition Pathway?

Capabilities

- Do the CEO and senior leadership team have the talent and capabilities to successfully implement the emissions-mitigation plan?
- Does the company have the resources needed to implement the mitigation plan successfully?
- Does management have the effective skills and expertise to achieve its net zero targets primarily through eco-efficiency?
- Does management have access to the financial resources for capital investments in, for example, the carbon-capture technologies that will be required?
- Does management have the technology capabilities needed to improve continually the efficiency of their business processes and reduce costs?

Commitment

- Are CEO and executive compensation targets and metrics aligned with the mitigation strategies and targets?
- Are the short-term and long-term incentive plan components aligned with the time frames in the mitigation plan?
- Are employees engaged and supportive of the net zero targets and timelines?

- Are supply chain partners selected on the basis of their alignment with the company's eco-efficiency and carbon cost reduction programs and are they reducing their emissions in line with the company's targets?
- What are investors' perceptions of the company's approach to climate change in particular and ESG matters in general? Do they support the net zero targets, timeline, and CapEx implications?

Tracking, Reporting, and Learning

- Does the company have a data collection and analytics strategy to track and manage its emissions data?
- Are appropriate measurement systems and metrics in place and being reported internally for management and board monitoring of progress in executing the mitigation plan?
- Is external reporting to investors and other stakeholders about progress and performance on Pathway One (e.g., about strategy, risk, and mitigation as well as governance oversight and commercial success) trusted by investors and other users, and in line with current reporting requirements and guidance?

- Are internal controls and disclosure controls in place to ensure the reliability of the climate-related data and information that is reported externally as well as internally?

APPENDIX 7.1 Some Questions Pathway Two Company Boards and Investors Might Ask and for Management to Consider

Purpose, Vision, Customers, and Competition

- Based on how we see the global economy's transition to net zero emissions in 2030, 2040, and 2050, what do we think a net zero economy will look like, what characteristics will it have, and what do we think this all means for our industry? What is the compelling overarching vision and purpose for our company that will sustain our focus on the business model and strategies needed for our transformation to a net zero enterprise?

- How will the needs, attitudes, and expectations of our customers and potential customers (markets) change during the transition to a net zero economy? Who will be the most valuable and high-influencer customers? What must industry leaders do to create value for customers and exceed their expectations in a zero emissions economy?

- Where will we compete (e.g., industries, geographies, categories, channels, etc.)? Where are our best opportunities for success in a net zero economy and in the transition to it?

- How will we compete, gain market share, and win? How will our current formula for competitive success have to change? What changes are needed to our current product and service offerings, and to our business model?

- What are our competitors' net zero transition strategies? What is the potential for a disruptor to appear and eat our lunch with a net zero business model that is better aligned with emerging customer needs and expectations?

Business Model and Strategy

- What are the dimensions and size of the gap between our aspirations and our current state? Do we agree that the transition strategies and changes to our business model recommended by management to transform our company and close that gap are likely to succeed within the necessary timeframes?

- Has management stress tested the business model against various carbon price escalation levels and changing regulatory scenarios?
- What are the stress test impacts on key metrics like total emissions, metric tons of CO_2e emissions per $1 million of revenue, GAAP earnings, economic income, return on invested capital, and free cash flow?
- What factors or metrics would indicate we need to augment our strategy of transforming our products to also transform our fundamental business model?
- What factors or metrics would indicate we need to transcend Pathway Two and consider a transition to Pathway Four?

Commitment

- What communication, training, and performance management processes are we using to build and sustain a long-term commitment to our transformation strategies and targets from key players (e.g., board, CEO, senior management, employees)?
- How will we gain the support of our customers, suppliers, business partners, and other key stakeholders (e.g., media, communities) to our net zero transformation strategy and targets?
- Are our executive compensation systems aligned with execution of a multiyear/decade transition to net zero?
- Do our investors and other capital market actors support our net zero transition approach, including, for example, long-term vision, business model changes, strategy, CapEx needs, and capital allocation decisions?

Capabilities

- Do we have the CEO and management talent and skills needed to design, launch, and lead a successful transition to becoming a net zero enterprise?
- Do we have the executive talent development systems in place to develop the second and third generations of management with the skills to continue to lead and execute the transition?
- Do we have the financial resources for the capital investments needed during the timeframe of the transition plan? Do our capital allocation strategies and processes take account of what our transition plan calls for?
- What other resource and relationship capabilities (e.g., physical, technological, intellectual, relationships, access to resources, etc.) are required? Do we have these? If not, what is to be done?

Tracking, Reporting, Learning

- Are appropriate measurement systems and metrics in place for reliable, timely reporting internally for management purposes and for board monitoring of progress against targets and strategic objectives?
- Is external reporting about progress and performance in Pathway Two in line with current reporting requirements, disclosure standards, and guidance, and is it trusted by and useful to investors?
- Is external reporting to other stakeholders about progress and performance in Pathway Two building their trust and in line with current reporting frameworks and guidance?
- Are internal controls and disclosure controls in place to ensure the reliability of climate-related data and information that is reported externally as well as internally?

APPENDIX 9.1 Some Questions Pathway Three Company Boards and Investors Might Ask and for Management to Consider

Success as a startup Pathway Three company, possibly as an industry disruptor, calls for value creation mindsets, processes, and skills that are very different from those needed for an established Pathway One or Two company's transition to net zero.

Purpose, Vision, Markets, and Competition

Based on how we see the global economy's transition to net zero emissions by 2050, what do we think a net zero economy will look like, and what we think this means for our industry and its markets:

- What is the compelling, overarching purpose and vision for our company that will inspire and sustain our focus on becoming an innovative leader in our industry while achieving net zero carbon emissions? What core values will be our North Star in building our business?
- How will the needs, attitudes, and expectations of our customers and potential customers (markets) change during the transition to a net zero economy? Who will be the most valuable and high-influencer customers? As potential industry leaders, how will we uniquely create value for customers and exceed their expectations in a zero-emissions economy?
- What are the distinctive characteristics of the brand we will build? What are the inherent as well as explicit promises we will make about our brand?
- Where will we compete (e.g., industries, geographies, categories, channels, etc.)? Where are our best opportunities for success in a net zero economy and in the transition to it?

- How will we compete and gain market share from established companies in our industry, and from other startups similar to us? What are our competitors' net zero transition strategies? What is the potential for us to be a disruptor with products, services, and a net zero business model that is better aligned with emerging customer needs and expectations?

Business Model and Strategy

- Has management stress tested our business model against various carbon price escalation levels and changing regulatory scenarios?
- What are the stress test impacts on key metrics like future total emissions, carbon intensity, GAAP earnings, economic income, return on invested capital, and free cash flow?
- Do we have a compelling narrative and business case that will appeal to investors, bankers, and other suppliers of capital?

Commitment

- What communication, training, and performance management processes are we using to build and sustain a long-term commitment from key players (e.g., board, CEO, senior management, employees) to our business plan and targets?
- How will we gain support for our business plan from our customers, suppliers, business partners, and other key stakeholders (e.g., media, communities)?
- Are our executive compensation systems aligned with execution of our business plan over the early years of start up as well as longer term to achievement of net zero?

- Do our investors and other capital market actors support our vision and business plan including, for example, business model, strategy, CapEx needs, and capital allocation decisions?

Capabilities

- Do we have the CEO, management, and innovation talent and skills needed to plan, launch, and lead a successful startup that creates and markets innovative technologies to help customers' transitions to net zero, while achieving net zero ourselves?
- Do we have the executive talent development systems in place to develop the second and third generations of management with the skills to continue to lead the company beyond the startup phase?
- Do we have the financial resources to support the startup and development phases, including necessary R&D and capital investments, until cash flow from operations is adequate?
- What other resource and relationship capabilities (e.g., physical, technological, human relationships, access to resources, etc.) are required? Are these available to us?
- What innovation and knowledge ecosystems does the company participate in?
- Have we obtained patent protection for the technologies we have developed and brought to market or may in future decide to do so?

Tracking, Reporting, Learning

- Are appropriate measurement systems and metrics in place for reliable, timely reporting internally for management purposes and for board monitoring of progress against targets and strategic objectives?

- Is external reporting about our progress and performance in line with current reporting requirements, disclosure standards, and guidance, and is it trusted by and useful to investors?
- Is external reporting to other stakeholders about progress and performance in this Pathway building their trust and in line with current reporting frameworks and guidance?
- Are internal controls and disclosure controls in place to ensure the reliability of climate-related data and information that is reported externally as well as internally?

APPENDIX 10.1 **Some Questions Pathway Four Company Boards and Investors Might Ask and for Management to Consider**

What is the level of carbon emissions and carbon intensity across the industry? What is the level of urgency and commitment in the industry to address the net zero goals set forth in the COP21 Paris Agreement?

- Is there a common view on what the industry of the future will look like? What forces are driving and shaping the future of the industry? What role will the transition to net zero play in shaping the future of the industry?
- What are the industry-wide net zero transition opportunities, potential benefits, and risks? What is the level of capital investment required?
- What is the industry's overall reputation with respect to dealing with environment and climate change? How do investors, regulators, politicians, and consumers view the industry's reputation and brand for dealing with climate change? How will this impact the industry's ability to successfully transition to net zero?
- Is there a company that is leading, or emerging as a leader, with respect to the industry's transition to net zero? What first-mover advantages will accrue to a net zero industry leader?
- Who are the individuals who are leading the net zero transformation in particular companies and in the industry? Do they have the capabilities to help lead an industry transformation?
- Does this company have the capabilities, or can they build the capabilities, to play a leading role in the industry's transition to net zero? What advantages would accrue to the company and its stakeholders?
- Are there areas where companies in the industry can cooperate and share knowledge with respect to the net zero transition without impairing their ability to compete or violating anti-trust legislation?

- What is the level of trust between government policy setters, regulators, and the industry? How effective is the industry working with the government in developing meaningful regulations and facilitating an orderly transition to net zero?
- Are there areas where the industry should pursue public-private partnerships or similar working arrangements?
- What can be done within the industry and working with governments to help retrain people whose jobs are lost in the transition to a net zero economy?
- What is the level of transparency and quality of climate change reporting across the industry?

APPENDIX 12.1 Possible Questions About Corporate Transformations

The Leader

- How will the transformation affect you as a leader?
- How might you need to alter your leadership style to model new behaviors to support our desired culture?
- How might you need to alter your mindset, beliefs, or assumptions?
- What new activities can you imagine you will need to engage as a change leader to drive the transformation?
- How might you need to engage your team differently?
- What new work or change leadership practices might be needed of you personally?

Change Leadership Team

- How will your team need to change how it works to support the initiative?
- How will work, deliverables, and timetables need to be reprioritized?
- How will you allocate resources to support the transformation?
- How will you keep everyone informed?

Company

- What's our capacity to take on the transformation and succeed?
- How do we best develop our leadership capability and alignment to lead the transformation to fruition?
- How do we communicate to and engage our workforce?
- How do we change our culture?
- How do we course correct?
- How do we maintain focus, energy, and commitment until our desired outcome is achieved and is sustainable?

Preparing to Ask for Leadership Commitment

- Who: From which leaders do you need commitment?
- What: The ask. What specific commitment are you looking for?
- Inform: What information will you share to create buy-in?
- Impacts: What impact areas will you explore?
- What deeper issues might there be?
- What first action will you ask the team to do?

APPENDIX 13.1 World and North American Power Generation Mix

Continental Grid Region	Population 2021	Grid Country / Independent System Operator	Coal Generation	Natural Gas Turbines + Other Fossil Fuel Generation	Total Fossil Fuel Power Generation	Hydro and Geothermal	Atomic Power	Intermittent Wind, Solar with / without Energy Storage	Total Carbon-Free Energy Generation
North America	375.0 MM				52.0%	34.7%	18.5%	9.9%	44.6%
		Quebec Hydro	0%	0%	0%	89.0%	0.0%	11.0%	100.0%
		Ontario – ISO	0%	6.3%	6.3%	51.5%	32.0%	9.0%	92.5%
		CAMX – California	2.7%	37.1%	39.8%	25.8%	2.0%	24.3%	52.1%
		Texas – ERCOT	19.0%	42.0%	61.0%	6.0%	4.0%	25%	35.0%
		RFC Grid – including Ohio, Michigan, NJ, PA, WV, DC	29.6%	34.1%	64.6%	18.3%	14.0%	3.0%	35.3%
Europe	748.0 MM	EU = Total			36.6%	7.5%	12.0%	19.5%	39.0%
		Iceland			0%	100%	0.0%	0%	100.0%
		Sweden			.5%	57.2%	17.0%	17.4%	91.6%
		Norway			1.3%	92.0%	0.0%	6.5%	98.5%
		France			8.6%	30.1%	49.0%	10%	89.1%
		Denmark			15.7%	.1%	0.0%	61.9%	62.0%

(Continued)

APPENDIX 13.1 (Continued)

Continental Grid Region	Population 2021	Grid Country / Independent System Operator	Coal Generation	Natural Gas Turbines + Other Fossil Fuel Generation	Total Fossil Fuel Power Generation	Hydro and Geothermal	Atomic Power	Intermittent Wind, Solar with / without Energy Storage	Total Carbon-Free Energy Generation
		Spain			32.9%	27.0%	8.0%	29.3%	64.3%
		Germany			42.6%	12.7%	3.0%	31.6%	47.3%
		Ireland			56.4%	3.8%	0.0%	36.0%	39.8%
		Italy			56.7%	17.7%	0.0%	15.6%	33.3%
		Greece			63.3%	7.1%	0.0%	28.5%	35.6%
		Netherlands			68.3%	1.3%	2.0%	19.6%	22.9%
		Poland			81.3%	1.9%	0.0%	11.2%	13.1%
Taiwan	23.5 MM		45.0%	35.7%	80.7%	4.2%	7.0%	5.4%	16.6%
Korea	77.0 MM		35.6%	26.4%	62.0%	9.3%	21.0%	5.9%	36.2%
China	1.4 B		69.0%	0.0%	69.0%	19.0%	4.0%	9.0%	32.0%
India	1.4 B		74.0%	0.0%	74.0%	0.0%	2.0%	20.0%	20.0%
World	7.9 B		36.7%	26.6%	63.3%	16.2%	10.0%	8.0%	30.2%

Source: FutureZero analysis with data from 2019/2020/2021, EU – EuroStat, U.S. EPA, StatsCan, World Population Review 2019, BP Statistical Review 2020; S&PCAPIQ with Power; China Electricity Council.

APPENDIX 13.2 The North American Power Grid

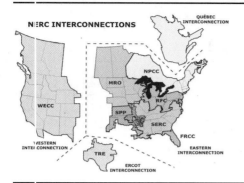

- The largest machine in the world
- Comprised of 3 large interconnections:
    - East
    - West
    - ERCOT - Texas
- 8 Reliability Councils

Source: FutureZero.

APPENDIX 14.1 Worksheet for Carbon-Free Energy

Power Type – by MWh and MWh % of Total Power Mix	3-Year Lookback LFY Minus 3	Current Performance Latest Fiscal Year	5-Year Ahead LFY Plus 5-Year Target	2030 Target Range
Total Power in MWh	?	?	?	?
Direct Power % Carbon-Free Energy (CFE)				
1. Onsite / offsite self generated clean energy power + storage – complete off grid – MWh %				
2. Onsite / offsite self generated clean power – with utility power grid backed-up				
Intermittent – RE Purchased Power / Power Offsets % of Generation Mix				
Grid mix offset max = fossil energy total being mixed with the below intermittent clean energy purchased power offsets = grey electrons mixed on the power grid				
3. Power Purchase Agreement to a specific clean power / energy asset – PPA or virtual PPA				
4. Energy Attribute Certificate / Renewable Energy Credit (REC)				
5. Clean energy power products from utility and grid delivered – wind, solar, storage				
Default Grid Power %				
NA Grid default mix – fossil energy total	60%	52%	?	?
6. Default electrical power from the power grids based on default power generation mix including Renewable Portfolio and Energy Attribution Certificates / Renewable Energy Credits				
Total Enterprise Net Carbon-Free Energy (CFE) after RE power offsets – MWh %				
Total MWh				

Source: FutureZero.

The Eco-Efficiency components of the Net Zero Transition Plan and summary table for actions and foundation for a credible plan.

APPENDIX 14.2 Worksheet for Eco-Efficiency

NZBM Innovation Strategy for Net Zero Business Model	3-Year Lookback LFY Minus 3	Current Performance Latest Fiscal Year	5-Year Ahead LFY Plus 5-Year Target	2030 Target Range
GHG tons Scope 1 and 2				
GHG tons Scope 3				
Total Net GHG Emissions				
Carbon credit and offsets				
Electric Power				
Total enterprise MWh				
Carbon-free energy MWh %				
Fossil fuel MWh energy %				
Transportation				
Number of vehicles owned or leased				
Number zero-emission vehicles owned				
SMART zero-emission fleet plan + targets				
Buildings and Processes				
Number of FTE employees				
% of FTE working remotely				
Number of facilities owned or leased				
Energy efficiency improvement & conservation plans for process optimization (including energy audits)				
SMART LEED Zero buildings or ISO 50001 EMS Standard				
$ CAPEX for eco-efficiency plan implementation				

Source: FutureZero.

Innovation and growth for sustainability including zero-carbon products, net zero business model, net zero industry ecosystems.

APPENDIX 14.3 Worksheet for Innovation

NZBM Strategy Summary – Eco-Efficiency Plans and Targets	3-Year Lookback LFY Minus 3	Current Performance Latest Fiscal Year	5-Year Ahead LFY Plus 5-Year Target	2030 Target Range
Net Zero Business Model		Declared Net Zero		
Revenue				
Tons CO_2e / $1 million revenue				
% Revenue for new products launched in the last 5 years				
% Revenue from zero carbon / sustainable products				
% Product revenue for circular designed products / services				
Return on Capital				
P/E ratio				
Number technology platforms				
Number of patents				
C-Suite – Succession readiness rate for Net Zero Business Model transformation				
3-year total compensation of regrettable talent losses				
Total R&D in				
Total R&D % revenues				
R&D for zero-emission products services % of R&D $$				
R&D for Industry Transformation % of R&D $$				
CAPEX total in $				
CAPEX zero-emission operating assets %				
CAPEX for nature-based climate solutions %				
CAPEX fossil maintain %				
M&A – clean / zero-emission / sustainable $				
$ for Industry Eco-System(s) collaboration and standards setting for Net Zero Industry transformation				
Number of Government submissions for policies and regulators related to innovation, carbon pricing, GHG reduction incentives, clean power incentives – influence rules of the game and required disclosures				

Source: FutureZero.

Credible Net Zero Transition Plan Best Practices Compared to Guidance for Net Zero

X = fully part of guidance, x = partially aligned, Blank field = KPI and plan not requested

APPENDIX 14.4 Gap Analysis of Net Zero Business Model Disclosures Missing from Guidance Frameworks

Requested Disclosures for Credible Net Zero Transition and Detailed Plans For:	TCFD	GFANZ	ISSB	CA-100	TPI
GHG Reduction Targets – 2030, 2040, 2050	X	X	X	X	X
% Total Power – MWh from Electricity Grids					
Carbon-Free Energy (CFE) power plans and % CFE as a total of all MWhs consumed and 100 % CFE MWh target by when					
Energy efficiency improvement plans for process innovation and existing product design improvement (including energy audits)					
Zero-Emission SMART transportation fleet % with target and plan					
Zero-Emission SMART sustainable buildings / facilities % with target and plan					
Return on Invested Capital (capacity to fund transition)					
Carbon Adjusted Return on Capital Stress tested $100 / Ton CO_2e – sensitivity analysis	x	x			
Total R&D in $$					
Total R&D % revenues					
% R&D for zero-emission & sustainable products and services					
Total CAPEX total in $					
% CAPEX for zero-emission operating assets	X	X	X	X	X
% CAPEX for nature based GHG climate solutions					
% CAPEX fossil maintain (including pipelines for future hydrogen and CO_2)					
% CAPEX Fossil New					
% Revenues from Products & Services that are Zero Carbon / Sustainable					
% Product Portfolio Operating Income from for Zero-Emission / Sustainable Products				x	

Requested Disclosures for Credible Net Zero Transition and Detailed Plans For:	TCFD	GFANZ	ISSB	CA-100	TPI
% Products that are circular in design including renewable product content					
Industry Sector(s) Engagement to develop plans for industry eco-system(s) and value chain(s) transformation to Net Zero Industry		x			
Incentives Aligned with Net Zero / Sustainable Business Model	X	X		X	X
Skills Required for Development & Execution of Net Zero Transition Plan (Board & Executive Management)			x	x	
C-Suite – Succession Readiness Rate for Business Model Transformation					

Source: FutureZero.

TCFD = Task Force for Climate Financial Disclosure,
GFANZ = Glasgow Financial Alliance for Net Zero,
ISSB = International Sustainability Standards Board,
CA – 100 = Climate Action 100,
TPI = Transition Pathway Initiative

ACKNOWLEDGMENTS

We deeply appreciate everyone who supported the process of writing *Net Zero Business Models*.

We wish to thank Bartley (Bart) Madden, the former Managing Director of Credit Suisse HOLT®, and author of several books about innovation life cycles, investment, and return on capital, for connecting our team at FutureZero with the team at Credit Suisse HOLT®. Bart's framework for innovation and the return on capital life cycle provided the key ideas in Chapter 11, A Foundational Framework to Choose a Pathway. Bart championed the need for *Net Zero Business Models* and introduced Mark to Bill Falloon, Executive Editor, Finance and Investments at Wiley.

We also appreciate our publicist, Mary Bisbee-Beek, for her help and encouragement in preparing the Wiley book proposal, and Harry Max for suggesting we write a useful book and directing us to *Write Useful Books* by Rob Fitzpatrick.[1] We also acknowledge Dr. Raj Thamotheram, former head of Corporate Governance at the USS pension fund and at AXA Investment Managers, who encouraged Mark to come out of early retirement, which then resulted in setting up FutureZero, recruiting a new team, and developing this book.

We thank the Credit Suisse HOLT® team in London and Chicago for providing us with access to their Credit Suisse HOLT® database and for assisting us with our preliminary analysis of the effect of a carbon tax of $75 per metric ton on over 14,000 public companies with reported emissions data. The analysis and carbon shock stress-testing confirmed the need for *Net Zero Business Models* by showing that many public companies were ill-prepared for a real cost of carbon and its financial impact on their operating performance. We acknowledge the contributions of Lori Mattes and Teresa Betts, Directors of Analytics at FutureZero, who led our carbon shock stress-testing and strategic analytic research.

We especially wish to acknowledge James (Jim) Goodfellow, FCPA, FCA, and Alan Willis, FCPA, FCA, whose contributions to *Net Zero Business Models*, and particularly to developing and elucidating its stars— the four Pathways—were extraordinary. Jim and Alan brought camaraderie to the writing process. Their wit and humor kept us moving forward during the more difficult parts of drafting this book.

Jim and Alan's breadth of expertise and experience made enormous contributions to the book.

Jim's extensive experience in the automotive, retail, and high-tech sectors together with his experience as Vice Chairman of Deloitte Canada and as a corporate director was invaluable in articulating for boards of directors and executive management the strategic implications of adopting a net zero business model and in interpreting the Tesla story in Chapter 10. As the former Chairman of the Canadian Accounting Standards Committee and former Chairman of the Canadian Performance Reporting Board, Jim also brought a keen financial and analytic perspective to the book.

Having been a member of the founding steering committee of the Global Reporting Initiative, a member of the working group for the International Integrated Reporting Council, an advisory council member of the Sustainability Accounting Standards Board, and the author of several white papers on sustainability reporting, Alan's expertise in sustainability accounting and reporting standards significantly enhanced Chapter 14, Telling the Net Zero Story.

We acknowledge Denise Bonte, FutureZero's Director of Visual Presentation and Design, for creating the illustrations in *Net Zero Business Models*. Denise's beautiful work was indispensable in bringing the book to life through more than 60 illustrations.

We are particularly grateful for all the people who shared their wisdom and experience at numerous educational events with a net zero business models theme, which allowed us to introduce and to stress test the key ideas of *Net Zero Business Models*.

Tamara Close, Managing Partner of CGC Consulting, and Betty Jiang, America's Managing Director, ESG Research at Credit Suisse, were both instrumental in shaping our thinking regarding the capital markets and ESG. Chris Colbert, CFA, Chief Strategy Officer, and Robert Temple, General Counsel, of NuScale Power Corporation, shared strategic foresight that shaped our thinking on how power grids need to evolve to deliver 100% carbon-free energy. We thank Karina Litvack for sharing her journey toward net zero on the board of directors at Eni in Italy.

We thank Matt Orsagh, CFA, Senior Director, Capital Markets Policy at the CFA Institute for hosting us on his sustainability podcasts leading up to COP26. Henrik Jeppesen, CFA, Head of Investor Outreach at Carbon Tracker, and Co-Chair, CFA Society New York, Sustainable Investing Group, hosted a special event about net zero business models for CFA Society members. We are grateful to Anne Simpson, Global Head of Sustainable Investments at Franklin Templeton Investments, who shared her insights about net zero during a "Fireside Chat" with Mark at the CFA Society New York special event. We also thank Russell Longmuir, CEO of EFQM, for hosting multiple events about *Net Zero Business Models* for EFQM members around the world.

We are particularly grateful for all the people who shared their wisdom and experience about the transition from a global energy system based on fossil fuels to one that produces carbon-free energy. This includes Richard Manley, Chief Sustainability Officer and Head of Sustainable Investments; Martha Hall Finlay, Chief Climate Officer of Suncor; and Michael Rubio, General Manager, ESG and Sustainability at Chevron, for sharing their insights on the energy transition on a panel moderated by Betty Jiang at the Credit Suisse Global Energy Conference. We are particularly grateful to Chuck Williamson, former CEO of Unocal, former Chairman of the Board at Talisman Energy and Weyerhaeuser Company, and former lead independent director at PACCAR, for sharing key insights on the realities of the energy transition.

Janet Carrig, John Ballow, John McCormack, Sundeep Bajikar, Keith Johnson, Ken McNeil, Keith Ambachsteer, Claude Lamoureux, Jon Lukomnik, Hamish Stewart, Julien Morgan, Susan Winchester, Peter Harder, and Diana Fox Carney provided key insights that were critical in framing the complexity, change management challenges, and scale of the transition to a global net zero emissions economy from the perspective of the C-Suite, the board of directors, and institutional investors.

Terry Seigel, former Director of Nuclear Fuel Handling of Ontario Power Generation and former chairman of the board of two municipal utilities; Jack Joyce, with over 30 years of experience in the power industry including key positions at GE Power Systems, Siemens, and the Electric Power Research Institute; and Amelia Badders, Senior Director, Strategic Pricing of CPS Energy and former Chief of Staff to the CEO, all shared frontline experience and insights about the real challenges facing the electric power sector to produce 100% carbon free energy with 24/7 reliability.

We thank Renae Kezar, Vice President Global Sustainability and Regulatory Affairs at Johnson Controls, Chris Librie, ESG Director, at Applied Materials, and other senior sustainability leaders at Ikea Group, Velux, Signify, Schlumberger, Salesforce.com, Google, and 3M for validating the five eco-efficiency processes and systems outlined in Chapter 5, which form the foundation of every company's net zero transition plan.

We acknowledge the contributions of FutureZero's extended global team and network, including John Swannick, Sandy Miles, Andrei Stepanov, Fabiaan Van Vrekhem, Amanda Boyden, Remi Morel, Martin Sutherland, Brett Mulder, James Hipkin, and Bonnie Conrad to the research, the video, and to *Net Zero Business Models*.

We are indebted to Dr. T Owen Jacobs. Dr. J., the former head of 'Strategic Leadership' research at the Industrial College of the Armed Forces and National Defense University of the United States, whose work and over 40 years of research in the U.S. Armed Forces provided the basis of our framework on the three domains of systems thinking in Chapter 13.

We also acknowledge Joseph Jaworski for his magnificent works and for encouraging us to write the book from the "U." Most of the book emerged from a remarkable eight-week burst of creativity from within the "U." John's wife, Margareth Mayr, helped mightily in holding open the "U" during the creative process. Mark's life partner, Susan (Francis) Van Clieaf, an expert in educational technology and former Global Director of Training and Development at Scotiabank, provided an ongoing critique of key ideas in the book to ensure they would resonate in the C-Suite.

We received wonderful ideas and feedback from our readers, whose insights and encouragement were invaluable. This included insightful input from Jan Lewis, Bill Montgomery, Sanjay Kapoor, Mark Feenstra, Karen Alonardo, Fernando Agudelo-Silva, Michael Putz, Parker Montgomery, Dean Anderson, and Linda Anderson. We wish to acknowledge Dean Anderson's and Linda Anderson's life work in the field of change leadership and corporate transformation, which provided many of the key ideas in Chapter 12, Preparing to Lead the Transformation.

Finally, we thank our Executive Editor Bill Falloon, and his team at Wiley, Purvi Patel, Managing Editor, and Samantha Wu, Editorial Assistant, for their guidance in bringing *Net Zero Business Models* to market in an accelerated manner. We also thank our copyeditor, Julie Kerr, for polishing the book with her thoughtful edits.

NOTE

1. Fitzpatrick, R. (2021). *Write Useful Books: A Modern Approach to Designing and Refining Recommendable Nonfiction*. Useful Books Ltd.

INDEX